Congo Democratic Republic

Business Law Handbook

by **Cram101**

Table of Contents

Index: Answers

Just The Facts101

Exam Prep for

Congo Democratic Republic Business
Law Handbook

Just The Facts101 Exam Prep is your link from
the textbook and lecture to your exams.

**Just The Facts101 Exam Preps are unauthorized and comprehensive reviews
of your textbooks.**

All material provided by CTI Publications (c) 2019

Textbook publishers and textbook authors do not participate in or contribute to these reviews.

Just The Facts101 Exam Prep

eAIN 444535

Foundations of Business

A business, also known as an enterprise, agency or a firm, is an entity involved in the provision of goods and/or services to consumers. Businesses are prevalent in capitalist economies, where most of them are privately owned and provide goods and services to customers in exchange for other goods, services, or money.

:: Business terms ::

A _____ is a short statement of why an organization exists, what its overall goal is, identifying the goal of its operations: what kind of product or service it provides, its primary customers or market, and its geographical region of operation. It may include a short statement of such fundamental matters as the organization's values or philosophies, a business's main competitive advantages, or a desired future state—the "vision".

Exam Probability: **Medium**

1. *Answer choices:*

(see index for correct answer)

- a. noncommercial
- b. Owner Controlled Insurance Program
- c. centralization
- d. Mission statement

Guidance: level 1

:: Environmental economics ::

_____ is the process of people maintaining change in a balanced environment, in which the exploitation of resources, the direction of investments, the orientation of technological development and institutional change are all in harmony and enhance both current and future potential to meet human needs and aspirations. For many in the field, _____ is defined through the following interconnected domains or pillars: environment, economic and social, which according to Fritjof Capra is based on the principles of Systems Thinking. Sub-domains of sustainable development have been considered also: cultural, technological and political. While sustainable development may be the organizing principle for _____ for some, for others, the two terms are paradoxical . Sustainable development is the development that meets the needs of the present without compromising the ability of future generations to meet their own needs. Brundtland Report for the World Commission on Environment and Development introduced the term of sustainable development.

Exam Probability: **Medium**

2. *Answer choices:*

(see index for correct answer)

- a. Steering tax
- b. Environmental enterprise
- c. Sustainability
- d. Good Country Index

Guidance: level 1

:: Project management ::

Some scenarios associate "this kind of planning" with learning "life skills". _____ s are necessary, or at least useful, in situations where individuals need to know what time they must be at a specific location to receive a specific service, and where people need to accomplish a set of goals within a set time period.

Exam Probability: **High**

3. *Answer choices:*

(see index for correct answer)

- a. Value of work done
- b. Schedule
- c. Project appraisal
- d. Project blog

Guidance: level 1

:: ::

_____ is an abstract concept of management of complex systems according to a set of rules and trends. In systems theory, these types of rules exist in various fields of biology and society, but the term has slightly different meanings according to context. For example.

Exam Probability: **Medium**

4. *Answer choices:*

(see index for correct answer)

- a. information systems assessment
- b. Regulation
- c. similarity-attraction theory
- d. process perspective

Guidance: level 1

:: Commercial item transport and distribution ::

A _____ is a commitment or expectation to perform some action in general or if certain circumstances arise. A _____ may arise from a system of ethics or morality, especially in an honor culture. Many duties are created by law, sometimes including a codified punishment or liability for non-performance. Performing one`s _____ may require some sacrifice of self-interest.

Exam Probability: **Low**

5. *Answer choices:*

(see index for correct answer)

- a. Cargo scanning
- b. Toll Global Forwarding
- c. Duty
- d. Aeroscraft

:: Globalization-related theories ::

_____ is the process in which a nation is being improved in the sector of the economic, political, and social well-being of its people. The term has been used frequently by economists, politicians, and others in the 20th and 21st centuries. The concept, however, has been in existence in the West for centuries. "Modernization, "westernization", and especially "industrialization" are other terms often used while discussing _____ . _____ has a direct relationship with the environment and environmental issues. _____ is very often confused with industrial development, even in some academic sources.

Exam Probability: **High**

6. *Answer choices:*

(see index for correct answer)

- a. post-industrial
- b. postmodernism
- c. Economic Development

:: Business ::

_____ is a trade policy that does not restrict imports or exports; it can also be understood as the free market idea applied to international trade. In government, _____ is predominantly advocated by political parties that hold liberal economic positions while economically left-wing and nationalist political parties generally support protectionism, the opposite of _____ .

Exam Probability: **Low**

7. *Answer choices:*

(see index for correct answer)

- a. Crowdsourcing
- b. Business tourism
- c. Counter trade
- d. OrderUp

Guidance: level 1

:: Market research ::

_____ is "the process or set of processes that links the producers, customers, and end users to the marketer through information used to identify and define marketing opportunities and problems; generate, refine, and evaluate marketing actions; monitor marketing performance; and improve understanding of marketing as a process. _____ specifies the information required to address these issues, designs the method for collecting information, manages and implements the data collection process, analyzes the results, and communicates the findings and their implications."

8. *Answer choices:*

(see index for correct answer)

- a. Marketing research
- b. Market surveillance
- c. Global environmental analysis
- d. Advertising Research Foundation

Guidance: level 1

:: Management ::

In business, a _____ is the attribute that allows an organization to outperform its competitors. A _____ may include access to natural resources, such as high-grade ores or a low-cost power source, highly skilled labor, geographic location, high entry barriers, and access to new technology.

Exam Probability: **High**

9. *Answer choices:*

(see index for correct answer)

- a. Overtime rate
- b. Defensive expenditures
- c. Business rule

- d. Competitive advantage

:: Stock market ::

_____ is freedom from, or resilience against, potential harm caused by others. Beneficiaries of _____ may be of persons and social groups, objects and institutions, ecosystems or any other entity or phenomenon vulnerable to unwanted change by its environment.

Exam Probability: **High**

10. *Answer choices:*

(see index for correct answer)

- a. stock price
- b. Security
- c. Stockjobber
- d. Witching hour

:: Mathematical finance ::

In economics and finance, _____ , also known as present discounted value, is the value of an expected income stream determined as of the date of valuation. The _____ is always less than or equal to the future value because money has interest-earning potential, a characteristic referred to as the time value of money, except during times of negative interest rates, when the _____ will be more than the future value. Time value can be described with the simplified phrase, "A dollar today is worth more than a dollar tomorrow". Here, `worth more` means that its value is greater. A dollar today is worth more than a dollar tomorrow because the dollar can be invested and earn a day's worth of interest, making the total accumulate to a value more than a dollar by tomorrow. Interest can be compared to rent. Just as rent is paid to a landlord by a tenant without the ownership of the asset being transferred, interest is paid to a lender by a borrower who gains access to the money for a time before paying it back. By letting the borrower have access to the money, the lender has sacrificed the exchange value of this money, and is compensated for it in the form of interest. The initial amount of the borrowed funds is less than the total amount of money paid to the lender.

Exam Probability: **High**

11. *Answer choices:*

(see index for correct answer)

- a. Time-weighted return
- b. Sonkin enterprise multiple
- c. Statistical arbitrage
- d. Present value

Guidance: level 1

:: Organizational theory ::

_____ is the process of groups of organisms working or acting together for common, mutual, or some underlying benefit, as opposed to working in competition for selfish benefit. Many animal and plant species cooperate both with other members of their own species and with members of other species .

Exam Probability: **Medium**

12. *Answer choices:*

(see index for correct answer)

- a. Organization development
- b. Goat rodeo
- c. Cooperation
- d. Organizational change fatigue

Guidance: level 1

:: Project management ::

_____ is the right to exercise power, which can be formalized by a state and exercised by way of judges, appointed executives of government, or the ecclesiastical or priestly appointed representatives of a God or other deities.

Exam Probability: **Medium**

13. *Answer choices:*

(see index for correct answer)

- a. Advanced Integrated Practice
- b. Authority
- c. Product-based planning
- d. Responsibility assignment matrix

Guidance: level 1

:: Quality management ::

_____ ensures that an organization, product or service is consistent. It has four main components: quality planning, quality assurance, quality control and quality improvement. _____ is focused not only on product and service quality, but also on the means to achieve it. _____ , therefore, uses quality assurance and control of processes as well as products to achieve more consistent quality. What a customer wants and is willing to pay for it determines quality. It is written or unwritten commitment to a known or unknown consumer in the market . Thus, quality can be defined as fitness for intended use or, in other words, how well the product performs its intended function

Exam Probability: **Low**

14. *Answer choices:*

(see index for correct answer)

- a. Test bay
- b. Informal Methods
- c. Quality Management Maturity Grid

- d. Quality management

Guidance: level 1

:: Marketing ::

_____ is the percentage of a market accounted for by a specific entity. In a survey of nearly 200 senior marketing managers, 67% responded that they found the revenue- "dollar _____ " metric very useful, while 61% found "unit _____ " very useful.

Exam Probability: **Low**

15. *Answer choices:*

(see index for correct answer)

- a. Lingerie party
- b. societal marketing
- c. Market share
- d. Primary research

Guidance: level 1

:: Competition (economics) ::

_____ arises whenever at least two parties strive for a goal which cannot be shared: where one`s gain is the other`s loss .

Exam Probability: **Low**

16. *Answer choices:*

- a. Currency competition
- b. Wantrapreneur
- c. Competition
- d. Blindspots analysis

Guidance: level 1

:: Regression analysis ::

A _____ often refers to a set of documented requirements to be satisfied by a material, design, product, or service. A _____ is often a type of technical standard.

Exam Probability: **High**

17. *Answer choices:*

- a. Least squares
- b. Unit-weighted regression
- c. Heckman correction
- d. Zero-inflated model

Guidance: level 1

:: International trade ::

_____ or globalisation is the process of interaction and integration among people, companies, and governments worldwide. As a complex and multifaceted phenomenon, _____ is considered by some as a form of capitalist expansion which entails the integration of local and national economies into a global, unregulated market economy. _____ has grown due to advances in transportation and communication technology. With the increased global interactions comes the growth of international trade, ideas, and culture. _____ is primarily an economic process of interaction and integration that's associated with social and cultural aspects. However, conflicts and diplomacy are also large parts of the history of _____, and modern _____ .

Exam Probability: **Medium**

18. *Answer choices:*

(see index for correct answer)

- a. Flying geese paradigm
- b. Globalization
- c. Trade commissioner

- d. Westline

Guidance: level 1

:: International relations ::

A _____ is any event that is going to lead to an unstable and dangerous situation affecting an individual, group, community, or whole society. Crises are deemed to be negative changes in the security, economic, political, societal, or environmental affairs, especially when they occur abruptly, with little or no warning. More loosely, it is a term meaning "a testing time" or an "emergency event".

Exam Probability: **Medium**

19. *Answer choices:*

(see index for correct answer)

- a. Foreign agent
- b. Monetization of U.S. in-kind food aid
- c. Arctic policy of Russia
- d. Duties Beyond Borders

Guidance: level 1

:: Management ::

A _____ is a method or technique that has been generally accepted as superior to any alternatives because it produces results that are superior to those achieved by other means or because it has become a standard way of doing things, e.g., a standard way of complying with legal or ethical requirements.

Exam Probability: **Low**

20. *Answer choices:*

(see index for correct answer)

- a. Sensemaking
- b. Project cost management
- c. Discovery-driven planning
- d. Best practice

Guidance: level 1

:: Business process ::

A _____ or business method is a collection of related, structured activities or tasks by people or equipment which in a specific sequence produce a service or product for a particular customer or customers. _____ es occur at all organizational levels and may or may not be visible to the customers. A _____ may often be visualized as a flowchart of a sequence of activities with interleaving decision points or as a process matrix of a sequence of activities with relevance rules based on data in the process. The benefits of using _____ es include improved customer satisfaction and improved agility for reacting to rapid market change. Process-oriented organizations break down the barriers of structural departments and try to avoid functional silos.

Exam Probability: **Medium**

21. *Answer choices:*

(see index for correct answer)

- a. Business Motivation Model
- b. Value process management
- c. Information technology outsourcing
- d. Business process reengineering

Guidance: level 1

:: Information science ::

A _____ is a written, drawn, presented, or memorialized representation of thought. a _____ is a form, or written piece that trains a line of thought or as in history, a significant event. The word originates from the Latin _____ um, which denotes a "teaching" or "lesson": the verb doceo denotes "to teach". In the past, the word was usually used to denote a written proof useful as evidence of a truth or fact. In the computer age, " _____ " usually denotes a primarily textual computer file, including its structure and format, e.g. fonts, colors, and images. Contemporarily, " _____ " is not defined by its transmission medium, e.g., paper, given the existence of electronic _____ s. " _____ ation" is distinct because it has more denotations than " _____ ". _____ s are also distinguished from "realia", which are three-dimensional objects that would otherwise satisfy the definition of " _____ " because they memorialize or represent thought; _____ s are considered more as 2 dimensional representations. While _____ s are able to have large varieties of customization, all _____ s are able to be shared freely, and have the right to do so, creativity can be represented by _____ s, also. History, events, examples, opinion, etc. all can be expressed in _____ s.

Exam Probability: **Medium**

22. *Answer choices:*

(see index for correct answer)

- a. Document
- b. BioCreative
- c. Sound and music computing
- d. Information

Guidance: level 1

In regulatory jurisdictions that provide for it , _____ is a group of laws and organizations designed to ensure the rights of consumers as well as fair trade, competition and accurate information in the marketplace. The laws are designed to prevent the businesses that engage in fraud or specified unfair practices from gaining an advantage over competitors. They may also provides additional protection for those most vulnerable in society. _____ laws are a form of government regulation that aim to protect the rights of consumers. For example, a government may require businesses to disclose detailed information about products—particularly in areas where safety or public health is an issue, such as food.

Exam Probability: **Medium**

23. *Answer choices:*

(see index for correct answer)

- a. levels of analysis
- b. open system
- c. corporate values
- d. Consumer Protection

Guidance: level 1

:: Fraud ::

In law, _____ is intentional deception to secure unfair or unlawful gain, or to deprive a victim of a legal right. _____ can violate civil law, a criminal law, or it may cause no loss of money, property or legal right but still be an element of another civil or criminal wrong. The purpose of _____ may be monetary gain or other benefits, for example by obtaining a passport, travel document, or driver's license, or mortgage _____, where the perpetrator may attempt to qualify for a mortgage by way of false statements.

Exam Probability: **Low**

24. *Answer choices:*

(see index for correct answer)

- a. Deceptive advertising
- b. Welfare queen
- c. Fraud
- d. Hijacked journal

Guidance: level 1

:: Management ::

The _____ is a strategy performance management tool – a semi-standard structured report, that can be used by managers to keep track of the execution of activities by the staff within their control and to monitor the consequences arising from these actions.

25. *Answer choices:*

(see index for correct answer)

- a. Backsourcing
- b. Supplier performance management
- c. Topple rate
- d. Balanced scorecard

Guidance: level 1

:: ::

An _____ is the production of goods or related services within an economy. The major source of revenue of a group or company is the indicator of its relevant _____ . When a large group has multiple sources of revenue generation, it is considered to be working in different industries.
Manufacturing _____ became a key sector of production and labour in European and North American countries during the Industrial Revolution, upsetting previous mercantile and feudal economies. This came through many successive rapid advances in technology, such as the production of steel and coal.

Exam Probability: **Medium**

26. *Answer choices:*

(see index for correct answer)

- a. deep-level diversity
- b. cultural
- c. surface-level diversity
- d. corporate values

Guidance: level 1

:: Industrial design ::

In physics and mathematics, the _____ of a mathematical space is informally defined as the minimum number of coordinates needed to specify any point within it. Thus a line has a _____ of one because only one coordinate is needed to specify a point on it for example, the point at 5 on a number line. A surface such as a plane or the surface of a cylinder or sphere has a _____ of two because two coordinates are needed to specify a point on it for example, both a latitude and longitude are required to locate a point on the surface of a sphere. The inside of a cube, a cylinder or a sphere is three-_____ al because three coordinates are needed to locate a point within these spaces.

Exam Probability: **Low**

27. *Answer choices:*

(see index for correct answer)

- a. Dimension
- b. Projection augmented model
- c. Industrial design
- d. Objectified

:: Information technology ::

_____ is the use of computers to store, retrieve, transmit, and manipulate data, or information, often in the context of a business or other enterprise. IT is considered to be a subset of information and communications technology . An _____ system is generally an information system, a communications system or, more specifically speaking, a computer system – including all hardware, software and peripheral equipment – operated by a limited group of users.

Exam Probability: **High**

28. *Answer choices:*

(see index for correct answer)

- a. Information technology
- b. Data center infrastructure management
- c. CIO-plus
- d. VSoft Technologies Private Limited

:: Business law ::

A _____ is a group of people who jointly supervise the activities of an organization, which can be either a for-profit business, nonprofit organization, or a government agency. Such a board's powers, duties, and responsibilities are determined by government regulations and the organization's own constitution and bylaws. These authorities may specify the number of members of the board, how they are to be chosen, and how often they are to meet.

Exam Probability: **Low**

29. *Answer choices:*

(see index for correct answer)

- a. Whitewash waiver
- b. Double ticketing
- c. Single business enterprise
- d. Board of directors

Guidance: level 1

:: Monopoly (economics) ::

A _____ is a form of intellectual property that gives its owner the legal right to exclude others from making, using, selling, and importing an invention for a limited period of years, in exchange for publishing an enabling public disclosure of the invention. In most countries _____ rights fall under civil law and the _____ holder needs to sue someone infringing the _____ in order to enforce his or her rights. In some industries _____ s are an essential form of competitive advantage; in others they are irrelevant.

Exam Probability: **High**

30. *Answer choices:*

(see index for correct answer)

- a. Bilateral monopoly
- b. Motion Picture Patents Company
- c. Herfindahl index
- d. Public utility

Guidance: level 1

:: Management ::

A _____ is when two or more people come together to discuss one or more topics, often in a formal or business setting, but _____ s also occur in a variety of other environments. Many various types of _____ s exist.

Exam Probability: **High**

31. *Answer choices:*

(see index for correct answer)

- a. PDCA
- b. Meeting
- c. Gemba
- d. I-VMS

Guidance: level 1

:: Stock market ::

A shareholder is an individual or institution that legally owns one or more shares of stock in a public or private corporation. _____ may be referred to as members of a corporation. Legally, a person is not a shareholder in a corporation until their name and other details are entered in the corporation's register of _____ or members.

Exam Probability: **Medium**

32. *Answer choices:*

(see index for correct answer)

- a. Voting interest
- b. Shareholders
- c. Common stock
- d. Green sheet

:: Packaging ::

In work place, _____ or job _____ means good ranking with the hypothesized conception of requirements of a role. There are two types of job _____ s: contextual and task. Task _____ is related to cognitive ability while contextual _____ is dependent upon personality. Task _____ are behavioral roles that are recognized in job descriptions and by remuneration systems, they are directly related to organizational _____ , whereas, contextual _____ are value based and additional behavioral roles that are not recognized in job descriptions and covered by compensation; they are extra roles that are indirectly related to organizational _____ . Citizenship _____ like contextual _____ means a set of individual activity/contribution that supports the organizational culture.

Exam Probability: **Low**

33. *Answer choices:*

(see index for correct answer)

- a. Record sleeve
- b. Performance
- c. Flexography
- d. Cold foil printing

:: Project management ::

A _____ is a source or supply from which a benefit is produced and it has some utility. _____ s can broadly be classified upon their availability—they are classified into renewable and non-renewable _____ s.Examples of non renewable _____ s are coal ,crude oil natural gas nuclear energy etc. Examples of renewable _____ s are air,water,wind,solar energy etc. They can also be classified as actual and potential on the basis of level of development and use, on the basis of origin they can be classified as biotic and abiotic, and on the basis of their distribution, as ubiquitous and localized . An item becomes a _____ with time and developing technology. Typically, _____ s are materials, energy, services, staff, knowledge, or other assets that are transformed to produce benefit and in the process may be consumed or made unavailable. Benefits of _____ utilization may include increased wealth, proper functioning of a system, or enhanced well-being. From a human perspective a natural _____ is anything obtained from the environment to satisfy human needs and wants. From a broader biological or ecological perspective a _____ satisfies the needs of a living organism .

Exam Probability: **Medium**

34. *Answer choices:*

(see index for correct answer)

- a. Resource
- b. Collaborative project management
- c. Project governance
- d. Multidisciplinary approach

Guidance: level 1

:: Corporate crime ::

_____ LLP, based in Chicago, was an American holding company. Formerly one of the "Big Five" accounting firms , the firm had provided auditing, tax, and consulting services to large corporations. By 2001, it had become one of the world's largest multinational companies.

Exam Probability: **Low**

35. *Answer choices:*
(see index for correct answer)

- a. Titan Corporation
- b. NatWest Three
- c. Langbar International
- d. Arthur Andersen

Guidance: level 1

:: ::

_____ or accountancy is the measurement, processing, and communication of financial information about economic entities such as businesses and corporations. The modern field was established by the Italian mathematician Luca Pacioli in 1494. _____ , which has been called the "language of business", measures the results of an organization's economic activities and conveys this information to a variety of users, including investors, creditors, management, and regulators. Practitioners of _____ are known as accountants. The terms " _____ " and "financial reporting" are often used as synonyms.

Exam Probability: **Low**

36. *Answer choices:*

(see index for correct answer)

- a. information systems assessment
- b. cultural
- c. Accounting
- d. functional perspective

Guidance: level 1

:: Customs duties ::

A _____ is a tax on imports or exports between sovereign states. It is a form of regulation of foreign trade and a policy that taxes foreign products to encourage or safeguard domestic industry. _____ s are the simplest and oldest instrument of trade policy. Traditionally, states have used them as a source of income. Now, they are among the most widely used instruments of protection, along with import and export quotas.

Exam Probability: **High**

37. *Answer choices:*

(see index for correct answer)

- a. Immigration tariff
- b. Court of Exchequer
- c. Tariff
- d. Specific rate duty

Guidance: level 1

:: Organizational structure ::

An _____ defines how activities such as task allocation, coordination, and supervision are directed toward the achievement of organizational aims.

Exam Probability: **Low**

38. *Answer choices:*

(see index for correct answer)

- a. Automated Bureaucracy
- b. Organization of the New York City Police Department
- c. Unorganisation
- d. Organizational structure

Guidance: level 1

:: Systems theory ::

A _____ is a group of interacting or interrelated entities that form a unified whole. A _____ is delineated by its spatial and temporal boundaries, surrounded and influenced by its environment, described by its structure and purpose and expressed in its functioning.

Exam Probability: **Low**

39. *Answer choices:*

(see index for correct answer)

- a. equifinality
- b. System
- c. Viable System Model
- d. subsystem

Guidance: level 1

:: Project management ::

Contemporary business and science treat as a _____ any undertaking, carried out individually or collaboratively and possibly involving research or design, that is carefully planned to achieve a particular aim.

Exam Probability: **Low**

40. *Answer choices:*

(see index for correct answer)

- a. Hart Mason Index
- b. Extreme project management
- c. Project
- d. Project management 2.0

Guidance: level 1

:: Rhetoric ::

_____ is the pattern of narrative development that aims to make vivid a place, object, character, or group. _____ is one of four rhetorical modes , along with exposition, argumentation, and narration. In practice it would be difficult to write literature that drew on just one of the four basic modes.

41. *Answer choices:*

(see index for correct answer)

- a. Diacope
- b. Belgrade Competition in Oratory
- c. Jeremiad
- d. Description

Guidance: level 1

:: Organizational behavior ::

_____ is the state or fact of exclusive rights and control over property, which may be an object, land/real estate or intellectual property. _____ involves multiple rights, collectively referred to as title, which may be separated and held by different parties.

Exam Probability: **High**

42. *Answer choices:*

(see index for correct answer)

- a. Ownership
- b. Group behaviour
- c. Positive organizational behavior

- d. Civic virtue

Guidance: level 1

:: Legal terms ::

_____ , a form of alternative dispute resolution , is a way to resolve disputes outside the courts. The dispute will be decided by one or more persons , which renders the " _____ award". An _____ award is legally binding on both sides and enforceable in the courts.

Exam Probability: **High**

43. *Answer choices:*

(see index for correct answer)

- a. Duplicity
- b. Possession proceedings
- c. Arbitration
- d. Empty chair

Guidance: level 1

:: Problem solving ::

In other words, _____ is a situation where a group of people meet to generate new ideas and solutions around a specific domain of interest by removing inhibitions. People are able to think more freely and they suggest as many spontaneous new ideas as possible. All the ideas are noted down and those ideas are not criticized and after _____ session the ideas are evaluated. The term was popularized by Alex Faickney Osborn in the 1953 book Applied Imagination.

Exam Probability: **High**

44. *Answer choices:*

(see index for correct answer)

- a. Brainstorming
- b. Nursing process
- c. Puzzle
- d. Analytical skill

Guidance: level 1

:: Marketing ::

_____ is based on a marketing concept which can be adopted by an organization as a strategy for business expansion. Where implemented, a franchisor licenses its know-how, procedures, intellectual property, use of its business model, brand, and rights to sell its branded products and services to a franchisee. In return the franchisee pays certain fees and agrees to comply with certain obligations, typically set out in a Franchise Agreement.

45. *Answer choices:*

(see index for correct answer)

- a. Target market
- b. Editorial calendar
- c. Impulse purchase
- d. Franchising

Guidance: level 1

:: Management ::

A _____ is an idea of the future or desired result that a person or a group of people envisions, plans and commits to achieve. People endeavor to reach _____ s within a finite time by setting deadlines.

Exam Probability: **Low**

46. *Answer choices:*

(see index for correct answer)

- a. Goal
- b. Scrum
- c. Failure demand
- d. Quick response manufacturing

:: Stock market ::

A _____ , securities exchange or bourse, is a facility where stock brokers and traders can buy and sell securities, such as shares of stock and bonds and other financial instruments. _____ s may also provide for facilities the issue and redemption of such securities and instruments and capital events including the payment of income and dividends. Securities traded on a _____ include stock issued by listed companies, unit trusts, derivatives, pooled investment products and bonds. _____ s often function as "continuous auction" markets with buyers and sellers consummating transactions via open outcry at a central location such as the floor of the exchange or by using an electronic trading platform.

Exam Probability: **Medium**

47. *Answer choices:*

(see index for correct answer)

- a. Stock market bubble
- b. First Prudential Markets
- c. Security
- d. Stock exchange

:: Management accounting ::

In economics, _____ s, indirect costs or overheads are business expenses that are not dependent on the level of goods or services produced by the business. They tend to be time-related, such as interest or rents being paid per month, and are often referred to as overhead costs. This is in contrast to variable costs, which are volume-related and unknown at the beginning of the accounting year. For a simple example, such as a bakery, the monthly rent for the baking facilities, and the monthly payments for the security system and basic phone line are _____ s, as they do not change according to how much bread the bakery produces and sells. On the other hand, the wage costs of the bakery are variable, as the bakery will have to hire more workers if the production of bread increases. Economists reckon _____ as a entry barrier for new entrepreneurs.

48. *Answer choices:*

(see index for correct answer)

- a. Contribution margin
- b. Pre-determined overhead rate
- c. Certified Management Accountant
- d. Direct material total variance

Guidance: level 1

:: Strategic alliances ::

A _____ is an agreement between two or more parties to pursue a set of agreed upon objectives needed while remaining independent organizations. A _____ will usually fall short of a legal partnership entity, agency, or corporate affiliate relationship. Typically, two companies form a _____ when each possesses one or more business assets or have expertise that will help the other by enhancing their businesses. _____ s can develop in outsourcing relationships where the parties desire to achieve long-term win-win benefits and innovation based on mutually desired outcomes.

Exam Probability: **Medium**

49. *Answer choices:*

(see index for correct answer)

- a. Defensive termination
- b. Cross-licensing
- c. Bridge Alliance
- d. Strategic alliance

Guidance: level 1

:: Shareholders ::

A _____ is a payment made by a corporation to its shareholders, usually as a distribution of profits. When a corporation earns a profit or surplus, the corporation is able to re-invest the profit in the business and pay a proportion of the profit as a _____ to shareholders. Distribution to shareholders may be in cash or, if the corporation has a _____ reinvestment plan, the amount can be paid by the issue of further shares or share repurchase. When _____ s are paid, shareholders typically must pay income taxes, and the corporation does not receive a corporate income tax deduction for the _____ payments.

Exam Probability: **Low**

50. *Answer choices:*

(see index for correct answer)

- a. Friedman doctrine
- b. Proxy statement
- c. Dividend
- d. Shareholder Protection Act

Guidance: level 1

:: ::

Some scenarios associate "this kind of planning" with learning "life skills".Schedules are necessary, or at least useful, in situations where individuals need to know what time they must be at a specific location to receive a specific service, and where people need to accomplish a set of goals within a set time period.

51. *Answer choices:*

(see index for correct answer)

- a. corporate values
- b. Scheduling
- c. deep-level diversity
- d. process perspective

Guidance: level 1

:: Office administration ::

An _____ is generally a room or other area where an organization's employees perform administrative work in order to support and realize objects and goals of the organization. The word " _____ " may also denote a position within an organization with specific duties attached to it ; the latter is in fact an earlier usage, _____ as place originally referring to the location of one's duty. When used as an adjective, the term " _____ " may refer to business-related tasks. In law, a company or organization has _____ s in any place where it has an official presence, even if that presence consists of a storage silo rather than an establishment with desk-and-chair. An _____ is also an architectural and design phenomenon: ranging from a small _____ such as a bench in the corner of a small business of extremely small size , through entire floors of buildings, up to and including massive buildings dedicated entirely to one company. In modern terms an _____ is usually the location where white-collar workers carry out their functions. As per James Stephenson, " _____ is that part of business enterprise which is devoted to the direction and co-ordination of its various activities."

52. *Answer choices:*

(see index for correct answer)

- a. Inter departmental communication
- b. Office administration
- c. Activity management
- d. Office

Guidance: level 1

:: Business law ::

A _____ is a business entity created by two or more parties, generally characterized by shared ownership, shared returns and risks, and shared governance. Companies typically pursue _____ s for one of four reasons: to access a new market, particularly emerging markets; to gain scale efficiencies by combining assets and operations; to share risk for major investments or projects; or to access skills and capabilities.

53. *Answer choices:*

(see index for correct answer)

- a. Consignment agreement
- b. Business valuation

- c. Power harassment
- d. Joint venture

Guidance: level 1

:: Auditing ::

_____ , as defined by accounting and auditing, is a process for assuring of an organization's objectives in operational effectiveness and efficiency, reliable financial reporting, and compliance with laws, regulations and policies. A broad concept, _____ involves everything that controls risks to an organization.

Exam Probability: **High**

54. *Answer choices:*
(see index for correct answer)

- a. Certified Quality Auditor
- b. audit log
- c. Provided by client
- d. Internal control

Guidance: level 1

:: Stock market ::

The _____ of a corporation is all of the shares into which ownership of the corporation is divided. In American English, the shares are commonly known as " _____ s". A single share of the _____ represents fractional ownership of the corporation in proportion to the total number of shares. This typically entitles the _____ holder to that fraction of the company's earnings, proceeds from liquidation of assets , or voting power, often dividing these up in proportion to the amount of money each _____ holder has invested. Not all _____ is necessarily equal, as certain classes of _____ may be issued for example without voting rights, with enhanced voting rights, or with a certain priority to receive profits or liquidation proceeds before or after other classes of shareholders.

Exam Probability: **Low**

55. *Answer choices:*

(see index for correct answer)

- a. NewConnect
- b. Box spread
- c. Erie War
- d. Stock

Guidance: level 1

:: ::

_____ is the means to see, hear, or become aware of something or someone through our fundamental senses. The term _____ derives from the Latin word perceptio, and is the organization, identification, and interpretation of sensory information in order to represent and understand the presented information, or the environment.

Exam Probability: **Low**

56. *Answer choices:*

(see index for correct answer)

- a. imperative
- b. Perception
- c. information systems assessment
- d. personal values

Guidance: level 1

:: Business law ::

A _____ is an arrangement where parties, known as partners, agree to cooperate to advance their mutual interests. The partners in a _____ may be individuals, businesses, interest-based organizations, schools, governments or combinations. Organizations may partner to increase the likelihood of each achieving their mission and to amplify their reach. A _____ may result in issuing and holding equity or may be only governed by a contract.

Exam Probability: **High**

57. *Answer choices:*

(see index for correct answer)

- a. Partnership
- b. Chattel mortgage
- c. Business license
- d. Finance lease

Guidance: level 1

:: Human resource management ::

_____ are the people who make up the workforce of an organization, business sector, or economy. "Human capital" is sometimes used synonymously with " _____ ", although human capital typically refers to a narrower effect . Likewise, other terms sometimes used include manpower, talent, labor, personnel, or simply people.

Exam Probability: **High**

58. *Answer choices:*

(see index for correct answer)

- a. Cross-functional team
- b. Human resources
- c. Aspiring Minds
- d. Work activity management

:: Materials ::

A _____ , also known as a feedstock, unprocessed material, or primary commodity, is a basic material that is used to produce goods, finished products, energy, or intermediate materials which are feedstock for future finished products. As feedstock, the term connotes these materials are bottleneck assets and are highly important with regard to producing other products. An example of this is crude oil, which is a _____ and a feedstock used in the production of industrial chemicals, fuels, plastics, and pharmaceutical goods; lumber is a _____ used to produce a variety of products including all types of furniture. The term " _____ " denotes materials in minimally processed or unprocessed in states; e.g., raw latex, crude oil, cotton, coal, raw biomass, iron ore, air, logs, or water i.e. "...any product of agriculture, forestry, fishing and any other mineral that is in its natural form or which has undergone the transformation required to prepare it for internationally marketing in substantial volumes."

Exam Probability: **High**

59. *Answer choices:*

(see index for correct answer)

- a. Raw material
- b. Noil
- c. Ion Gel
- d. Three-dimensional quartz phenolic

Management

Management is the administration of an organization, whether it is a business, a not-for-profit organization, or government body. Management includes the activities of setting the strategy of an organization and coordinating the efforts of its employees (or of volunteers) to accomplish its objectives through the application of available resources, such as financial, natural, technological, and human resources.

:: Project management ::

_____ is the right to exercise power, which can be formalized by a state and exercised by way of judges, appointed executives of government, or the ecclesiastical or priestly appointed representatives of a God or other deities.

1. *Answer choices:*

(see index for correct answer)

- a. A Guide to the Project Management Body of Knowledge
- b. Authority
- c. Association for Project Management
- d. Gantt chart

Guidance: level 1

:: ::

_____ is the process of making predictions of the future based on past and present data and most commonly by analysis of trends. A commonplace example might be estimation of some variable of interest at some specified future date. Prediction is a similar, but more general term. Both might refer to formal statistical methods employing time series, cross-sectional or longitudinal data, or alternatively to less formal judgmental methods. Usage can differ between areas of application: for example, in hydrology the terms "forecast" and " _____ " are sometimes reserved for estimates of values at certain specific future times, while the term "prediction" is used for more general estimates, such as the number of times floods will occur over a long period.

2. *Answer choices:*

(see index for correct answer)

- a. process perspective
- b. Character
- c. hierarchical perspective
- d. Forecasting

Guidance: level 1

:: Project management ::

A _____ is a type of bar chart that illustrates a project schedule, named after its inventor, Henry Gantt , who designed such a chart around the years 1910–1915. Modern _____ s also show the dependency relationships between activities and current schedule status.

Exam Probability: **Medium**

3. *Answer choices:*

(see index for correct answer)

- a. Gantt chart
- b. Karol Adamiecki
- c. Social project management
- d. Kickoff meeting

Guidance: level 1

:: Electronic feedback ::

_____ occurs when outputs of a system are routed back as inputs as part of a chain of cause-and-effect that forms a circuit or loop. The system can then be said to feed back into itself. The notion of cause-and-effect has to be handled carefully when applied to _____ systems.

Exam Probability: **Low**

4. *Answer choices:*

(see index for correct answer)

- a. Positive feedback
- b. Feedback

Guidance: level 1

:: Management ::

A _____ is someone who engages in facilitation—any activity that makes a social process easy or easier. A _____ often helps a group of people to understand their common objectives and assists them to plan how to achieve these objectives; in doing so, the _____ remains "neutral", meaning he/she does not take a particular position in the discussion. Some _____ tools will try to assist the group in achieving a consensus on any disagreements that preexist or emerge in the meeting so that it has a strong basis for future action.

5. *Answer choices:*

(see index for correct answer)

- a. Board of governors
- b. Social business model
- c. Mushroom management
- d. Facilitator

Guidance: level 1

:: Mereology ::

_____ , in the abstract, is what belongs to or with something, whether as an attribute or as a component of said thing. In the context of this article, it is one or more components , whether physical or incorporeal, of a person's estate; or so belonging to, as in being owned by, a person or jointly a group of people or a legal entity like a corporation or even a society. Depending on the nature of the _____ , an owner of _____ has the right to consume, alter, share, redefine, rent, mortgage, pawn, sell, exchange, transfer, give away or destroy it, or to exclude others from doing these things, as well as to perhaps abandon it; whereas regardless of the nature of the _____ , the owner thereof has the right to properly use it , or at the very least exclusively keep it.

Exam Probability: **High**

6. *Answer choices:*

(see index for correct answer)

- a. Mereotopology
- b. Property
- c. Mereology
- d. Gunk

Guidance: level 1

:: Lean manufacturing ::

A continual improvement process, also often called a _____ process , is an ongoing effort to improve products, services, or processes. These efforts can seek "incremental" improvement over time or "breakthrough" improvement all at once. Delivery processes are constantly evaluated and improved in the light of their efficiency, effectiveness and flexibility.

Exam Probability: **High**

7. *Answer choices:*

(see index for correct answer)

- a. Overall Labor Effectiveness
- b. Continuous improvement
- c. Failure mode and effects analysis
- d. Fixed Repeating Schedule

:: Management ::

The _____ is a strategy performance management tool – a semi-standard structured report, that can be used by managers to keep track of the execution of activities by the staff within their control and to monitor the consequences arising from these actions.

Exam Probability: **Low**

8. *Answer choices:*

(see index for correct answer)

- a. Tata Management Training Centre
- b. Process management
- c. Balanced scorecard
- d. Critical path method

:: Supply chain management terms ::

In business and finance, _____ is a system of organizations, people, activities, information, and resources involved in moving a product or service from supplier to customer. _____ activities involve the transformation of natural resources, raw materials, and components into a finished product that is delivered to the end customer. In sophisticated _____ systems, used products may re-enter the _____ at any point where residual value is recyclable. _____ s link value chains.

Exam Probability: **Medium**

9. *Answer choices:*

(see index for correct answer)

- a. inventory management
- b. Direct shipment
- c. Supply chain
- d. Capital spare

Guidance: level 1

:: Operations research ::

_____ is a method to achieve the best outcome in a mathematical model whose requirements are represented by linear relationships. _____ is a special case of mathematical programming .

Exam Probability: **Low**

10. *Answer choices:*

- a. European Working Group on Multiple Criteria Decision Aiding
- b. Open-shop scheduling
- c. Linear programming
- d. Energy minimization

Guidance: level 1

:: Game theory ::

_____ is the idea that rationality is limited when individuals make decisions: by the tractability of the decision problem, the cognitive limitations of the mind, and the time available to make the decision. Decision-makers, in this view, act as satisficers, seeking a satisfactory solution rather than an optimal one.

Exam Probability: **Medium**

11. *Answer choices:*

- a. Rational agent
- b. Small-numbers game
- c. Mean field game theory
- d. Bounded rationality

:: Autonomy ::

In developmental psychology and moral, political, and bioethical philosophy, _____ is the capacity to make an informed, uncoerced decision. Autonomous organizations or institutions are independent or self-governing. _____ can also be defined from a human resources perspective, where it denotes a level of discretion granted to an employee in his or her work. In such cases, _____ is known to generally increase job satisfaction. _____ is a term that is also widely used in the field of medicine — personal _____ is greatly recognized and valued in health care.

Exam Probability: **Low**

12. *Answer choices:*

(see index for correct answer)

- a. Self-governance
- b. Accountable autonomy
- c. Autonomy
- d. Consent

:: International trade ::

_____ involves the transfer of goods or services from one person or entity to another, often in exchange for money. A system or network that allows _____ is called a market.

Exam Probability: **High**

13. *Answer choices:*

(see index for correct answer)

- a. Business English
- b. Trade commissioner
- c. Balassa index
- d. Trade

Guidance: level 1

:: ::

An _____ is, most an organized examination or formal evaluation exercise. In engineering activities _____ involves the measurements, tests, and gauges applied to certain characteristics in regard to an object or activity. The results are usually compared to specified requirements and standards for determining whether the item or activity is in line with these targets, often with a Standard _____ Procedure in place to ensure consistent checking. _____ s are usually non-destructive.

Exam Probability: **Low**

14. *Answer choices:*

(see index for correct answer)

- a. cultural
- b. similarity-attraction theory
- c. hierarchical
- d. Inspection

Guidance: level 1

:: Classification systems ::

_____ is the practice of comparing business processes and performance metrics to industry bests and best practices from other companies. Dimensions typically measured are quality, time and cost.

Exam Probability: **High**

15. *Answer choices:*

(see index for correct answer)

- a. Structural Classification of Proteins database
- b. Benchmarking
- c. Alpine Club classification of the Eastern Alps
- d. Classification of Instructional Programs

Guidance: level 1

:: International trade ::

_____ or globalisation is the process of interaction and integration among people, companies, and governments worldwide. As a complex and multifaceted phenomenon, _____ is considered by some as a form of capitalist expansion which entails the integration of local and national economies into a global, unregulated market economy. _____ has grown due to advances in transportation and communication technology. With the increased global interactions comes the growth of international trade, ideas, and culture. _____ is primarily an economic process of interaction and integration that's associated with social and cultural aspects. However, conflicts and diplomacy are also large parts of the history of _____ , and modern _____ .

Exam Probability: **High**

16. *Answer choices:*

(see index for correct answer)

- a. Bill of lading
- b. Trans-Saharan trade
- c. Hilton Quota
- d. Nordic Innovation

Guidance: level 1

:: Industrial design ::

In physics and mathematics, the _____ of a mathematical space is informally defined as the minimum number of coordinates needed to specify any point within it. Thus a line has a _____ of one because only one coordinate is needed to specify a point on it for example, the point at 5 on a number line. A surface such as a plane or the surface of a cylinder or sphere has a _____ of two because two coordinates are needed to specify a point on it for example, both a latitude and longitude are required to locate a point on the surface of a sphere. The inside of a cube, a cylinder or a sphere is three- _____ al because three coordinates are needed to locate a point within these spaces.

Exam Probability: **High**

17. *Answer choices:*

(see index for correct answer)

- a. Japanese design law
- b. Sky-Sailor
- c. Design patent
- d. Dimension

Guidance: level 1

:: Marketing ::

_____ is the percentage of a market accounted for by a specific entity. In a survey of nearly 200 senior marketing managers, 67% responded that they found the revenue- "dollar _____ " metric very useful, while 61% found "unit _____ " very useful.

18. *Answer choices:*

(see index for correct answer)

- a. Fixed value-added resource
- b. Discounts and allowances
- c. Price umbrella
- d. Market share

Guidance: level 1

:: ::

_____ or haggling is a type of negotiation in which the buyer and seller of a good or service debate the price and exact nature of a transaction. If the _____ produces agreement on terms, the transaction takes place. _____ is an alternative pricing strategy to fixed prices. Optimally, if it costs the retailer nothing to engage and allow _____ , s/he can divine the buyer's willingness to spend. It allows for capturing more consumer surplus as it allows price discrimination, a process whereby a seller can charge a higher price to one buyer who is more eager . Haggling has largely disappeared in parts of the world where the cost to haggle exceeds the gain to retailers for most common retail items. However, for expensive goods sold to uninformed buyers such as automobiles, _____ can remain commonplace.

Exam Probability: **Medium**

19. *Answer choices:*

(see index for correct answer)

- a. levels of analysis
- b. interpersonal communication
- c. deep-level diversity
- d. similarity-attraction theory

Guidance: level 1

:: Production economics ::

_____ is the joint use of a resource or space. It is also the process of dividing and distributing. In its narrow sense, it refers to joint or alternating use of inherently finite goods, such as a common pasture or a shared residence. Still more loosely, " _____ " can actually mean giving something as an outright gift: for example, to "share" one's food really means to give some of it as a gift. _____ is a basic component of human interaction, and is responsible for strengthening social ties and ensuring a person's well-being.

Exam Probability: **High**

20. *Answer choices:*
(see index for correct answer)

- a. Division of work
- b. Synergy
- c. Sharing

- d. Marginal rate of technical substitution

Guidance: level 1

:: Industrial relations ::

_____ or employee satisfaction is a measure of workers' contentedness with their job, whether or not they like the job or individual aspects or facets of jobs, such as nature of work or supervision. _____ can be measured in cognitive , affective , and behavioral components. Researchers have also noted that _____ measures vary in the extent to which they measure feelings about the job . or cognitions about the job .

Exam Probability: **Medium**

21. *Answer choices:*

(see index for correct answer)

- a. Industrial violence
- b. Injury prevention
- c. European Journal of Industrial Relations
- d. Workforce Investment Board

Guidance: level 1

:: Organizational behavior ::

_____ is the term now used more commonly in business management, particularly human resource management. _____ refers to the number of subordinates a supervisor has.

Exam Probability: **Low**

22. *Answer choices:*

(see index for correct answer)

- a. Organizational Expedience
- b. Organizational behavior management
- c. Span of control
- d. Managerial grid model

Guidance: level 1

:: Project management ::

In economics, _____ is the assignment of available resources to various uses. In the context of an entire economy, resources can be allocated by various means, such as markets or central planning.

Exam Probability: **Low**

23. *Answer choices:*

(see index for correct answer)

- a. Time horizon
- b. Social project management
- c. Gold plating
- d. Resource allocation

Guidance: level 1

:: ::

_____ is the amount of time someone works beyond normal working hours. The term is also used for the pay received for this time. Normal hours may be determined in several ways.

Exam Probability: **High**

24. *Answer choices:*

(see index for correct answer)

- a. interpersonal communication
- b. corporate values
- c. process perspective
- d. Overtime

Guidance: level 1

:: Rhetoric ::

_____ is the pattern of narrative development that aims to make vivid a place, object, character, or group. _____ is one of four rhetorical modes , along with exposition, argumentation, and narration. In practice it would be difficult to write literature that drew on just one of the four basic modes.

Exam Probability: **High**

25. *Answer choices:*

(see index for correct answer)

- a. Keywords
- b. Description
- c. Word play
- d. Rhetrickery

Guidance: level 1

:: Employee relations ::

_____ ownership, or employee share ownership, is an ownership interest in a company held by the company's workforce. The ownership interest may be facilitated by the company as part of employees' remuneration or incentive compensation for work performed, or the company itself may be employee owned.

Exam Probability: **Medium**

26. *Answer choices:*

(see index for correct answer)

- a. Employee surveys
- b. Employee motivation
- c. Employee stock
- d. Employee morale

Guidance: level 1

:: Organizational theory ::

_____ refers to both a body of non-elective government officials and an administrative policy-making group. Historically, a _____ was a government administration managed by departments staffed with non-elected officials. Today, _____ is the administrative system governing any large institution, whether publicly owned or privately owned. The public administration in many countries is an example of a _____ , but so is the centralized hierarchical structure of a business firm.

Exam Probability: **High**

27. *Answer choices:*

(see index for correct answer)

- a. Identity negotiation
- b. Strategic Choice Theory
- c. Bureaucracy
- d. Organizational theory

:: Management occupations ::

_____ is the process of designing, launching and running a new business, which is often initially a small business. The people who create these businesses are called entrepreneurs.

Exam Probability: **Low**

28. *Answer choices:*

(see index for correct answer)

- a. Legal management
- b. Corporate trainer
- c. Comptroller
- d. Entrepreneurship

:: Project management ::

_____ and Theory Y are theories of human work motivation and management. They were created by Douglas McGregor while he was working at the MIT Sloan School of Management in the 1950s, and developed further in the 1960s. McGregor's work was rooted in motivation theory alongside the works of Abraham Maslow, who created the hierarchy of needs. The two theories proposed by McGregor describe contrasting models of workforce motivation applied by managers in human resource management, organizational behavior, organizational communication and organizational development. _____ explains the importance of heightened supervision, external rewards, and penalties, while Theory Y highlights the motivating role of job satisfaction and encourages workers to approach tasks without direct supervision. Management use of _____ and Theory Y can affect employee motivation and productivity in different ways, and managers may choose to implement strategies from both theories into their practices.

Exam Probability: **Low**

29. *Answer choices:*

(see index for correct answer)

- a. Graphical path method
- b. Theory X
- c. Flexible product development
- d. Direct changeover

Guidance: level 1

:: Cognitive biases ::

The _____ is a type of immediate judgement discrepancy, or cognitive bias, where a person making an initial assessment of another person, place, or thing will assume ambiguous information based upon concrete information. A simplified example of the _____ is when an individual noticing that the person in the photograph is attractive, well groomed, and properly attired, assumes, using a mental heuristic, that the person in the photograph is a good person based upon the rules of that individual's social concept. This constant error in judgment is reflective of the individual's preferences, prejudices, ideology, aspirations, and social perception. The _____ is an evaluation by an individual and can affect the perception of a decision, action, idea, business, person, group, entity, or other whenever concrete data is generalized or influences ambiguous information.

Exam Probability: **Low**

30. *Answer choices:*

(see index for correct answer)

- a. Fundamental attribution error
- b. Affect heuristic
- c. Hot-hand fallacy
- d. Halo effect

Guidance: level 1

:: Human resource management ::

A _____ is a group of people with different functional expertise working toward a common goal. It may include people from finance, marketing, operations, and human resources departments. Typically, it includes employees from all levels of an organization. Members may also come from outside an organization .

Exam Probability: **High**

31. *Answer choices:*

(see index for correct answer)

- a. Cross-functional team
- b. Contextual performance
- c. Herrmann Brain Dominance Instrument
- d. Perceived organizational support

Guidance: level 1

:: Human resource management ::

_____ are the people who make up the workforce of an organization, business sector, or economy. "Human capital" is sometimes used synonymously with " _____ ", although human capital typically refers to a narrower effect . Likewise, other terms sometimes used include manpower, talent, labor, personnel, or simply people.

Exam Probability: **Low**

32. *Answer choices:*

- a. Human resources
- b. Employeeship
- c. Employee relationship management
- d. Illness rate

Guidance: level 1

:: Outsourcing ::

_____ is the relocation of a business process from one country to another—typically an operational process, such as manufacturing, or supporting processes, such as accounting. Typically this refers to a company business, although state governments may also employ _____ . More recently, technical and administrative services have been offshored.

Exam Probability: **High**

33. *Answer choices:*

- a. Offshoring
- b. Divestment
- c. Shared services center
- d. Sourcing agent

:: Decision theory ::

Within economics the concept of _____ is used to model worth or value, but its usage has evolved significantly over time. The term was introduced initially as a measure of pleasure or satisfaction within the theory of utilitarianism by moral philosophers such as Jeremy Bentham and John Stuart Mill. But the term has been adapted and reapplied within neoclassical economics, which dominates modern economic theory, as a _____ function that represents a consumer's preference ordering over a choice set. As such, it is devoid of its original interpretation as a measurement of the pleasure or satisfaction obtained by the consumer from that choice.

Exam Probability: **Low**

34. *Answer choices:*

(see index for correct answer)

- a. VIKOR method
- b. Utility
- c. Rademacher complexity
- d. Applied information economics

:: Business process ::

A _____ or business method is a collection of related, structured activities or tasks by people or equipment which in a specific sequence produce a service or product for a particular customer or customers. _____ es occur at all organizational levels and may or may not be visible to the customers. A _____ may often be visualized as a flowchart of a sequence of activities with interleaving decision points or as a process matrix of a sequence of activities with relevance rules based on data in the process. The benefits of using _____ es include improved customer satisfaction and improved agility for reacting to rapid market change. Process-oriented organizations break down the barriers of structural departments and try to avoid functional silos.

Exam Probability: **High**

35. *Answer choices:*

(see index for correct answer)

- a. Business Motivation Model
- b. ADONIS
- c. Business process
- d. Business process outsourcing

Guidance: level 1

:: Socialism ::

In sociology, _____ is the process of internalizing the norms and ideologies of society. _____ encompasses both learning and teaching and is thus "the means by which social and cultural continuity are attained".

36. *Answer choices:*

(see index for correct answer)

- a. Project Cybersyn
- b. Tory socialism
- c. Commanding heights of the economy
- d. Socialization

Guidance: level 1

:: Credit cards ::

The _____ Company, also known as Amex, is an American multinational financial services corporation headquartered in Three World Financial Center in New York City. The company was founded in 1850 and is one of the 30 components of the Dow Jones Industrial Average. The company is best known for its charge card, credit card, and traveler's cheque businesses.

Exam Probability: **Low**

37. *Answer choices:*

(see index for correct answer)

- a. American Express
- b. CardIt

- c. Gravity Payments
- d. Payments as a service

Guidance: level 1

:: Poker strategy ::

_____ is any measure taken to guard a thing against damage caused by outside forces. _____ can be provided to physical objects, including organisms, to systems, and to intangible things like civil and political rights. Although the mechanisms for providing _____ vary widely, the basic meaning of the term remains the same. This is illustrated by an explanation found in a manual on electrical wiring.

Exam Probability: **High**

38. *Answer choices:*
(see index for correct answer)

- a. M-ratio
- b. Protection
- c. Position
- d. Steal

Guidance: level 1

:: Evaluation ::

_____ solving consists of using generic or ad hoc methods in an orderly manner to find solutions to _____ s. Some of the _____ -solving techniques developed and used in philosophy, artificial intelligence, computer science, engineering, mathematics, or medicine are related to mental _____ -solving techniques studied in psychology.

Exam Probability: **Low**

39. *Answer choices:*

(see index for correct answer)

- a. Narrative evaluation
- b. Evaluation Assurance Level
- c. SPECpower
- d. Transferable skills analysis

Guidance: level 1

:: Discrimination ::

In social psychology, a _____ is an over-generalized belief about a particular category of people. _____ s are generalized because one assumes that the _____ is true for each individual person in the category. While such generalizations may be useful when making quick decisions, they may be erroneous when applied to particular individuals. _____ s encourage prejudice and may arise for a number of reasons.

Exam Probability: **Medium**

40. *Answer choices:*

(see index for correct answer)

- a. Stereotype
- b. Anti-Americanism
- c. Elitism

Guidance: level 1

:: ::

_____ , known in Europe as research and technological development , refers to innovative activities undertaken by corporations or governments in developing new services or products, or improving existing services or products. _____ constitutes the first stage of development of a potential new service or the production process.

Exam Probability: **Medium**

41. *Answer choices:*

(see index for correct answer)

- a. cultural
- b. corporate values
- c. Research and development
- d. hierarchical perspective

:: ::

A _____ or sample _____ is a single measure of some attribute of a sample . It is calculated by applying a function to the values of the items of the sample, which are known together as a set of data.

Exam Probability: **High**

42. *Answer choices:*

(see index for correct answer)

- a. interpersonal communication
- b. Sarbanes-Oxley act of 2002
- c. Statistic
- d. functional perspective

:: Telecommuting ::

_____ , also called telework, teleworking, working from home, mobile work, remote work, and flexible workplace, is a work arrangement in which employees do not commute or travel to a central place of work, such as an office building, warehouse, or store. Teleworkers in the 21st century often use mobile telecommunications technology such as Wi-Fi-equipped laptop or tablet computers and smartphones to work from coffee shops; others may use a desktop computer and a landline phone at their home. According to a Reuters poll, approximately "one in five workers around the globe, particularly employees in the Middle East, Latin America and Asia, telecommute frequently and nearly 10 percent work from home every day." In the 2000s, annual leave or vacation in some organizations was seen as absence from the workplace rather than ceasing work, and some office employees used telework to continue to check work e-mails while on vacation.

Exam Probability: **Medium**

43. *Answer choices:*

(see index for correct answer)

- a. Telecommuting
- b. TalkPoint
- c. VWorker
- d. VenueGen

Guidance: level 1

:: Workplace ::

A _____ , also referred to as a performance review, performance evaluation, development discussion, or employee appraisal is a method by which the job performance of an employee is documented and evaluated. _____ s are a part of career development and consist of regular reviews of employee performance within organizations.

Exam Probability: **Medium**

44. *Answer choices:*

(see index for correct answer)

- a. Performance appraisal
- b. Toxic workplace
- c. Workplace spirituality
- d. Workplace harassment

Guidance: level 1

:: Television commercials ::

_____ is a phenomenon whereby something new and somehow valuable is formed. The created item may be intangible or a physical object .

Exam Probability: **High**

45. *Answer choices:*

(see index for correct answer)

- a. Swimblack
- b. Cheer Up!
- c. Creativity
- d. Lamp

Guidance: level 1

:: ::

_____ is the moral stance, political philosophy, ideology, or social outlook that emphasizes the moral worth of the individual. Individualists promote the exercise of one's goals and desires and so value independence and self-reliance and advocate that interests of the individual should achieve precedence over the state or a social group, while opposing external interference upon one's own interests by society or institutions such as the government. _____ is often defined in contrast to totalitarianism, collectivism, and more corporate social forms.

Exam Probability: **High**

46. *Answer choices:*

(see index for correct answer)

- a. imperative
- b. Individualism
- c. Sarbanes-Oxley act of 2002
- d. surface-level diversity

:: Business planning ::

_____ is an organization's process of defining its strategy, or direction, and making decisions on allocating its resources to pursue this strategy. It may also extend to control mechanisms for guiding the implementation of the strategy. _____ became prominent in corporations during the 1960s and remains an important aspect of strategic management. It is executed by strategic planners or strategists, who involve many parties and research sources in their analysis of the organization and its relationship to the environment in which it competes.

Exam Probability: **Low**

47. *Answer choices:*

(see index for correct answer)

- a. Gap analysis
- b. Strategic planning
- c. Stakeholder management
- d. operational planning

:: Management ::

_____ is a process by which entities review the quality of all factors involved in production. ISO 9000 defines _____ as "A part of quality management focused on fulfilling quality requirements".

Exam Probability: **Low**

48. *Answer choices:*

(see index for correct answer)

- a. Quality control
- b. Records manager
- c. Investment control
- d. Identity formation

Guidance: level 1

:: Meetings ::

A _____ is a body of one or more persons that is subordinate to a deliberative assembly. Usually, the assembly sends matters into a _____ as a way to explore them more fully than would be possible if the assembly itself were considering them. _____ s may have different functions and their type of work differ depending on the type of the organization and its needs.

Exam Probability: **High**

49. *Answer choices:*

(see index for correct answer)

- a. Stammtisch
- b. Committee
- c. Ex officio member
- d. Chatham House Rule

Guidance: level 1

:: Human resource management ::

An organizational chart is a diagram that shows the structure of an organization and the relationships and relative ranks of its parts and positions/jobs. The term is also used for similar diagrams, for example ones showing the different elements of a field of knowledge or a group of languages.

Exam Probability: **Medium**

50. *Answer choices:*

(see index for correct answer)

- a. Up or out
- b. Talascend
- c. Organization chart
- d. Voluntary redundancy

:: Marketing ::

_____ , in marketing, manufacturing, call centres and management, is the use of flexible computer-aided manufacturing systems to produce custom output. Such systems combine the low unit costs of mass production processes with the flexibility of individual customization.

Exam Probability: **High**

51. *Answer choices:*
(see index for correct answer)

- a. Price umbrella
- b. Advertising media selection
- c. Mass customization
- d. Gift suite

:: ::

In sales, commerce and economics, a _____ is the recipient of a good, service, product or an idea - obtained from a seller, vendor, or supplier via a financial transaction or exchange for money or some other valuable consideration.

Exam Probability: **Low**

52. *Answer choices:*

(see index for correct answer)

- a. Customer
- b. Character
- c. corporate values
- d. co-culture

Guidance: level 1

:: Workplace ::

A _____ is a process through which feedback from an employee's subordinates, colleagues, and supervisor, as well as a self-evaluation by the employee themselves is gathered. Such feedback can also include, when relevant, feedback from external sources who interact with the employee, such as customers and suppliers or other interested stakeholders. _____ is so named because it solicits feedback regarding an employee's behavior from a variety of points of view . It therefore may be contrasted with "downward feedback" , or "upward feedback" delivered to supervisory or management employees by subordinates only.

53. *Answer choices:*

(see index for correct answer)

- a. Performance appraisal
- b. Open allocation
- c. Staff turnover
- d. 360-degree feedback

Guidance: level 1

:: Industrial Revolution ::

The _____ , now also known as the First _____ , was the transition to new manufacturing processes in Europe and the US, in the period from about 1760 to sometime between 1820 and 1840. This transition included going from hand production methods to machines, new chemical manufacturing and iron production processes, the increasing use of steam power and water power, the development of machine tools and the rise of the mechanized factory system. The _____ also led to an unprecedented rise in the rate of population growth.

Exam Probability: **High**

54. *Answer choices:*

(see index for correct answer)

- a. Factory system

- b. Roberts Loom
- c. Ironbridge Gorge
- d. Stocking frame

Guidance: level 1

:: ::

An _____ is a contingent motivator. Traditional _____ s are extrinsic motivators which reward actions to yield a desired outcome. The effectiveness of traditional _____ s has changed as the needs of Western society have evolved. While the traditional _____ model is effective when there is a defined procedure and goal for a task, Western society started to require a higher volume of critical thinkers, so the traditional model became less effective. Institutions are now following a trend in implementing strategies that rely on intrinsic motivations rather than the extrinsic motivations that the traditional _____ s foster.

Exam Probability: **Low**

55. *Answer choices:*

(see index for correct answer)

- a. deep-level diversity
- b. similarity-attraction theory
- c. Incentive
- d. information systems assessment

Guidance: level 1

:: ::

_____ is the process of collecting, analyzing and/or reporting information regarding the performance of an individual, group, organization, system or component. _____ is not a new concept, some of the earliest records of human activity relate to the counting or recording of activities.

Exam Probability: **Low**

56. *Answer choices:*

(see index for correct answer)

- a. surface-level diversity
- b. functional perspective
- c. cultural
- d. corporate values

Guidance: level 1

:: ::

A _____ is a professional who provides expert advice in a particular area such as security , management, education, accountancy, law, human resources, marketing , finance, engineering, science or any of many other specialized fields.

57. *Answer choices:*

(see index for correct answer)

- a. Consultant
- b. empathy
- c. hierarchical perspective
- d. surface-level diversity

Guidance: level 1

:: ::

_____ involves decision making. It can include judging the merits of multiple options and selecting one or more of them. One can make a _____ between imagined options or between real options followed by the corresponding action. For example, a traveler might choose a route for a journey based on the preference of arriving at a given destination as soon as possible. The preferred route can then follow from information such as the length of each of the possible routes, traffic conditions, etc. The arrival at a _____ can include more complex motivators such as cognition, instinct, and feeling.

Exam Probability: **Low**

58. *Answer choices:*

(see index for correct answer)

- a. functional perspective
- b. open system
- c. levels of analysis
- d. hierarchical

Guidance: level 1

:: Management ::

_____ is an area of management concerned with designing and controlling the process of production and redesigning business operations in the production of goods or services. It involves the responsibility of ensuring that business operations are efficient in terms of using as few resources as needed and effective in terms of meeting customer requirements. _____ is primarily concerned with planning, organizing and supervising in the contexts of production, manufacturing or the provision of services.

Exam Probability: **Low**

59. *Answer choices:*

(see index for correct answer)

- a. Design management
- b. Value migration
- c. Responsible autonomy
- d. Operations management

Guidance: level 1

Business law

Corporate law (also known as business law) is the body of law governing the rights, relations, and conduct of persons, companies, organizations and businesses. It refers to the legal practice relating to, or the theory of corporations. Corporate law often describes the law relating to matters which derive directly from the life-cycle of a corporation. It thus encompasses the formation, funding, governance, and death of a corporation.

:: Abuse of the legal system ::

_____ occurs when a person is restricted in their personal movement within any area without justification or consent. Actual physical restraint is not necessary for _____ to occur. A _____ claim may be made based upon private acts, or upon wrongful governmental detention. For detention by the police, proof of _____ provides a basis to obtain a writ of habeas corpus.

Exam Probability: **High**

1. *Answer choices:*

(see index for correct answer)

- a. False imprisonment
- b. False arrest
- c. Forum shopping

Guidance: level 1

:: Legal doctrines and principles ::

_____ is a doctrine that a party is responsible for acts of their agents. For example, in the United States, there are circumstances when an employer is liable for acts of employees performed within the course of their employment. This rule is also called the master-servant rule, recognized in both common law and civil law jurisdictions.

Exam Probability: **High**

2. *Answer choices:*

(see index for correct answer)

- a. Respondeat superior
- b. Mutual mistake
- c. Contributory negligence
- d. Acquiescence

:: Contract law ::

Offer and acceptance analysis is a traditional approach in contract law. The offer and acceptance formula, developed in the 19th century, identifies a moment of formation when the parties are of one mind. This classical approach to contract formation has been modified by developments in the law of estoppel, misleading conduct, misrepresentation and unjust enrichment.

Exam Probability: **Low**

3. *Answer choices:*

(see index for correct answer)

- a. Flexible contracts
- b. South African contract law
- c. Subcontractor
- d. Principles of European Contract Law

:: Business law ::

A _____ is a legal right granted by a debtor to a creditor over the debtor's property which enables the creditor to have recourse to the property if the debtor defaults in making payment or otherwise performing the secured obligations. One of the most common examples of a _____ is a mortgage: When person, by the action of an expressed conveyance, pledges by a promise to pay a certain sum of money, with certain conditions, on a said date or dates for a said period, that action on the page with wet ink applied on the part of the one wishing the exchange creates the original funds and negotiable Instrument. That action of pledging conveys a promise binding upon the mortgagee which creates a face value upon the Instrument of the amount of currency being asked for in exchange. It is therein in good faith offered to the Bank in exchange for local currency from the Bank to buy a house. The particular country's Bank Acts usually requires the Banks to deliver such fund bearing negotiable instruments to the Countries Main Bank such as is the case in Canada. This creates a _____ in the land the house sits on for the Bank and they file a caveat at land titles on the house as evidence of that _____ . If the mortgagee fails to pay defaulting in his promise to repay the exchange, the bank then applies to the court to for-close on your property to eventually sell the house and apply the proceeds to the outstanding exchange.

Exam Probability: **High**

4. *Answer choices:*

(see index for correct answer)

- a. Retroactive overtime
- b. European Patent Convention
- c. Limited liability
- d. Security interest

Guidance: level 1

:: Contract law ::

_____ is a legal cause of action and a type of civil wrong, in which a binding agreement or bargained-for exchange is not honored by one or more of the parties to the contract by non-performance or interference with the other party's performance. Breach occurs when a party to a contract fails to fulfill its obligation as described in the contract, or communicates an intent to fail the obligation or otherwise appears not to be able to perform its obligation under the contract. Where there is _____ , the resulting damages will have to be paid by the party breaching the contract to the aggrieved party.

Exam Probability: **Low**

5. *Answer choices:*

(see index for correct answer)

- a. Oral contract
- b. Breach of contract
- c. Extended warranty
- d. Offeree

Guidance: level 1

:: ::

_____ Corporation was an American energy, commodities, and services company based in Houston, Texas. It was founded in 1985 as a merger between Houston Natural Gas and InterNorth, both relatively small regional companies. Before its bankruptcy on December 3, 2001, _____ employed approximately 29,000 staff and was a major electricity, natural gas, communications and pulp and paper company, with claimed revenues of nearly $101 billion during 2000. Fortune named _____ "America's Most Innovative Company" for six consecutive years.

Exam Probability: **High**

6. *Answer choices:*

(see index for correct answer)

- a. empathy
- b. Sarbanes-Oxley act of 2002
- c. functional perspective
- d. Enron

Guidance: level 1

:: ::

The _____ is an intergovernmental organization that is concerned with the regulation of international trade between nations. The WTO officially commenced on 1 January 1995 under the Marrakesh Agreement, signed by 124 nations on 15 April 1994, replacing the General Agreement on Tariffs and Trade , which commenced in 1948. It is the largest international economic organization in the world.

7. *Answer choices:*

(see index for correct answer)

- a. cultural
- b. imperative
- c. World Trade Organization
- d. hierarchical

Guidance: level 1

:: Judgment (law) ::

In law, a _____ is a judgment entered by a court for one party and against another party summarily, i.e., without a full trial. Such a judgment may be issued on the merits of an entire case, or on discrete issues in that case.

Exam Probability: **Medium**

8. *Answer choices:*

(see index for correct answer)

- a. judgment as a matter of law
- b. Summary judgment

:: ::

_____ is the collection of techniques, skills, methods, and processes used in the production of goods or services or in the accomplishment of objectives, such as scientific investigation. _____ can be the knowledge of techniques, processes, and the like, or it can be embedded in machines to allow for operation without detailed knowledge of their workings. Systems applying _____ by taking an input, changing it according to the system`s use, and then producing an outcome are referred to as _____ systems or technological systems.

Exam Probability: **Medium**

9. *Answer choices:*

(see index for correct answer)

- a. empathy
- b. Character
- c. Sarbanes-Oxley act of 2002
- d. co-culture

:: ::

_____ is a type of government support for the citizens of that society. _____ may be provided to people of any income level, as with social security , but it is usually intended to ensure that the poor can meet their basic human needs such as food and shelter. _____ attempts to provide poor people with a minimal level of well-being, usually either a free- or a subsidized-supply of certain goods and social services, such as healthcare, education, and vocational training.

Exam Probability: **Low**

10. *Answer choices:*

(see index for correct answer)

- a. open system
- b. Character
- c. functional perspective
- d. Welfare

Guidance: level 1

:: ::

_____ , often abbreviated cert. in the United States, is a process for seeking judicial review and a writ issued by a court that agrees to review. A _____ is issued by a superior court, directing an inferior court, tribunal, or other public authority to send the record of a proceeding for review.

11. *Answer choices:*

(see index for correct answer)

- a. Certiorari
- b. interpersonal communication
- c. surface-level diversity
- d. functional perspective

Guidance: level 1

:: ::

_____ is a judicial device in common law legal systems whereby a court may prevent, or "estop" a person from making assertions or from going back on his or her word; the person being sanctioned is "estopped". _____ may prevent someone from bringing a particular claim. Legal doctrines of _____ are based in both common law and equity.

Exam Probability: **High**

12. *Answer choices:*

(see index for correct answer)

- a. co-culture
- b. Estoppel

- c. open system
- d. interpersonal communication

Guidance: level 1

:: Law ::

_____ is a body of law which defines the role, powers, and structure of different entities within a state, namely, the executive, the parliament or legislature, and the judiciary; as well as the basic rights of citizens and, in federal countries such as the United States and Canada, the relationship between the central government and state, provincial, or territorial governments.

Exam Probability: **High**

13. *Answer choices:*

(see index for correct answer)

- a. Legal case
- b. Comparative law

Guidance: level 1

:: Services management and marketing ::

A _____ or servicemark is a trademark used in the United States and several other countries to identify a service rather than a product.

Exam Probability: **Medium**

14. *Answer choices:*

(see index for correct answer)

- a. Integrated customer management
- b. Service provider
- c. Service delivery framework
- d. Industrialization of services business model

Guidance: level 1

:: Clauses of the United States Constitution ::

The _____ describes an enumerated power listed in the United States Constitution . The clause states that the United States Congress shall have power "To regulate Commerce with foreign Nations, and among the several States, and with the Indian Tribes." Courts and commentators have tended to discuss each of these three areas of commerce as a separate power granted to Congress. It is common to see the individual components of the _____ referred to under specific terms: the Foreign _____ , the Interstate _____ , and the Indian _____ .

Exam Probability: **Low**

15. *Answer choices:*

(see index for correct answer)

- a. Full Faith and Credit Clause
- b. Double Jeopardy Clause
- c. Full faith and credit

Guidance: level 1

:: Commercial item transport and distribution ::

_____ s may be negotiable or non-negotiable. Negotiable _____ s allow transfer of ownership of that commodity without having to deliver the physical commodity. See Delivery order.

Exam Probability: **Medium**

16. *Answer choices:*

(see index for correct answer)

- a. Bulkhaul Limited
- b. Warehouse receipt
- c. Shipbroking
- d. NORPASS

Guidance: level 1

A _____ is an organization, usually a group of people or a company, authorized to act as a single entity and recognized as such in law. Early incorporated entities were established by charter . Most jurisdictions now allow the creation of new _____ s through registration.

Exam Probability: **Low**

17. *Answer choices:*

(see index for correct answer)

- a. co-culture
- b. Character
- c. information systems assessment
- d. deep-level diversity

Guidance: level 1

:: Legal terms ::

A _____ is any "lesser" criminal act in some common law legal systems. _____ s are generally punished less severely than felonies, but theoretically more so than administrative infractions and regulatory offences. Many _____ s are punished with monetary fines.

Exam Probability: **High**

18. *Answer choices:*

(see index for correct answer)

- a. Foral
- b. Advisory jury
- c. Ministerial act
- d. Additur

Guidance: level 1

:: ::

Industrial espionage, _____ , corporate spying or corporate espionage is a form of espionage conducted for commercial purposes instead of purely national security. While _____ is conducted or orchestrated by governments and is international in scope, industrial or corporate espionage is more often national and occurs between companies or corporations.

Exam Probability: **Medium**

19. *Answer choices:*

(see index for correct answer)

- a. Economic espionage
- b. imperative
- c. deep-level diversity
- d. Sarbanes-Oxley act of 2002

:: Legal terms ::

_____ , a form of alternative dispute resolution , is a way to resolve disputes outside the courts. The dispute will be decided by one or more persons , which renders the " _____ award". An _____ award is legally binding on both sides and enforceable in the courts.

Exam Probability: **Medium**

20. *Answer choices:*

(see index for correct answer)

- a. Arbitrariness
- b. Integration clause
- c. Pain and suffering
- d. Actual notice

:: ::

A _____ is an aggregate of fundamental principles or established precedents that constitute the legal basis of a polity, organisation or other type of entity, and commonly determine how that entity is to be governed.

Exam Probability: **High**

21. *Answer choices:*

(see index for correct answer)

- a. Constitution
- b. process perspective
- c. interpersonal communication
- d. surface-level diversity

Guidance: level 1

:: ::

_____ is the assignment of any responsibility or authority to another person to carry out specific activities. It is one of the core concepts of management leadership. However, the person who delegated the work remains accountable for the outcome of the delegated work. _____ empowers a subordinate to make decisions, i.e. it is a shifting of decision-making authority from one organizational level to a lower one. _____ , if properly done, is not fabrication. The opposite of effective _____ is micromanagement, where a manager provides too much input, direction, and review of delegated work. In general, _____ is good and can save money and time, help in building skills, and motivate people. On the other hand, poor _____ might cause frustration and confusion to all the involved parties. Some agents, however, do not favour a _____ and consider the power of making a decision rather burdensome.

Exam Probability: **Low**

22. *Answer choices:*

(see index for correct answer)

- a. corporate values
- b. similarity-attraction theory
- c. open system
- d. Delegation

Guidance: level 1

:: Contract law ::

A _____ is an event or state of affairs that is required before
something else will occur. In contract law, a _____ is an event which
must occur, unless its non-occurrence is excused, before performance under a
contract becomes due, i.e., before any contractual duty exists.

Exam Probability: **Low**

23. *Answer choices:*

(see index for correct answer)

- a. Principles of European Contract Law
- b. Frustration of purpose
- c. Condition precedent
- d. Talent holding deal

Guidance: level 1

:: ::

In financial markets, a share is a unit used as mutual funds, limited
partnerships, and real estate investment trusts. The owner of _____ in
the corporation/company is a shareholder of the corporation. A share is an
indivisible unit of capital, expressing the ownership relationship between the
company and the shareholder. The denominated value of a share is its face
value, and the total of the face value of issued _____ represent the
capital of a company, which may not reflect the market value of those
_____ .

24. *Answer choices:*

(see index for correct answer)

- a. cultural
- b. Shares
- c. imperative
- d. co-culture

Guidance: level 1

:: Commercial item transport and distribution ::

A _____ in common law countries is a person or company that transports goods or people for any person or company and that is responsible for any possible loss of the goods during transport. A _____ offers its services to the general public under license or authority provided by a regulatory body. The regulatory body has usually been granted "ministerial authority" by the legislation that created it. The regulatory body may create, interpret, and enforce its regulations upon the _____ with independence and finality, as long as it acts within the bounds of the enabling legislation.

Exam Probability: **Low**

25. *Answer choices:*

(see index for correct answer)

- a. Common carrier
- b. Human mail
- c. Second stage manufacturer
- d. Cargo

Guidance: level 1

:: Business law ::

_____ is where a person's financial liability is limited to a fixed sum, most commonly the value of a person's investment in a company or partnership. If a company with _____ is sued, then the claimants are suing the company, not its owners or investors. A shareholder in a limited company is not personally liable for any of the debts of the company, other than for the amount already invested in the company and for any unpaid amount on the shares in the company, if any. The same is true for the members of a _____ partnership and the limited partners in a limited partnership. By contrast, sole proprietors and partners in general partnerships are each liable for all the debts of the business .

Exam Probability: **Medium**

26. *Answer choices:*

(see index for correct answer)

- a. Unfair competition
- b. Limited liability
- c. Arbitration clause
- d. Whitewash waiver

:: Investment ::

In finance, the benefit from an _____ is called a return. The return may consist of a gain realised from the sale of property or an _____, unrealised capital appreciation , or _____ income such as dividends, interest, rental income etc., or a combination of capital gain and income. The return may also include currency gains or losses due to changes in foreign currency exchange rates.

Exam Probability: **Medium**

27. *Answer choices:*

(see index for correct answer)

- a. Investment
- b. VISTA
- c. Private equity
- d. Index fund

:: ::

The U.S. _____ is an independent agency of the United States federal government. The SEC holds primary responsibility for enforcing the federal securities laws, proposing securities rules, and regulating the securities industry, the nation's stock and options exchanges, and other activities and organizations, including the electronic securities markets in the United States.

Exam Probability: **Medium**

28. *Answer choices:*
(see index for correct answer)

- a. process perspective
- b. Character
- c. Securities and Exchange Commission
- d. similarity-attraction theory

Guidance: level 1

:: Contract law ::

_____ is a legal process for collecting a monetary judgment on behalf of a plaintiff from a defendant. _____ allows the plaintiff to take the money or property of the debtor from the person or institution that holds that property . A similar legal mechanism called execution allows the seizure of money or property held directly by the debtor.

Exam Probability: **Medium**

29. *Answer choices:*

(see index for correct answer)

- a. Oral contract
- b. Garnishment
- c. Fixed-price contract
- d. Warranty

Guidance: level 1

:: Commercial item transport and distribution ::

A _____ is a commitment or expectation to perform some action in general or if certain circumstances arise. A _____ may arise from a system of ethics or morality, especially in an honor culture. Many duties are created by law, sometimes including a codified punishment or liability for non-performance. Performing one's _____ may require some sacrifice of self-interest.

Exam Probability: **Medium**

30. *Answer choices:*

(see index for correct answer)

- a. EUR-pallet
- b. Duty
- c. Hold
- d. Steam wagon

:: Contract law ::

In common law jurisdictions, an _____ is a contract law term for certain assurances that are presumed to be made in the sale of products or real property, due to the circumstances of the sale. These assurances are characterized as warranties irrespective of whether the seller has expressly promised them orally or in writing. They include an _____ of fitness for a particular purpose, an _____ of merchantability for products, _____ of workmanlike quality for services, and an _____ of habitability for a home.

Exam Probability: **High**

31. *Answer choices:*

(see index for correct answer)

- a. Fundamental breach
- b. Beneficial interest
- c. Implied warranty
- d. Co-signing

:: Insolvency ::

_____ is a legal process through which people or other entities who cannot repay debts to creditors may seek relief from some or all of their debts. In most jurisdictions, _____ is imposed by a court order, often initiated by the debtor.

Exam Probability: **High**

32. *Answer choices:*

(see index for correct answer)

- a. Bankruptcy
- b. Insolvency law of Russia
- c. Debt consolidation
- d. George Samuel Ford

Guidance: level 1

:: ::

Competition arises whenever at least two parties strive for a goal which cannot be shared: where one's gain is the other's loss .

Exam Probability: **Medium**

33. *Answer choices:*

(see index for correct answer)

- a. process perspective
- b. Competitor
- c. corporate values
- d. hierarchical

Guidance: level 1

:: ::

_____ is property that is movable. In common law systems, _____ may also be called chattels or personalty. In civil law systems, _____ is often called movable property or movables – any property that can be moved from one location to another.

Exam Probability: **High**

34. *Answer choices:*

(see index for correct answer)

- a. surface-level diversity
- b. personal values
- c. co-culture
- d. corporate values

Guidance: level 1

In regulatory jurisdictions that provide for it , _____ is a group of laws and organizations designed to ensure the rights of consumers as well as fair trade, competition and accurate information in the marketplace. The laws are designed to prevent the businesses that engage in fraud or specified unfair practices from gaining an advantage over competitors. They may also provides additional protection for those most vulnerable in society. _____ laws are a form of government regulation that aim to protect the rights of consumers. For example, a government may require businesses to disclose detailed information about products—particularly in areas where safety or public health is an issue, such as food.

Exam Probability: **Low**

35. *Answer choices:*

(see index for correct answer)

- a. Consumer protection
- b. Sarbanes-Oxley act of 2002
- c. functional perspective
- d. levels of analysis

Guidance: level 1

:: Fair use ::

_____ is a doctrine in the law of the United States that permits limited use of copyrighted material without having to first acquire permission from the copyright holder. _____ is one of the limitations to copyright intended to balance the interests of copyright holders with the public interest in the wider distribution and use of creative works by allowing as a defense to copyright infringement claims certain limited uses that might otherwise be considered infringement.

Exam Probability: **High**

36. *Answer choices:*

(see index for correct answer)

- a. FAIR USE Act
- b. Fair Use Project
- c. Fair use
- d. Derivative work

Guidance: level 1

:: Patent law ::

A _____ is generally any statement intended to specify or delimit the scope of rights and obligations that may be exercised and enforced by parties in a legally recognized relationship. In contrast to other terms for legally operative language, the term _____ usually implies situations that involve some level of uncertainty, waiver, or risk.

37. *Answer choices:*

(see index for correct answer)

- a. Double patenting
- b. Patent thicket
- c. PatentFreedom
- d. Patent watch

Guidance: level 1

:: Contract law ::

_____ , also called an anticipatory breach, is a term in the law of contracts that describes a declaration by the promising party to a contract that he or she does not intend to live up to his or her obligations under the contract.

Exam Probability: **Low**

38. *Answer choices:*

(see index for correct answer)

- a. South African contract law
- b. Terms of service
- c. Anticipatory repudiation

- d. Executory contract

Guidance: level 1

:: Treaties ::

A _____ is an agreement under international law entered into by actors in international law, namely sovereign states and international organizations. A _____ may also be known as an agreement, protocol, covenant, convention, pact, or exchange of letters, among other terms. Regardless of terminology, all of these forms of agreements are, under international law, equally considered treaties and the rules are the same.

Exam Probability: **Low**

39. *Answer choices:*

(see index for correct answer)

- a. Jus tractatuum
- b. Clausula rebus sic stantibus
- c. Treaty
- d. Quasi alliance

Guidance: level 1

:: Contract law ::

_____ is an equitable remedy in the law of contract, whereby a court issues an order requiring a party to perform a specific act, such as to complete performance of the contract. It is typically available in the sale of land, but otherwise is not generally available if damages are an appropriate alternative. _____ is almost never available for contracts of personal service, although performance may also be ensured through the threat of proceedings for contempt of court.

Exam Probability: **Low**

40. *Answer choices:*

(see index for correct answer)

- a. South African contract law
- b. Interconnect agreement
- c. Morals clause
- d. Specific performance

Guidance: level 1

:: Business law ::

A _____ is a document guaranteeing the payment of a specific amount of money, either on demand, or at a set time, with the payer usually named on the document. More specifically, it is a document contemplated by or consisting of a contract, which promises the payment of money without condition, which may be paid either on demand or at a future date. The term can have different meanings, depending on what law is being applied and what country and context it is used in.

41. *Answer choices:*

(see index for correct answer)

- a. Finance lease
- b. Negotiable instrument
- c. Consularization
- d. Tacit relocation

Guidance: level 1

:: Consumer theory ::

A _____ is a technical term in psychology, economics and philosophy usually used in relation to choosing between alternatives. For example, someone prefers A over B if they would rather choose A than B.

Exam Probability: **Low**

42. *Answer choices:*

(see index for correct answer)

- a. Consumer sovereignty
- b. Elasticity of substitution
- c. Joint demand
- d. Price elasticity of demand

:: Labour relations ::

_____ is a field of study that can have different meanings depending on the context in which it is used. In an international context, it is a subfield of labor history that studies the human relations with regard to work – in its broadest sense – and how this connects to questions of social inequality. It explicitly encompasses unregulated, historical, and non-Western forms of labor. Here, _____ define "for or with whom one works and under what rules. These rules determine the type of work, type and amount of remuneration, working hours, degrees of physical and psychological strain, as well as the degree of freedom and autonomy associated with the work."

Exam Probability: **Medium**

43. *Answer choices:*

(see index for correct answer)

- a. Association of German Chambers of Industry and Commerce
- b. Labor relations
- c. United Students Against Sweatshops
- d. Impasse

:: Contract law ::

_____ are damages whose amount the parties designate during the formation of a contract for the injured party to collect as compensation upon a specific breach .

44. *Answer choices:*

(see index for correct answer)

- a. enforceable
- b. Morals clause
- c. Liquidated damages
- d. Substantial performance

Guidance: level 1

:: Contract law ::

In the United States, the _____ rule refers to the legal right for a buyer of goods to insist upon " _____ " by the seller. In a contract for the sale of goods, if the goods fail to conform exactly to the description in the contract the buyer may nonetheless accept the goods, or reject the goods, or reject the nonconforming part of the tender and accept the conforming part. The buyer does not have an unfettered ability to reject tender.

45. *Answer choices:*

(see index for correct answer)

- a. Fair Food Program
- b. Proprietary estoppel
- c. Bonus clause
- d. Perfect tender

Guidance: level 1

:: Legal doctrines and principles ::

_____ is a failure to exercise appropriate and or ethical ruled care expected to be exercised amongst specified circumstances. The area of tort law known as _____ involves harm caused by failing to act as a form of carelessness possibly with extenuating circumstances. The core concept of _____ is that people should exercise reasonable care in their actions, by taking account of the potential harm that they might foreseeably cause to other people or property.

Exam Probability: **Low**

46. *Answer choices:*

(see index for correct answer)

- a. Caveat emptor
- b. unconscionable contract
- c. Proximate cause

- d. Negligence

Guidance: level 1

:: ::

The _____ is one of the several United States Uniform Acts proposed by the National Conference of Commissioners on Uniform State Laws . Forty-seven states, the District of Columbia, and the U.S. Virgin Islands have adopted the UETA. Its purpose is to harmonize state laws concerning retention of paper records and the validity of electronic signatures.

Exam Probability: **Medium**

47. *Answer choices:*

(see index for correct answer)

- a. Uniform Electronic Transactions Act
- b. interpersonal communication
- c. levels of analysis
- d. empathy

Guidance: level 1

:: ::

The _____ to the United States Constitution prevents the government from making laws which respect an establishment of religion, prohibit the free exercise of religion, or abridge the freedom of speech, the freedom of the press, the right to peaceably assemble, or the right to petition the government for redress of grievances. It was adopted on December 15, 1791, as one of the ten amendments that constitute the Bill of Rights.

Exam Probability: **High**

48. *Answer choices:*

(see index for correct answer)

- a. interpersonal communication
- b. process perspective
- c. First Amendment
- d. hierarchical

Guidance: level 1

:: ::

An _____ is a formal or official change made to a law, contract, constitution, or other legal document. It is based on the verb to amend, which means to change for better. _____ s can add, remove, or update parts of these agreements. They are often used when it is better to change the document than to write a new one.

Exam Probability: **Low**

49. *Answer choices:*

(see index for correct answer)

- a. cultural
- b. levels of analysis
- c. Amendment
- d. co-culture

Guidance: level 1

:: Legal procedure ::

_____ , adjective law, or rules of court comprises the rules by which a court hears and determines what happens in civil, lawsuit, criminal or administrative proceedings. The rules are designed to ensure a fair and consistent application of due process or fundamental justice to all cases that come before a court.

Exam Probability: **Medium**

50. *Answer choices:*

(see index for correct answer)

- a. Procedural law
- b. Opening statement
- c. Closing argument
- d. appellate

:: Parental leave ::

_____ is a type of employment discrimination that occurs when expectant women are fired, not hired, or otherwise discriminated against due to their pregnancy or intention to become pregnant. Common forms of _____ include not being hired due to visible pregnancy or likelihood of becoming pregnant, being fired after informing an employer of one's pregnancy, being fired after maternity leave, and receiving a pay dock due to pregnancy. Convention on the Elimination of All Forms of Discrimination against Women prohibits dismissal on the grounds of maternity or pregnancy and ensures right to maternity leave or comparable social benefits. The Maternity Protection Convention C 183 proclaims adequate protection for pregnancy as well. Though women have some protection in the United States because of the _____ Act of 1978, it has not completely curbed the incidence of _____ . The Equal Rights Amendment could ensure more robust sex equality ensuring that women and men could both work and have children at the same time.

Exam Probability: **High**

51. *Answer choices:*

(see index for correct answer)

- a. Pregnant Workers Directive
- b. Cleveland Board of Education v. LaFleur
- c. Parental leave economics
- d. Equal Opportunities Commission v Secretary of State for Trade and Industry

---

:: ::

_____ is that part of a civil law legal system which is part of the jus commune that involves relationships between individuals, such as the law of contracts or torts , and the law of obligations . It is to be distinguished from public law, which deals with relationships between both natural and artificial persons and the state, including regulatory statutes, penal law and other law that affects the public order. In general terms, _____ involves interactions between private citizens, whereas public law involves interrelations between the state and the general population.

Exam Probability: **Low**

52. *Answer choices:*

(see index for correct answer)

- a. imperative
- b. Private law
- c. Character
- d. deep-level diversity

:: Working time ::

Labour law is the area of law most commonly relating to the relationship between trade unions, employers and the government.

Exam Probability: **Medium**

53. *Answer choices:*

(see index for correct answer)

- a. Eight-hour day
- b. Bank Holidays Act 1871
- c. Employment law
- d. Blue laws in the United States

Guidance: level 1

:: ::

_____ is the practice of protecting the natural environment by individuals, organizations and governments. Its objectives are to conserve natural resources and the existing natural environment and, where possible, to repair damage and reverse trends.

Exam Probability: **High**

54. *Answer choices:*

(see index for correct answer)

- a. Environmental Protection
- b. hierarchical perspective
- c. interpersonal communication
- d. levels of analysis

Guidance: level 1

:: ::

At common law, _____ are a remedy in the form of a monetary award to be paid to a claimant as compensation for loss or injury. To warrant the award, the claimant must show that a breach of duty has caused foreseeable loss. To be recognised at law, the loss must involve damage to property, or mental or physical injury; pure economic loss is rarely recognised for the award of _____ .

Exam Probability: **Medium**

55. *Answer choices:*

(see index for correct answer)

- a. process perspective
- b. Damages
- c. corporate values
- d. interpersonal communication

Guidance: level 1

:: Finance ::

_____ is the investigation or exercise of care that a reasonable business or person is expected to take before entering into an agreement or contract with another party, or an act with a certain standard of care.

Exam Probability: **High**

56. *Answer choices:*

(see index for correct answer)

- a. Due diligence
- b. Financial Secrecy Index
- c. Magic formula investing
- d. Subordinated debt

Guidance: level 1

:: ::

In the law of evidence, a _____ of a particular fact can be made without the aid of proof in some situations. The invocation of a _____ shifts the burden of proof from one party to the opposing party in a court trial.

Exam Probability: **Medium**

57. *Answer choices:*

(see index for correct answer)

- a. interpersonal communication
- b. deep-level diversity
- c. functional perspective
- d. Presumption

Guidance: level 1

:: ::

The _____ of 1933, also known as the 1933 Act, the _____ , the Truth in _____ , the Federal _____ , and the `33 Act, was enacted by the United States Congress on May 27, 1933, during the Great Depression, after the stock market crash of 1929. Legislated pursuant to the Interstate Commerce Clause of the Constitution, it requires every offer or sale of securities that uses the means and instrumentalities of interstate commerce to be registered with the SEC pursuant to the 1933 Act, unless an exemption from registration exists under the law. The term "means and instrumentalities of interstate commerce" is extremely broad and it is virtually impossible to avoid the operation of the statute by attempting to offer or sell a security without using an "instrumentality" of interstate commerce. Any use of a telephone, for example, or the mails would probably be enough to subject the transaction to the statute.

Exam Probability: **High**

58. *Answer choices:*

(see index for correct answer)

- a. Securities Act
- b. co-culture
- c. personal values
- d. surface-level diversity

Guidance: level 1

:: ::

_____ is the production of products for use or sale using labour and machines, tools, chemical and biological processing, or formulation. The term may refer to a range of human activity, from handicraft to high tech, but is most commonly applied to industrial design, in which raw materials are transformed into finished goods on a large scale. Such finished goods may be sold to other manufacturers for the production of other, more complex products, such as aircraft, household appliances, furniture, sports equipment or automobiles, or sold to wholesalers, who in turn sell them to retailers, who then sell them to end users and consumers.

Exam Probability: **High**

59. *Answer choices:*

(see index for correct answer)

- a. deep-level diversity
- b. interpersonal communication
- c. surface-level diversity
- d. process perspective

Guidance: level 1

Finance

Finance is a field that is concerned with the allocation (investment) of assets and liabilities over space and time, often under conditions of risk or uncertainty. Finance can also be defined as the science of money management. Participants in the market aim to price assets based on their risk level, fundamental value, and their expected rate of return. Finance can be split into three sub-categories: public finance, corporate finance and personal finance.

:: Financial risk ::

_____ is any of various types of risk associated with financing, including financial transactions that include company loans in risk of default. Often it is understood to include only downside risk, meaning the potential for financial loss and uncertainty about its extent.

1. *Answer choices:*

(see index for correct answer)

- a. Financial risk management
- b. Trading room
- c. Government risk
- d. Risk management in Indian banks

Guidance: level 1

:: Asset ::

In accounting, a _____ is any asset which can reasonably be expected to be sold, consumed, or exhausted through the normal operations of a business within the current fiscal year or operating cycle . Typical _____ s include cash, cash equivalents, short-term investments , accounts receivable, stock inventory, supplies, and the portion of prepaid liabilities which will be paid within a year.In simple words, assets which are held for a short period are known as _____ s. Such assets are expected to be realised in cash or consumed during the normal operating cycle of the business.

2. *Answer choices:*

(see index for correct answer)

- a. Asset
- b. Current asset

Guidance: level 1

:: Mereology ::

_____ , in the abstract, is what belongs to or with something, whether as an attribute or as a component of said thing. In the context of this article, it is one or more components , whether physical or incorporeal, of a person's estate; or so belonging to, as in being owned by, a person or jointly a group of people or a legal entity like a corporation or even a society. Depending on the nature of the _____ , an owner of _____ has the right to consume, alter, share, redefine, rent, mortgage, pawn, sell, exchange, transfer, give away or destroy it, or to exclude others from doing these things, as well as to perhaps abandon it; whereas regardless of the nature of the _____ , the owner thereof has the right to properly use it , or at the very least exclusively keep it.

Exam Probability: **High**

3. *Answer choices:*

(see index for correct answer)

- a. Mereological nihilism
- b. Mereology
- c. Mereotopology
- d. Non-wellfounded mereology

:: Monopoly (economics) ::

A _____ is a form of intellectual property that gives its owner the legal right to exclude others from making, using, selling, and importing an invention for a limited period of years, in exchange for publishing an enabling public disclosure of the invention. In most countries _____ rights fall under civil law and the _____ holder needs to sue someone infringing the _____ in order to enforce his or her rights. In some industries _____ s are an essential form of competitive advantage; in others they are irrelevant.

Exam Probability: **Medium**

4. *Answer choices:*

(see index for correct answer)

- a. Competition Commission
- b. Chamberlinian monopolistic competition
- c. Rate-of-return regulation
- d. Patent portfolio

:: Investment ::

_____ , and investment appraisal, is the planning process used to determine whether an organization's long term investments such as new machinery, replacement of machinery, new plants, new products, and research development projects are worth the funding of cash through the firm's capitalization structure . It is the process of allocating resources for major capital, or investment, expenditures. One of the primary goals of _____ investments is to increase the value of the firm to the shareholders.

Exam Probability: **Medium**

5. *Answer choices:*

(see index for correct answer)

- a. The Investment Answer
- b. Global assets under management
- c. Emerging market
- d. Capital budgeting

Guidance: level 1

:: Debt ::

A _____ is a monetary amount owed to a creditor that is unlikely to be paid and, or which the creditor is not willing to take action to collect for various reasons, often due to the debtor not having the money to pay, for example due to a company going into liquidation or insolvency. There are various technical definitions of what constitutes a _____ , depending on accounting conventions, regulatory treatment and the institution provisioning. In the USA, bank loans with more than ninety days' arrears become "problem loans". Accounting sources advise that the full amount of a _____ be written off to the profit and loss account or a provision for _____ s as soon as it is foreseen.

Exam Probability: **High**

6. *Answer choices:*

(see index for correct answer)

- a. Perpetual subordinated debt
- b. Bad debt
- c. Zombie company
- d. Default trap

Guidance: level 1

:: Asset ::

_____ s, also known as tangible assets or property, plant and equipment , is a term used in accounting for assets and property that cannot easily be converted into cash. This can be compared with current assets such as cash or bank accounts, described as liquid assets. In most cases, only tangible assets are referred to as fixed. IAS 16 defines _____ s as assets whose future economic benefit is probable to flow into the entity, whose cost can be measured reliably. _____ s belong to one of 2 types:"Freehold Assets" – assets which are purchased with legal right of ownership and used,and "Leasehold Assets" – assets used by owner without legal right for a particular period of time.

Exam Probability: **Low**

7. *Answer choices:*

(see index for correct answer)

- a. Fixed asset
- b. Current asset

Guidance: level 1

:: Stock market ::

A share price is the price of a single share of a number of saleable stocks of a company, derivative or other financial asset.In layman's terms, the _____ is the highest amount someone is willing to pay for the stock, or the lowest amount that it can be bought for.

Exam Probability: **High**

8. *Answer choices:*

(see index for correct answer)

- a. China Concepts Stock
- b. Public offering without listing
- c. Wash trade
- d. Stock price

Guidance: level 1

:: Materials ::

A _____ , also known as a feedstock, unprocessed material, or primary commodity, is a basic material that is used to produce goods, finished products, energy, or intermediate materials which are feedstock for future finished products. As feedstock, the term connotes these materials are bottleneck assets and are highly important with regard to producing other products. An example of this is crude oil, which is a _____ and a feedstock used in the production of industrial chemicals, fuels, plastics, and pharmaceutical goods; lumber is a _____ used to produce a variety of products including all types of furniture. The term "_____" denotes materials in minimally processed or unprocessed in states; e.g., raw latex, crude oil, cotton, coal, raw biomass, iron ore, air, logs, or water i.e. "...any product of agriculture, forestry, fishing and any other mineral that is in its natural form or which has undergone the transformation required to prepare it for internationally marketing in substantial volumes."

Exam Probability: **Low**

9. *Answer choices:*

(see index for correct answer)

- a. Cellulose fiber
- b. Exotic material
- c. Solid surface
- d. Raw material

Guidance: level 1

:: Financial ratios ::

The _____ or dividend-price ratio of a share is the dividend per share, divided by the price per share. It is also a company's total annual dividend payments divided by its market capitalization, assuming the number of shares is constant. It is often expressed as a percentage.

Exam Probability: **Low**

10. *Answer choices:*

(see index for correct answer)

- a. Quick ratio
- b. Dividend yield
- c. Average accounting return
- d. Calmar ratio

Guidance: level 1

The _____ of a function of a real variable measures the sensitivity to change of the function value with respect to a change in its argument . _____ s are a fundamental tool of calculus. For example, the _____ of the position of a moving object with respect to time is the object's velocity: this measures how quickly the position of the object changes when time advances.

Exam Probability: **Low**

11. *Answer choices:*

(see index for correct answer)

- a. Sarbanes-Oxley act of 2002
- b. cultural
- c. corporate values
- d. Derivative

Guidance: level 1

:: Hazard analysis ::

Broadly speaking, a _____ is the combined effort of 1. identifying and analyzing potential events that may negatively impact individuals, assets, and/or the environment ; and 2. making judgments "on the tolerability of the risk on the basis of a risk analysis" while considering influencing factors . Put in simpler terms, a _____ analyzes what can go wrong, how likely it is to happen, what the potential consequences are, and how tolerable the identified risk is. As part of this process, the resulting determination of risk may be expressed in a quantitative or qualitative fashion. The _____ is an inherent part of an overall risk management strategy, which attempts to, after a _____ , "introduce control measures to eliminate or reduce" any potential risk-related consequences.

Exam Probability: **High**

12. *Answer choices:*

(see index for correct answer)

- a. Hazardous Materials Identification System
- b. Swiss cheese model
- c. Risk assessment

Guidance: level 1

:: ::

_____ is the study and management of exchange relationships. _____ is the business process of creating relationships with and satisfying customers. With its focus on the customer, _____ is one of the premier components of business management.

13. *Answer choices:*

(see index for correct answer)

- a. Marketing
- b. personal values
- c. cultural
- d. similarity-attraction theory

Guidance: level 1

:: Debt ::

_____ , in finance and economics, is payment from a borrower or deposit-taking financial institution to a lender or depositor of an amount above repayment of the principal sum , at a particular rate. It is distinct from a fee which the borrower may pay the lender or some third party. It is also distinct from dividend which is paid by a company to its shareholders from its profit or reserve, but not at a particular rate decided beforehand, rather on a pro rata basis as a share in the reward gained by risk taking entrepreneurs when the revenue earned exceeds the total costs.

Exam Probability: **High**

14. *Answer choices:*

(see index for correct answer)

- a. Interest
- b. Debt
- c. Debtors Anonymous
- d. Charge-off

Guidance: level 1

:: Options (finance) ::

In finance, a put or _____ is a stock market device which gives the owner the right, but not the obligation, to sell an asset , at a specified price , by a predetermined date to a given party . The purchase of a _____ is interpreted as a negative sentiment about the future value of theunderlying stock. The term "put" comes from the fact that the owner has the right to "put up for sale" the stock or index.

Exam Probability: **Low**

15. *Answer choices:*

(see index for correct answer)

- a. Chicago Options Associates
- b. Compound option
- c. Put option
- d. Call option

Guidance: level 1

_____ is the quantity of three-dimensional space enclosed by a closed surface, for example, the space that a substance or shape occupies or contains. _____ is often quantified numerically using the SI derived unit, the cubic metre. The _____ of a container is generally understood to be the capacity of the container; i. e., the amount of fluid that the container could hold, rather than the amount of space the container itself displaces. Three dimensional mathematical shapes are also assigned _____ s. _____ s of some simple shapes, such as regular, straight-edged, and circular shapes can be easily calculated using arithmetic formulas. _____ s of complicated shapes can be calculated with integral calculus if a formula exists for the shape's boundary. One-dimensional figures and two-dimensional shapes are assigned zero _____ in the three-dimensional space.

Exam Probability: **High**

16. *Answer choices:*

(see index for correct answer)

- a. open system
- b. co-culture
- c. hierarchical
- d. Volume

Guidance: level 1

From an accounting perspective, _____ is crucial because _____ and _____ taxes considerably affect the net income of most companies and because they are subject to laws and regulations .

Exam Probability: **Low**

17. *Answer choices:*

(see index for correct answer)

- a. Payroll
- b. imperative
- c. similarity-attraction theory
- d. hierarchical

Guidance: level 1

:: Human resource management ::

_____ is the corporate management term for the act of reorganizing the legal, ownership, operational, or other structures of a company for the purpose of making it more profitable, or better organized for its present needs. Other reasons for _____ include a change of ownership or ownership structure, demerger, or a response to a crisis or major change in the business such as bankruptcy, repositioning, or buyout. _____ may also be described as corporate _____ , debt _____ and financial _____ .

Exam Probability: **Medium**

18. *Answer choices:*

(see index for correct answer)

- a. Restructuring
- b. Senior management
- c. Simultaneous recruiting of new graduates
- d. Workforce planning

Guidance: level 1

:: Generally Accepted Accounting Principles ::

_____ is the accounting classification of an account. It is part of double-entry book-keeping technique.

Exam Probability: **High**

19. *Answer choices:*

(see index for correct answer)

- a. Financial position of the United States
- b. Normal balance
- c. Depreciation
- d. Contributed capital

Guidance: level 1

:: Business law ::

_____ is where a person's financial liability is limited to a fixed sum, most commonly the value of a person's investment in a company or partnership. If a company with _____ is sued, then the claimants are suing the company, not its owners or investors. A shareholder in a limited company is not personally liable for any of the debts of the company, other than for the amount already invested in the company and for any unpaid amount on the shares in the company, if any. The same is true for the members of a _____ partnership and the limited partners in a limited partnership. By contrast, sole proprietors and partners in general partnerships are each liable for all the debts of the business .

Exam Probability: **Medium**

20. *Answer choices:*

(see index for correct answer)

- a. Duty of fair representation
- b. Ease of doing business index
- c. Limited liability
- d. Bulk sale

Guidance: level 1

:: Accounting terminology ::

_____ are liabilities that reflect expenses that have not yet been paid or logged under accounts payable during an accounting period; in other words, a company's obligation to pay for goods and services that have been provided for which invoices have not yet been received. Examples would include accrued wages payable, accrued sales tax payable, and accrued rent payable.

Exam Probability: **Medium**

21. *Answer choices:*

(see index for correct answer)

- a. Double-entry accounting
- b. Accrued liabilities
- c. Accounts receivable
- d. Internal auditing

Guidance: level 1

:: Management accounting ::

In finance, the _____ or net present worth applies to a series of cash flows occurring at different times. The present value of a cash flow depends on the interval of time between now and the cash flow. It also depends on the discount rate. NPV accounts for the time value of money. It provides a method for evaluating and comparing capital projects or financial products with cash flows spread over time, as in loans, investments, payouts from insurance contracts plus many other applications.

22. *Answer choices:*

(see index for correct answer)

- a. Variable cost
- b. Fixed assets management
- c. Net present value
- d. Customer profitability

Guidance: level 1

:: Cash flow ::

In corporate finance, _____ or _____ to firm is a way of looking at a business's cash flow to see what is available for distribution among all the securities holders of a corporate entity. This may be useful to parties such as equity holders, debt holders, preferred stock holders, and convertible security holders when they want to see how much cash can be extracted from a company without causing issues to its operations.

23. *Answer choices:*

(see index for correct answer)

- a. Free cash flow
- b. Invoice discounting

- c. Cash flow loan
- d. Cash flow forecasting

Guidance: level 1

:: Fixed income market ::

The _____ is a financial market where participants can issue new debt, known as the primary market, or buy and sell debt securities, known as the secondary market. This is usually in the form of bonds, but it may include notes, bills, and so on.

Exam Probability: **High**

24. *Answer choices:*

(see index for correct answer)

- a. Bond market
- b. Bond Exchange of South Africa
- c. Basis point
- d. Pool factor

Guidance: level 1

:: ::

In marketing, a _____ is a ticket or document that can be redeemed for a financial discount or rebate when purchasing a product.

Exam Probability: **High**

25. *Answer choices:*

(see index for correct answer)

- a. interpersonal communication
- b. cultural
- c. Coupon
- d. levels of analysis

Guidance: level 1

:: Generally Accepted Accounting Principles ::

In accounting, an economic item's _____ is the original nominal monetary value of that item. _____ accounting involves reporting assets and liabilities at their _____ s, which are not updated for changes in the items' values. Consequently, the amounts reported for these balance sheet items often differ from their current economic or market values.

Exam Probability: **Low**

26. *Answer choices:*

(see index for correct answer)

- a. Depreciation
- b. Deferred income
- c. net realisable value
- d. Reserve

Guidance: level 1

:: Financial economics ::

_____ , Inc. is an independent investment research and financial publishing firm based in New York City, New York, United States, founded in 1931 by Arnold Bernhard. _____ is best known for publishing The _____ Investment Survey, a stock analysis newsletter that is among the most highly regarded and widely used independent investment research resources in global investment and trading markets, tracking approximately 1,700 publicly traded stocks in over 99 industries.

Exam Probability: **Low**

27. *Answer choices:*

(see index for correct answer)

- a. Efficient-market hypothesis
- b. Consumer leverage ratio
- c. Value Line
- d. Journal of Financial and Quantitative Analysis

:: Marketing ::

A _____ is the quantity of payment or compensation given by one party to another in return for one unit of goods or services.. A _____ is influenced by both production costs and demand for the product. A _____ may be determined by a monopolist or may be imposed on the firm by market conditions.

Exam Probability: **Medium**

28. *Answer choices:*

(see index for correct answer)

- a. Price
- b. Bass diffusion model
- c. Law of primacy in persuasion
- d. Pitching engine

:: Management accounting ::

_____ , or dollar contribution per unit, is the selling price per unit minus the variable cost per unit. "Contribution" represents the portion of sales revenue that is not consumed by variable costs and so contributes to the coverage of fixed costs. This concept is one of the key building blocks of break-even analysis.

Exam Probability: Low

29. *Answer choices:*

(see index for correct answer)

- a. Contribution margin
- b. Management accounting in supply chains
- c. Cash and cash equivalents
- d. Direct material price variance

Guidance: level 1

:: Project management ::

Some scenarios associate "this kind of planning" with learning "life skills". _____ s are necessary, or at least useful, in situations where individuals need to know what time they must be at a specific location to receive a specific service, and where people need to accomplish a set of goals within a set time period.

Exam Probability: High

30. *Answer choices:*

(see index for correct answer)

- a. Schedule
- b. TargetProcess
- c. The Transformation Project
- d. Research program

Guidance: level 1

:: ::

An _____ is a contingent motivator. Traditional _____ s are extrinsic motivators which reward actions to yield a desired outcome. The effectiveness of traditional _____ s has changed as the needs of Western society have evolved. While the traditional _____ model is effective when there is a defined procedure and goal for a task, Western society started to require a higher volume of critical thinkers, so the traditional model became less effective. Institutions are now following a trend in implementing strategies that rely on intrinsic motivations rather than the extrinsic motivations that the traditional _____ s foster.

Exam Probability: **High**

31. *Answer choices:*

(see index for correct answer)

- a. Incentive
- b. similarity-attraction theory

- c. hierarchical perspective
- d. corporate values

Guidance: level 1

:: Loans ::

In corporate finance, a _____ is a medium- to long-term debt instrument used by large companies to borrow money, at a fixed rate of interest. The legal term " _____ " originally referred to a document that either creates a debt or acknowledges it, but in some countries the term is now used interchangeably with bond, loan stock or note. A _____ is thus like a certificate of loan or a loan bond evidencing the fact that the company is liable to pay a specified amount with interest and although the money raised by the _____ s becomes a part of the company's capital structure, it does not become share capital. Senior _____ s get paid before subordinate _____ s, and there are varying rates of risk and payoff for these categories.

Exam Probability: **Medium**

32. *Answer choices:*
(see index for correct answer)

- a. Asset-based loan
- b. SGE Loans
- c. PLUS Loan
- d. International lender of last resort

Guidance: level 1

:: Derivatives (finance) ::

_____ is any bodily activity that enhances or maintains physical fitness and overall health and wellness. It is performed for various reasons, to aid growth and improve strength, preventing aging, developing muscles and the cardiovascular system, honing athletic skills, weight loss or maintenance, improving health and also for enjoyment. Many individuals choose to _____ outdoors where they can congregate in groups, socialize, and enhance well-being.

Exam Probability: **Medium**

33. *Answer choices:*

(see index for correct answer)

- a. Non-deliverable forward
- b. Vertical spread
- c. Exercise
- d. Rolling turbo

Guidance: level 1

:: Notes (finance) ::

A _____ , sometimes referred to as a note payable, is a legal instrument , in which one party promises in writing to pay a determinate sum of money to the other , either at a fixed or determinable future time or on demand of the payee, under specific terms.

Exam Probability: **High**

34. *Answer choices:*

(see index for correct answer)

- a. Interest Bearing Note
- b. Large-sized note
- c. Promissory note
- d. Surplus note

Guidance: level 1

:: Derivatives (finance) ::

In finance, a _____ or simply a forward is a non-standardized contract between two parties to buy or to sell an asset at a specified future time at a price agreed upon today, making it a type of derivative instrument. The party agreeing to buy the underlying asset in the future assumes a long position, and the party agreeing to sell the asset in the future assumes a short position. The price agreed upon is called the delivery price, which is equal to the forward price at the time the contract is entered into.

Exam Probability: **Low**

35. *Answer choices:*

(see index for correct answer)

- a. Derivative and Commodity Exchange Nepal Ltd.
- b. Mexican Derivatives Exchange
- c. Single-stock
- d. Forward contract

Guidance: level 1

:: Real estate ::

Amortisation is paying off an amount owed over time by making planned, incremental payments of principal and interest. To amortise a loan means "to kill it off". In accounting, amortisation refers to charging or writing off an intangible asset`s cost as an operational expense over its estimated useful life to reduce a company`s taxable income.

Exam Probability: **Low**

36. *Answer choices:*

(see index for correct answer)

- a. The Registry
- b. Amortization
- c. Landed nobility
- d. County surveyor

:: Accounting systems ::

In bookkeeping, a _____ statement is a process that explains the difference on a specified date between the bank balance shown in an organization's bank statement, as supplied by the bank and the corresponding amount shown in the organization's own accounting records.

Exam Probability: **Low**

37. *Answer choices:*

(see index for correct answer)

- a. Bank reconciliation
- b. Single-entry bookkeeping
- c. Waste book
- d. Controlling account

:: Financial markets ::

A _____ is a market in which people trade financial securities and derivatives such as futures and options at low transaction costs. Securities include stocks and bonds, and precious metals.

38. *Answer choices:*

- a. Financial market
- b. Noise trader
- c. Arbitrage
- d. Market impact cost

Guidance: level 1

:: bad_topic ::

_____ refers to systematic approach to the governance and realization of value from the things that a group or entity is responsible for, over their whole life cycles. It may apply both to tangible assets and to intangible assets . _____ is a systematic process of developing, operating, maintaining, upgrading, and disposing of assets in the most cost-effective manner .

39. *Answer choices:*

(see index for correct answer)

- a. Wendy Levinson
- b. return period
- c. Liquidation preference
- d. Manuscript format

Guidance: level 1

:: Generally Accepted Accounting Principles ::

Financial statements prepared and presented by a company typically follow an external standard that specifically guides their preparation. These standards vary across the globe and are typically overseen by some combination of the private accounting profession in that specific nation and the various government regulators. Variations across countries may be considerable, making cross-country evaluation of financial data challenging.

Exam Probability: **Low**

40. *Answer choices:*

(see index for correct answer)

- a. Reserve
- b. Generally accepted accounting principles
- c. Chinese accounting standards
- d. Closing entries

:: Subprime mortgage crisis ::

The _____ Group, Inc., is an American multinational investment bank and financial services company headquartered in New York City. It offers services in investment management, securities, asset management, prime brokerage, and securities underwriting.

Exam Probability: **Medium**

41. *Answer choices:*

(see index for correct answer)

- a. Subprime mortgage crisis solutions debate
- b. Housing and Economic Recovery Act of 2008
- c. Goldman Sachs
- d. Homeowners Affordability and Stability Plan

:: Portfolio theories ::

In finance, the _____ is a model used to determine a theoretically appropriate required rate of return of an asset, to make decisions about adding assets to a well-diversified portfolio.

Exam Probability: **Low**

42. *Answer choices:*

- a. Maslowian portfolio theory
- b. Intertemporal portfolio choice
- c. Post-modern portfolio theory
- d. Efficient frontier

Guidance: level 1

:: ::

An _____ is an area of the production, distribution, or trade, and consumption of goods and services by different agents. Understood in its broadest sense, `The _____ is defined as a social domain that emphasize the practices, discourses, and material expressions associated with the production, use, and management of resources`. Economic agents can be individuals, businesses, organizations, or governments. Economic transactions occur when two parties agree to the value or price of the transacted good or service, commonly expressed in a certain currency. However, monetary transactions only account for a small part of the economic domain.

43. *Answer choices:*

(see index for correct answer)

- a. Character
- b. corporate values
- c. information systems assessment
- d. Economy

Guidance: level 1

:: Scheduling (computing) ::

Ageing or _____ is the process of becoming older. The term refers especially to human beings, many animals, and fungi, whereas for example bacteria, perennial plants and some simple animals are potentially biologically immortal. In the broader sense, ageing can refer to single cells within an organism which have ceased dividing or to the population of a species .

44. *Answer choices:*

(see index for correct answer)

- a. Aging
- b. Kernel preemption

- c. Affinity mask
- d. Idle

Guidance: level 1

:: Business law ::

A _____ is a group of people who jointly supervise the activities of an organization, which can be either a for-profit business, nonprofit organization, or a government agency. Such a board`s powers, duties, and responsibilities are determined by government regulations and the organization`s own constitution and bylaws. These authorities may specify the number of members of the board, how they are to be chosen, and how often they are to meet.

Exam Probability: **High**

45. *Answer choices:*

(see index for correct answer)

- a. Rules of origin
- b. Fraudulent trading
- c. Board of directors
- d. General assignment

Guidance: level 1

:: Business ethics ::

In accounting and in most Schools of economic thought, _____ is a rational and unbiased estimate of the potential market price of a good, service, or asset. It takes into account such objectivity factors as.

Exam Probability: **Low**

46. *Answer choices:*

(see index for correct answer)

- a. Impact investing
- b. Corporate sustainability
- c. Moral hazard
- d. Fair value

Guidance: level 1

:: Valuation (finance) ::

_____ refers to an assessment of the viability, stability, and profitability of a business, sub-business or project.

Exam Probability: **Low**

47. *Answer choices:*

(see index for correct answer)

- a. International Valuation Standards Council
- b. Expertization
- c. Russian Society of Appraisers
- d. Pre-money valuation

Guidance: level 1

:: Income ::

_____ is a ratio between the net profit and cost of investment resulting from an investment of some resources. A high ROI means the investment's gains favorably to its cost. As a performance measure, ROI is used to evaluate the efficiency of an investment or to compare the efficiencies of several different investments. In purely economic terms, it is one way of relating profits to capital invested. _____ is a performance measure used by businesses to identify the efficiency of an investment or number of different investments.

Exam Probability: **Low**

48. *Answer choices:*

(see index for correct answer)

- a. Return on investment
- b. Per capita income
- c. IRD asset

- d. Aggregate expenditure

Guidance: level 1

:: ::

An _____ is an asset that lacks physical substance. It is defined in opposition to physical assets such as machinery and buildings. An _____ is usually very hard to evaluate. Patents, copyrights, franchises, goodwill, trademarks, and trade names. The general interpretation also includes software and other intangible computer based assets are all examples of _____ s. _____ s generally—though not necessarily—suffer from typical market failures of non-rivalry and non-excludability.

Exam Probability: **High**

49. *Answer choices:*

(see index for correct answer)

- a. empathy
- b. surface-level diversity
- c. Intangible asset
- d. co-culture

Guidance: level 1

:: Accounting terminology ::

In accounting/accountancy, _____ are journal entries usually made at the end of an accounting period to allocate income and expenditure to the period in which they actually occurred. The revenue recognition principle is the basis of making _____ that pertain to unearned and accrued revenues under accrual-basis accounting. They are sometimes called Balance Day adjustments because they are made on balance day.

Exam Probability: **Low**

50. *Answer choices:*

(see index for correct answer)

- a. Double-entry accounting
- b. Accrued liabilities
- c. Adjusting entries
- d. Accounts payable

Guidance: level 1

:: Generally Accepted Accounting Principles ::

_____ , or non-current liabilities, are liabilities that are due beyond a year or the normal operation period of the company. The normal operation period is the amount of time it takes for a company to turn inventory into cash. On a classified balance sheet, liabilities are separated between current and _____ to help users assess the company's financial standing in short-term and long-term periods. _____ give users more information about the long-term prosperity of the company, while current liabilities inform the user of debt that the company owes in the current period. On a balance sheet, accounts are listed in order of liquidity, so _____ come after current liabilities. In addition, the specific long-term liability accounts are listed on the balance sheet in order of liquidity. Therefore, an account due within eighteen months would be listed before an account due within twenty-four months. Examples of _____ are bonds payable, long-term loans, capital leases, pension liabilities, post-retirement healthcare liabilities, deferred compensation, deferred revenues, deferred income taxes, and derivative liabilities.

Exam Probability: **Medium**

51. *Answer choices:*

(see index for correct answer)

- a. Earnings before interest, taxes and depreciation
- b. Deferred income
- c. Historical cost
- d. Long-term liabilities

Guidance: level 1

:: Actuarial science ::

The _____ is the greater benefit of receiving money now rather than an identical sum later. It is founded on time preference.

Exam Probability: **High**

52. *Answer choices:*

(see index for correct answer)

- a. Expected shortfall
- b. Actuarial science
- c. Extreme value theory
- d. Replicating portfolio

Guidance: level 1

:: Generally Accepted Accounting Principles ::

The first published description of the process is found in Luca Pacioli's 1494 work Summa de arithmetica, in the section titled Particularis de Computis et Scripturis. Although he did not use the term, he essentially prescribed a technique similar to a post-closing _____ .

Exam Probability: **High**

53. *Answer choices:*

(see index for correct answer)

- a. Trial balance
- b. Long-term liabilities
- c. Operating profit
- d. Cash method of accounting

Guidance: level 1

:: ::

In business, economics or investment, market _____ is a market's feature whereby an individual or firm can quickly purchase or sell an asset without causing a drastic change in the asset's price. _____ is about how big the trade-off is between the speed of the sale and the price it can be sold for. In a liquid market, the trade-off is mild: selling quickly will not reduce the price much. In a relatively illiquid market, selling it quickly will require cutting its price by some amount.

Exam Probability: **Low**

54. *Answer choices:*
(see index for correct answer)

- a. Liquidity
- b. process perspective
- c. cultural
- d. deep-level diversity

Guidance: level 1

:: Generally Accepted Accounting Principles ::

In accounting, _____ is the income that a business have from its normal business activities, usually from the sale of goods and services to customers. _____ is also referred to as sales or turnover.Some companies receive _____ from interest, royalties, or other fees. _____ may refer to business income in general, or it may refer to the amount, in a monetary unit, earned during a period of time, as in "Last year, Company X had _____ of $42 million". Profits or net income generally imply total _____ minus total expenses in a given period. In accounting, in the balance statement it is a subsection of the Equity section and _____ increases equity, it is often referred to as the "top line" due to its position on the income statement at the very top. This is to be contrasted with the "bottom line" which denotes net income .

Exam Probability: **High**

55. *Answer choices:*

(see index for correct answer)

- a. Revenue
- b. Gross income
- c. Generally Accepted Accounting Practice
- d. Deferral

Guidance: level 1

:: Debt ::

A _____ is a party that has a claim on the services of a second party. It is a person or institution to whom money is owed. The first party, in general, has provided some property or service to the second party under the assumption that the second party will return an equivalent property and service. The second party is frequently called a debtor or borrower. The first party is called the _____ , which is the lender of property, service, or money.

Exam Probability: **Low**

56. *Answer choices:*

(see index for correct answer)

- a. Creditor
- b. Legal liability
- c. Teacher Loan Forgiveness
- d. Debt adjustment

Guidance: level 1

:: Financial accounting ::

_____ in accounting is the process of treating investments in associate companies. Equity accounting is usually applied where an investor entity holds 20–50% of the voting stock of the associate company. The investor records such investments as an asset on its balance sheet. The investor`s proportional share of the associate company`s net income increases the investment , and proportional payments of dividends decrease it. In the investor's income statement, the proportional share of the investor's net income or net loss is reported as a single-line item.

Exam Probability: **Low**

57. *Answer choices:*

(see index for correct answer)

- a. Accelerated depreciation
- b. Asset swap
- c. Authorised capital
- d. Equity method

Guidance: level 1

:: Costs ::

In economics, _____ is the total economic cost of production and is made up of variable cost, which varies according to the quantity of a good produced and includes inputs such as labour and raw materials, plus fixed cost, which is independent of the quantity of a good produced and includes inputs that cannot be varied in the short term: fixed costs such as buildings and machinery, including sunk costs if any. Since cost is measured per unit of time, it is a flow variable.

Exam Probability: **Low**

58. *Answer choices:*

(see index for correct answer)

- a. Total cost
- b. Road Logistics Costing in South Africa
- c. Average variable cost
- d. Repugnancy costs

Guidance: level 1

:: Stock market ::

_____ is a form of stock which may have any combination of features not possessed by common stock including properties of both an equity and a debt instrument, and is generally considered a hybrid instrument. _____ s are senior to common stock, but subordinate to bonds in terms of claim and may have priority over common stock in the payment of dividends and upon liquidation. Terms of the _____ are described in the issuing company's articles of association or articles of incorporation.

59. *Answer choices:*

(see index for correct answer)

- a. Piqqem
- b. Preferred stock
- c. American depositary receipt
- d. Immediate or cancel

Guidance: level 1

Human resource management

Human resource (HR) management is the strategic approach to the effective management of organization workers so that they help the business gain a competitive advantage. It is designed to maximize employee performance in service of an employer's strategic objectives. HR is primarily concerned with the management of people within organizations, focusing on policies and on systems. HR departments are responsible for overseeing employee-benefits design, employee recruitment, training and development, performance appraisal, and rewarding (e.g., managing pay and benefit systems). HR also concerns itself with organizational change and industrial relations, that is, the balancing of organizational practices with requirements arising from collective bargaining and from governmental laws.

:: Recruitment ::

_____ is a specialized recruitment service which organizations pay to seek out and recruit highly qualified candidates for senior-level and executive jobs . Headhunters may also seek out and recruit other highly specialized and/or skilled positions in organizations for which there is strong competition in the job market for the top talent, such as senior data analysts or computer programmers. The method usually involves commissioning a third-party organization, typically an _____ firm, but possibly a standalone consultant or consulting firm, to research the availability of suitable qualified candidates working for competitors or related businesses or organizations. Having identified a shortlist of qualified candidates who match the client's requirements, the _____ firm may act as an intermediary to contact the individual and see if they might be interested in moving to a new employer. The _____ firm may also carry out initial screening of the candidate, negotiations on remuneration and benefits, and preparing the employment contract. In some markets there has been a move towards using _____ for lower positions driven by the fact that there are less candidates for some positions even on lower levels than executive.

Exam Probability: **Low**

1. *Answer choices:*

(see index for correct answer)

- a. Job fraud
- b. Internet recruiting
- c. Disclosure Scotland
- d. Background check

Guidance: level 1

:: ::

A _____ , medical practitioner, medical doctor, or simply doctor, is a professional who practises medicine, which is concerned with promoting, maintaining, or restoring health through the study, diagnosis, prognosis and treatment of disease, injury, and other physical and mental impairments.

_____ s may focus their practice on certain disease categories, types of patients, and methods of treatment—known as specialities—or they may assume responsibility for the provision of continuing and comprehensive medical care to individuals, families, and communities—known as general practice. Medical practice properly requires both a detailed knowledge of the academic disciplines, such as anatomy and physiology, underlying diseases and their treatment—the science of medicine—and also a decent competence in its applied practice—the art or craft of medicine.

Exam Probability: **Low**

2. *Answer choices:*

(see index for correct answer)

- a. levels of analysis
- b. functional perspective
- c. deep-level diversity
- d. interpersonal communication

Guidance: level 1

:: Systems thinking ::

Systems theory is the interdisciplinary study of systems. A system is a cohesive conglomeration of interrelated and interdependent parts that is either natural or man-made. Every system is delineated by its spatial and temporal boundaries, surrounded and influenced by its environment, described by its structure and purpose or nature and expressed in its functioning. In terms of its effects, a system can be more than the sum of its parts if it expresses synergy or emergent behavior. Changing one part of the system usually affects other parts and the whole system, with predictable patterns of behavior. For systems that are self-learning and self-adapting, the positive growth and adaptation depend upon how well the system is adjusted with its environment. Some systems function mainly to support other systems by aiding in the maintenance of the other system to prevent failure. The goal of systems theory is systematically discovering a system's dynamics, constraints, conditions and elucidating principles that can be discerned and applied to systems at every level of nesting, and in every field for achieving optimized equifinality.

Exam Probability: **Medium**

3. *Answer choices:*

(see index for correct answer)

- a. World Futures Studies Federation
- b. Ted Coombs
- c. Future history
- d. Interdependence

Guidance: level 1

:: ::

A _____ is a technical analysis of a biological specimen, for example urine, hair, blood, breath, sweat, and/or oral fluid/saliva—to determine the presence or absence of specified parent drugs or their metabolites. Major applications of _____ ing include detection of the presence of performance enhancing steroids in sport, employers and parole/probation officers screening for drugs prohibited by law and police officers testing for the presence and concentration of alcohol in the blood commonly referred to as BAC . BAC tests are typically administered via a breathalyzer while urinalysis is used for the vast majority of _____ ing in sports and the workplace. Numerous other methods with varying degrees of accuracy, sensitivity , and detection periods exist.

Exam Probability: **Low**

4. *Answer choices:*

(see index for correct answer)

- a. levels of analysis
- b. surface-level diversity
- c. empathy
- d. Drug test

Guidance: level 1

:: Sociological theories ::

A _____ is a systematic process for determining and addressing needs, or "gaps" between current conditions and desired conditions or "wants". The discrepancy between the current condition and wanted condition must be measured to appropriately identify the need. The need can be a desire to improve current performance or to correct a deficiency.

Exam Probability: **Low**

5. *Answer choices:*

(see index for correct answer)

- a. comfort zone
- b. social constructionism
- c. Needs assessment
- d. Compliance gaining

Guidance: level 1

:: Human resource management ::

Frederick Herzberg, an American psychologist, originally developed the concept of ` _____ ` in 1968, in an article that he published on pioneering studies at A T&T. The concept stemmed from Herzberg's motivator-hygiene theory, which is based on the premise that job attitude is a construct of two independent factors, namely job satisfaction and job dissatisfaction. Job satisfaction encompasses intrinsic factors that arise from the work itself, including achievement and advancement; whilst job dissatisfaction stems from factors external to the actual work, including company policy and the quality of supervision.

6. *Answer choices:*

- a. Talascend
- b. Income bracket
- c. Service record
- d. Job enrichment

Guidance: level 1

:: Validity (statistics) ::

In psychometrics, criterion or concrete validity is the extent to which a measure is related to an outcome. _____ is often divided into concurrent and predictive validity. Concurrent validity refers to a comparison between the measure in question and an outcome assessed at the same time. In Standards for Educational & Psychological Tests, it states, "concurrent validity reflects only the status quo at a particular time." Predictive validity, on the other hand, compares the measure in question with an outcome assessed at a later time. Although concurrent and predictive validity are similar, it is cautioned to keep the terms and findings separated. "Concurrent validity should not be used as a substitute for predictive validity without an appropriate supporting rationale."

Exam Probability: **Medium**

7. *Answer choices:*

(see index for correct answer)

- a. Validation
- b. Statistical conclusion
- c. Ecological validity
- d. Criterion validity

Guidance: level 1

:: Trade unions in the United States ::

The _____ is a labor union in the United States and Canada. Formed in 1903 by the merger of The Team Drivers International Union and The Teamsters National Union, the union now represents a diverse membership of blue-collar and professional workers in both the public and private sectors. The union had approximately 1.3 million members in 2013. Formerly known as the _____, Chauffeurs, Warehousemen and Helpers of America, the IBT is a member of the Change to Win Federation and Canadian Labour Congress.

Exam Probability: **High**

8. *Answer choices:*
(see index for correct answer)

- a. International Union of Bricklayers and Allied Craftworkers
- b. Association of Professional Flight Attendants
- c. Tennessee Nurses Association
- d. International Brotherhood of Teamsters

:: Management ::

_____ is a technique used by some employers to rotate their employees' assigned jobs throughout their employment. Employers practice this technique for a number of reasons. It was designed to promote flexibility of employees and to keep employees interested into staying with the company/organization which employs them. There is also research that shows how _____ s help relieve the stress of employees who work in a job that requires manual labor.

Exam Probability: **Medium**

9. *Answer choices:*

(see index for correct answer)

- a. Risk appetite
- b. Communities of innovation
- c. Event chain diagram
- d. Resource breakdown structure

:: Human resource management ::

_____ is athletic training in sports other than the athlete's usual sport. The goal is improving overall performance. It takes advantage of the particular effectiveness of one training method to negate the shortcomings of another.

10. *Answer choices:*

(see index for correct answer)

- a. Applicant tracking system
- b. Expense management
- c. Cross-training
- d. Public service motivation

Guidance: level 1

:: Employment compensation ::

Employee stock ownership, or employee share ownership, is an ownership interest in a company held by the company's workforce. The ownership interest may be facilitated by the company as part of employees' remuneration or incentive compensation for work performed, or the company itself may be employee owned.

11. *Answer choices:*

(see index for correct answer)

- a. Basic Income Earth Network
- b. Golden boot compensation
- c. Cost to company
- d. Agency Workers Regulations 2010

Guidance: level 1

:: Management education ::

_____ is the implementation of government policy and also an academic discipline that studies this implementation and prepares civil servants for working in the public service. As a "field of inquiry with a diverse scope" whose fundamental goal is to "advance management and policies so that government can function". Some of the various definitions which have been offered for the term are: "the management of public programs"; the "translation of politics into the reality that citizens see every day"; and "the study of government decision making, the analysis of the policies themselves, the various inputs that have produced them, and the inputs necessary to produce alternative policies."

Exam Probability: **Medium**

12. *Answer choices:*

(see index for correct answer)

- a. Public administration

- b. Institute of Computer and Management Sciences
- c. Peter F. Drucker and Masatoshi Ito Graduate School of Management
- d. Doctor of Business Administration

:: Human resource management ::

_____ are the people who make up the workforce of an organization, business sector, or economy. "Human capital" is sometimes used synonymously with " _____ ", although human capital typically refers to a narrower effect . Likewise, other terms sometimes used include manpower, talent, labor, personnel, or simply people.

Exam Probability: **Medium**

13. *Answer choices:*

(see index for correct answer)

- a. Technical performance measure
- b. Workplace mentoring
- c. Job description management
- d. Human resources

Educational technology is "the study and ethical practice of facilitating learning and improving performance by creating, using, and managing appropriate technological processes and resources".

Exam Probability: **High**

14. *Answer choices:*

(see index for correct answer)

- a. personal values
- b. similarity-attraction theory
- c. co-culture
- d. E-learning

Guidance: level 1

:: Employment ::

Onboarding, also known as _____ , is management jargon first created in 1988 that refers to the mechanism through which new employees acquire the necessary knowledge, skills, and behaviors in order to become effective organizational members and insiders.

Exam Probability: **High**

15. *Answer choices:*

(see index for correct answer)

- a. Social VAT
- b. Organizational socialization
- c. Cyberloafing
- d. Job Services Australia

Guidance: level 1

:: Training ::

_____ is the process of ensuring compliance with laws, regulations, rules, standards, or social norms. By enforcing laws and regulations, governments attempt to effectuate successful implementation of policies.

Exam Probability: **High**

16. *Answer choices:*

(see index for correct answer)

- a. Confidence-based learning
- b. Strength and conditioning coach
- c. Jeff Phillips
- d. Enforcement

Guidance: level 1

:: Human resource management ::

_____ involves improving the effectiveness of organizations and the individuals and teams within them. Training may be viewed as related to immediate changes in organizational effectiveness via organized instruction, while development is related to the progress of longer-term organizational and employee goals. While _____ technically have differing definitions, the two are oftentimes used interchangeably and/or together. _____ has historically been a topic within applied psychology but has within the last two decades become closely associated with human resources management, talent management, human resources development, instructional design, human factors, and knowledge management.

Exam Probability: **High**

17. *Answer choices:*

(see index for correct answer)

- a. Human resource accounting
- b. Training and development
- c. Managerial assessment of proficiency
- d. Contractor management

Guidance: level 1

:: ::

_____ is a form of development in which a person called a coach supports a learner or client in achieving a specific personal or professional goal by providing training and guidance. The learner is sometimes called a coachee. Occasionally, _____ may mean an informal relationship between two people, of whom one has more experience and expertise than the other and offers advice and guidance as the latter learns; but _____ differs from mentoring in focusing on specific tasks or objectives, as opposed to more general goals or overall development.

Exam Probability: **High**

18. *Answer choices:*

(see index for correct answer)

- a. Coaching
- b. deep-level diversity
- c. levels of analysis
- d. Character

Guidance: level 1

:: Persuasion techniques ::

_____ is a psychological technique in which an individual attempts to influence another person by becoming more likeable to their target. This term was coined by social psychologist Edward E. Jones, who further defined _____ as "a class of strategic behaviors illicitly designed to influence a particular other person concerning the attractiveness of one's personal qualities." _____ research has identified some specific tactics of employing _____ .

Exam Probability: **Medium**

19. *Answer choices:*

(see index for correct answer)

- a. Compliance
- b. Crocodile tears
- c. Ingratiation
- d. Modes of persuasion

Guidance: level 1

:: Organizational theory ::

Decentralisation is the process by which the activities of an organization, particularly those regarding planning and decision making, are distributed or delegated away from a central, authoritative location or group. Concepts of _____ have been applied to group dynamics and management science in private businesses and organizations, political science, law and public administration, economics, money and technology.

20. *Answer choices:*

(see index for correct answer)

- a. Swift trust
- b. Star Roles Model
- c. Interaction value analysis
- d. Institutional complementarity

Guidance: level 1

:: Business ethics cases ::

_____ , 477 U.S. 57 , is a US labor law case, where the United States Supreme Court, in a 9-0 decision, recognized sexual harassment as a violation of Title VII of the Civil Rights Act of 1964. The case was the first of its kind to reach the Supreme Court and would redefine sexual harassment in the workplace.

Exam Probability: **High**

21. *Answer choices:*

(see index for correct answer)

- a. Jenson v. Eveleth Taconite Co.
- b. Meritor Savings Bank v. Vinson

- c. Bank of Credit and Commerce International
- d. Firestone and Ford tire controversy

Guidance: level 1

:: Stochastic processes ::

_____ in its modern meaning is a "new idea, creative thoughts, new imaginations in form of device or method". _____ is often also viewed as the application of better solutions that meet new requirements, unarticulated needs, or existing market needs. Such _____ takes place through the provision of more-effective products, processes, services, technologies, or business models that are made available to markets, governments and society. An _____ is something original and more effective and, as a consequence, new, that "breaks into" the market or society. _____ is related to, but not the same as, invention, as _____ is more apt to involve the practical implementation of an invention to make a meaningful impact in the market or society, and not all _____s require an invention. _____ often manifests itself via the engineering process, when the problem being solved is of a technical or scientific nature. The opposite of _____ is exnovation.

Exam Probability: **Low**

22. *Answer choices:*

(see index for correct answer)

- a. Loss network
- b. Branching random walk
- c. Poisson point process
- d. Reflected Brownian motion

:: ::

An _____ is a person temporarily or permanently residing in a country other than their native country. In common usage, the term often refers to professionals, skilled workers, or artists taking positions outside their home country, either independently or sent abroad by their employers, who can be companies, universities, governments, or non-governmental organisations. Effectively migrant workers, they usually earn more than they would at home, and less than local employees. However, the term ` _____ ` is also used for retirees and others who have chosen to live outside their native country. Historically, it has also referred to exiles.

Exam Probability: **Medium**

23. *Answer choices:*

(see index for correct answer)

- a. levels of analysis
- b. deep-level diversity
- c. Expatriate
- d. surface-level diversity

:: ::

_____ is the administration of an organization, whether it is a business, a not-for-profit organization, or government body. _____ includes the activities of setting the strategy of an organization and coordinating the efforts of its employees to accomplish its objectives through the application of available resources, such as financial, natural, technological, and human resources. The term "_____" may also refer to those people who manage an organization.

Exam Probability: **Medium**

24. *Answer choices:*

(see index for correct answer)

- a. Management
- b. personal values
- c. similarity-attraction theory
- d. deep-level diversity

Guidance: level 1

:: Labour relations ::

_____ is a field of study that can have different meanings depending on the context in which it is used. In an international context, it is a subfield of labor history that studies the human relations with regard to work – in its broadest sense – and how this connects to questions of social inequality. It explicitly encompasses unregulated, historical, and non-Western forms of labor. Here, _____ define "for or with whom one works and under what rules. These rules determine the type of work, type and amount of remuneration, working hours, degrees of physical and psychological strain, as well as the degree of freedom and autonomy associated with the work."

Exam Probability: **High**

25. *Answer choices:*

(see index for correct answer)

- a. Disciplinary counseling
- b. Employee voice
- c. Labor relations
- d. Picketing

Guidance: level 1

:: ::

_____ is an enduring pattern of romantic or sexual attraction to persons of the opposite sex or gender, the same sex or gender, or to both sexes or more than one gender. These attractions are generally subsumed under heterosexuality, homosexuality, and bisexuality, while asexuality is sometimes identified as the fourth category.

26. *Answer choices:*

(see index for correct answer)

- a. open system
- b. Sexual orientation
- c. corporate values
- d. personal values

Guidance: level 1

:: Human resource management ::

_____ is the strategic approach to the effective management of people in an organization so that they help the business to gain a competitive advantage. It is designed to maximize employee performance in service of an employer's strategic objectives. HR is primarily concerned with the management of people within organizations, focusing on policies and on systems. HR departments are responsible for overseeing employee-benefits design, employee recruitment, training and development, performance appraisal, and Reward management . HR also concerns itself with organizational change and industrial relations, that is, the balancing of organizational practices with requirements arising from collective bargaining and from governmental laws.

Exam Probability: **Medium**

27. *Answer choices:*

(see index for correct answer)

- a. Job performance
- b. Induction programme
- c. Turnover
- d. Flextime

Guidance: level 1

:: Production and manufacturing ::

_____ is a set of techniques and tools for process improvement. Though as a shortened form it may be found written as 6S, it should not be confused with the methodology known as 6S .

Exam Probability: **High**

28. *Answer choices:*

(see index for correct answer)

- a. Miniaturization
- b. Workmanship
- c. Six Sigma
- d. Economic dispatch

Guidance: level 1

:: Financial terminology ::

_____ is the cost of maintaining a certain standard of living. Changes in the _____ over time are often operationalized in a cost-of-living index. _____ calculations are also used to compare the cost of maintaining a certain standard of living in different geographic areas. Differences in _____ between locations can also be measured in terms of purchasing power parity rates.

Exam Probability: **High**

29. *Answer choices:*

(see index for correct answer)

- a. Intermarket Spread
- b. Cost of living
- c. Prosperity consciousness
- d. Earnings test

Guidance: level 1

:: Labour relations ::

A _____ , also known as a post-entry closed shop, is a form of a union security clause. Under this, the employer agrees to either only hire labor union members or to require that any new employees who are not already union members become members within a certain amount of time. Use of the _____ varies widely from nation to nation, depending on the level of protection given trade unions in general.

30. *Answer choices:*

(see index for correct answer)

- a. Review Body
- b. Two-tier system
- c. Inflatable rat
- d. Union shop

Guidance: level 1

:: Organizational behavior ::

_____ is the state or fact of exclusive rights and control over property, which may be an object, land/real estate or intellectual property. _____ involves multiple rights, collectively referred to as title, which may be separated and held by different parties.

31. *Answer choices:*

(see index for correct answer)

- a. Positive organizational behavior
- b. Conformity
- c. Organizational Expedience

- d. Satisficing

Guidance: level 1

:: Employment compensation ::

_____ s is a method for companies to give their management or employees a bonus if the company performs well financially. Such a method is called a `plan`. SARs resemble employee stock options in that the holder/employee benefits from an increase in stock price. They differ from options in that the holder/employee does not have to purchase anything to receive the proceeds. They are not required to pay the exercise price, but just receive the amount of the increase in cash or stock.

Exam Probability: **High**

32. *Answer choices:*

(see index for correct answer)

- a. Stock appreciation right
- b. Employee stock ownership plan
- c. Lilly Ledbetter Fair Pay Act of 2009
- d. Employee stock purchase plan

Guidance: level 1

:: Sociological terminology ::

In moral and political philosophy, the _____ is a theory or model that originated during the Age of Enlightenment and usually concerns the legitimacy of the authority of the state over the individual. _____ arguments typically posit that individuals have consented, either explicitly or tacitly, to surrender some of their freedoms and submit to the authority in exchange for protection of their remaining rights or maintenance of the social order. The relation between natural and legal rights is often a topic of _____ theory. The term takes its name from The _____ , a 1762 book by Jean-Jacques Rousseau that discussed this concept. Although the antecedents of _____ theory are found in antiquity, in Greek and Stoic philosophy and Roman and Canon Law, the heyday of the _____ was the mid-17th to early 19th centuries, when it emerged as the leading doctrine of political legitimacy.

Exam Probability: **Medium**

33. *Answer choices:*

(see index for correct answer)

- a. McDonaldization
- b. Social contract
- c. Anticipatory socialization
- d. Enculturation

Guidance: level 1

:: Management ::

A _____ is a method or technique that has been generally accepted as superior to any alternatives because it produces results that are superior to those achieved by other means or because it has become a standard way of doing things, e.g., a standard way of complying with legal or ethical requirements.

Exam Probability: **Medium**

34. *Answer choices:*

(see index for correct answer)

- a. Business workflow analysis
- b. Best practice
- c. Advisory board
- d. Fall guy

Guidance: level 1

:: Unemployment by country ::

Unemployment benefits are payments made by back authorized bodies to unemployed people. In the United States, benefits are funded by a compulsory governmental insurance system, not taxes on individual citizens. Depending on the jurisdiction and the status of the person, those sums may be small, covering only basic needs, or may compensate the lost time proportionally to the previous earned salary.

Exam Probability: **Medium**

35. *Answer choices:*

(see index for correct answer)

- a. Unemployment insurance
- b. Unemployment in Brazil
- c. Unemployment in Spain

Guidance: level 1

:: Trade unions in the United States ::

The _____ is an American labor union representing over 670,000 employees of the federal government, about 5,000 employees of the District of Columbia, and a few hundred private sector employees, mostly in and around federal facilities. AFGE is the largest union for civilian, non-postal federal employees and the largest union for District of Columbia employees who report directly to the mayor . It is affiliated with the AFL-CIO.

Exam Probability: **High**

36. *Answer choices:*

(see index for correct answer)

- a. Glass, Molders, Pottery, Plastics and Allied Workers International Union
- b. American Federation of Government Employees
- c. National Emergency Medical Services Association
- d. United Nurses and Allied Professionals

:: Behaviorism ::

In behavioral psychology, _____ is a consequence applied that will strengthen an organism's future behavior whenever that behavior is preceded by a specific antecedent stimulus. This strengthening effect may be measured as a higher frequency of behavior , longer duration , greater magnitude , or shorter latency . There are two types of _____ , known as positive _____ and negative _____ ; positive is where by a reward is offered on expression of the wanted behaviour and negative is taking away an undesirable element in the persons environment whenever the desired behaviour is achieved.

Exam Probability: **Low**

37. *Answer choices:*

(see index for correct answer)

- a. social facilitation
- b. Matching Law
- c. Reinforcement
- d. contingency management

:: United States employment discrimination case law ::

_____ , 411 U.S. 792 , is a US employment law case by the United States Supreme Court regarding the burdens and nature of proof in proving a Title VII case and the order in which plaintiffs and defendants present proof. It was the seminal case in the McDonnell Douglas burden-shifting framework.

Exam Probability: **Low**

38. *Answer choices:*

(see index for correct answer)

- a. Ricci v. DeStefano
- b. McDonnell Douglas Corp. v. Green
- c. New York City Transit Authority v. Beazer
- d. Price Waterhouse v. Hopkins

Guidance: level 1

:: Asset ::

In financial accounting, an _____ is any resource owned by the business. Anything tangible or intangible that can be owned or controlled to produce value and that is held by a company to produce positive economic value is an _____ . Simply stated, _____ s represent value of ownership that can be converted into cash . The balance sheet of a firm records the monetary value of the _____ s owned by that firm. It covers money and other valuables belonging to an individual or to a business.

Exam Probability: **Low**

39. *Answer choices:*

(see index for correct answer)

- a. Fixed asset
- b. Asset

Guidance: level 1

:: Occupations ::

An _____ is a person who has a position of authority in a hierarchical organization. The term derives from the late Latin from officiarius, meaning "official".

Exam Probability: **High**

40. *Answer choices:*

(see index for correct answer)

- a. Elevator operator
- b. Language professional
- c. Officer
- d. Biologist

Guidance: level 1

:: Trade unions ::

A _____ , in North America, or union branch , in the United Kingdom and other countries, is a local branch of a usually national trade union. The terms used for sub-branches of _____ s vary from country to country and include "shop committee", "shop floor committee", "board of control", "chapel", and others.

Exam Probability: **High**

41. *Answer choices:*

(see index for correct answer)

- a. Local union
- b. Union democracy
- c. Public-sector trade union
- d. Recognition strike

Guidance: level 1

:: Financial statements ::

In financial accounting, a _____ or statement of financial position or statement of financial condition is a summary of the financial balances of an individual or organization, whether it be a sole proprietorship, a business partnership, a corporation, private limited company or other organization such as Government or not-for-profit entity. Assets, liabilities and ownership equity are listed as of a specific date, such as the end of its financial year. A _____ is often described as a "snapshot of a company's financial condition". Of the four basic financial statements, the _____ is the only statement which applies to a single point in time of a business' calendar year.

Exam Probability: **Medium**

42. *Answer choices:*

(see index for correct answer)

- a. quarterly report
- b. Balance sheet
- c. Financial report
- d. Statement on Auditing Standards No. 70: Service Organizations

Guidance: level 1

:: Human resource management ::

_____ , also known as organizational socialization, is management jargon first created in 1988 that refers to the mechanism through which new employees acquire the necessary knowledge, skills, and behaviors in order to become effective organizational members and insiders.

43. *Answer choices:*

(see index for correct answer)

- a. Experticity
- b. Management development
- c. Occupational Information Network
- d. Job performance

Guidance: level 1

:: Behavioral and social facets of systemic risk ::

_____ is the difficulty in understanding an issue and effectively making decisions when one has too much information about that issue. Generally, the term is associated with the excessive quantity of daily information. _____ most likely originated from information theory, which are studies in the storage, preservation, communication, compression, and extraction of information. The term, _____ , was first used in Bertram Gross' 1964 book, The Managing of Organizations, and it was further popularized by Alvin Toffler in his bestselling 1970 book Future Shock. Speier et al. stated.

44. *Answer choices:*

(see index for correct answer)

- a. Behavioral Finance
- b. Connectionism
- c. Information overload
- d. Gatekeeping

Guidance: level 1

:: Recruitment ::

Recruitment refers to the overall process of attracting, shortlisting, selecting and appointing suitable candidates for jobs within an organization. Recruitment can also refer to processes involved in choosing individuals for unpaid roles. Managers, human resource generalists and recruitment specialists may be tasked with carrying out recruitment, but in some cases public-sector employment agencies, commercial recruitment agencies, or specialist search consultancies are used to undertake parts of the process. Internet-based technologies which support all aspects of recruitment have become widespread.

Exam Probability: **High**

45. *Answer choices:*

(see index for correct answer)

- a. Peak earning years
- b. Haigui
- c. Employee referral
- d. NotchUp

:: Ethically disputed business practices ::

An _____ in US labor law refers to certain actions taken by employers or unions that violate the National Labor Relations Act of 1935 29 U.S.C. § 151–169 and other legislation. Such acts are investigated by the National Labor Relations Board .

Exam Probability: **High**

46. *Answer choices:*

(see index for correct answer)

- a. Wrongful dismissal
- b. Unfair labor practice
- c. Tobashi scheme
- d. Earnings management

:: Design of experiments ::

In the design of experiments, treatments are applied to experimental units in the treatment group. In comparative experiments, members of the complementary group, the _____ , receive either no treatment or a standard treatment.

Exam Probability: **High**

47. *Answer choices:*

(see index for correct answer)

- a. Latin square
- b. Minimisation
- c. Null hypothesis
- d. Control group

Guidance: level 1

:: Psychometrics ::

_____ is a dynamic, structured, interactive process where a neutral third party assists disputing parties in resolving conflict through the use of specialized communication and negotiation techniques. All participants in _____ are encouraged to actively participate in the process. _____ is a "party-centered" process in that it is focused primarily upon the needs, rights, and interests of the parties. The mediator uses a wide variety of techniques to guide the process in a constructive direction and to help the parties find their optimal solution. A mediator is facilitative in that she/he manages the interaction between parties and facilitates open communication. _____ is also evaluative in that the mediator analyzes issues and relevant norms , while refraining from providing prescriptive advice to the parties .

48. *Answer choices:*

(see index for correct answer)

- a. Mediation
- b. Linear-on-the-fly testing
- c. Intra-rater reliability
- d. Rating scale

Guidance: level 1

:: ::

The _____ of 1938 29 U.S.C. § 203 is a United States labor law that creates the right to a minimum wage, and "time-and-a-half" overtime pay when people work over forty hours a week. It also prohibits most employment of minors in "oppressive child labor". It applies to employees engaged in interstate commerce or employed by an enterprise engaged in commerce or in the production of goods for commerce, unless the employer can claim an exemption from coverage.

49. *Answer choices:*

(see index for correct answer)

- a. process perspective

- b. hierarchical perspective
- c. Fair Labor Standards Act
- d. similarity-attraction theory

Guidance: level 1

:: Network theory ::

A _____ is a social structure made up of a set of social actors , sets of dyadic ties, and other social interactions between actors. The _____ perspective provides a set of methods for analyzing the structure of whole social entities as well as a variety of theories explaining the patterns observed in these structures. The study of these structures uses _____ analysis to identify local and global patterns, locate influential entities, and examine network dynamics.

Exam Probability: **High**

50. *Answer choices:*
(see index for correct answer)

- a. Centrality
- b. Modularity
- c. Social network
- d. Clustering coefficient

Guidance: level 1

_____ refers to the overall process of attracting, shortlisting, selecting and appointing suitable candidates for jobs within an organization. _____ can also refer to processes involved in choosing individuals for unpaid roles. Managers, human resource generalists and _____ specialists may be tasked with carrying out _____ , but in some cases public-sector employment agencies, commercial _____ agencies, or specialist search consultancies are used to undertake parts of the process. Internet-based technologies which support all aspects of _____ have become widespread.

Exam Probability: **Low**

51. *Answer choices:*

(see index for correct answer)

- a. Recruitment
- b. Sarbanes-Oxley act of 2002
- c. process perspective
- d. open system

Guidance: level 1

:: Training ::

_____ is a phase of training needs analysis directed at identifying which individuals within an organization should receive training.

52. *Answer choices:*

(see index for correct answer)

- a. National sports team
- b. Enforcement
- c. Practicum
- d. Person Analysis

Guidance: level 1

:: Training ::

_____ refers to practicing newly acquired skills beyond the point of initial mastery. The term is also often used to refer to the pedagogical theory that this form of practice leads to automaticity or other beneficial consequences.

Exam Probability: **Medium**

53. *Answer choices:*

(see index for correct answer)

- a. Overlearning
- b. Hypoventilation training
- c. human resource development

- d. Confidence-based learning

:: Offshoring ::

Outsourcing is an agreement in which one company hires another company to be responsible for a planned or existing activity that is or could be done internally,and sometimes involves transferring employees and assets from one firm to another.

Exam Probability: **High**

54. *Answer choices:*

(see index for correct answer)

- a. Layoff
- b. Nearshoring
- c. Offshore custom software development
- d. TeleTech

:: Recruitment ::

A _____ is a quantitative research method commonly employed in survey research. The aim of this approach is to ensure that each interview is presented with exactly the same questions in the same order. This ensures that answers can be reliably aggregated and that comparisons can be made with confidence between sample subgroups or between different survey periods.

Exam Probability: **Low**

55. *Answer choices:*

(see index for correct answer)

- a. Audition
- b. Integrity Inventory
- c. Structured interview
- d. Internal labor market

Guidance: level 1

:: ::

According to Torrington, a _____ is usually developed by conducting a job analysis, which includes examining the tasks and sequences of tasks necessary to perform the job. The analysis considers the areas of knowledge and skills needed for the job. A job usually includes several roles. According to Hall, the _____ might be broadened to form a person specification or may be known as "terms of reference". The person/job specification can be presented as a stand-alone document, but in practice it is usually included within the _____ . A _____ is often used by employers in the recruitment process.

56. *Answer choices:*

(see index for correct answer)

- a. empathy
- b. Job description
- c. imperative
- d. information systems assessment

Guidance: level 1

:: Business ethics ::

_____ is a persistent pattern of mistreatment from others in the workplace that causes either physical or emotional harm. It can include such tactics as verbal, nonverbal, psychological, physical abuse and humiliation. This type of workplace aggression is particularly difficult because, unlike the typical school bully, workplace bullies often operate within the established rules and policies of their organization and their society. In the majority of cases, bullying in the workplace is reported as having been by someone who has authority over their victim. However, bullies can also be peers, and occasionally subordinates. Research has also investigated the impact of the larger organizational context on bullying as well as the group-level processes that impact on the incidence and maintenance of bullying behaviour. Bullying can be covert or overt. It may be missed by superiors; it may be known by many throughout the organization. Negative effects are not limited to the targeted individuals, and may lead to a decline in employee morale and a change in organizational culture. It can also take place as overbearing supervision, constant criticism, and blocking promotions.

57. *Answer choices:*

(see index for correct answer)

- a. Hypernorms
- b. Nishkam Karma
- c. Workplace bullying
- d. Anti-sweatshop movement

Guidance: level 1

:: ::

_____ is a common standard in United States labor law arbitration that is used in labor union contracts in the United States as a form of job security.

58. *Answer choices:*

(see index for correct answer)

- a. interpersonal communication
- b. Just cause
- c. deep-level diversity
- d. information systems assessment

:: Human resource management ::

_____ refers to the anticipation of required human capital for an organization and the planning to meet those needs. The field increased in popularity after McKinsey's 1997 research and the 2001 book on The War for Talent. _____ in this context does not refer to the management of entertainers.

Exam Probability: **Medium**

59. *Answer choices:*

(see index for correct answer)

- a. Talent management
- b. Leadership development
- c. Organizational behavior and human resources
- d. Human resource management in public administration

Information systems

Information systems (IS) are formal, sociotechnical, organizational systems designed to collect, process, store, and distribute information. In a sociotechnical perspective Information Systems are composed by four components: technology, process, people and organizational structure.

:: Telecommunications engineering ::

A _____ is a computer processor that incorporates the functions of a central processing unit on a single integrated circuit , or at most a few integrated circuits. The _____ is a multipurpose, clock driven, register based, digital integrated circuit that accepts binary data as input, processes it according to instructions stored in its memory and provides results as output. _____ s contain both combinational logic and sequential digital logic. _____ s operate on numbers and symbols represented in the binary number system.

Exam Probability: **High**

1. *Answer choices:*

(see index for correct answer)

- a. network architecture
- b. Computer network

Guidance: level 1

:: Information science ::

The United States National Forum on _____ defines _____ as "... the hyper ability to know when there is a need for information, to be able to identify, locate, evaluate, and effectively use that information for the issue or problem at hand." The American Library Association defines "_____ " as a set of abilities requiring individuals to "recognize when information is needed and have the ability to locate, evaluate, and use effectively the needed information. Other definitions incorporate aspects of "skepticism, judgement, free thinking, questioning, and understanding..." or incorporate competencies that an informed citizen of an information society ought to possess to participate intelligently and actively in that society.

Exam Probability: **High**

2. *Answer choices:*

(see index for correct answer)

- a. Data curation
- b. Information literacy
- c. Ontology engineering
- d. Memex

Guidance: level 1

:: Marketing ::

_____ is a business model in which consumers create value and businesses consume that value. For example, when a consumer writes reviews or when a consumer gives a useful idea for new product development then that consumer is creating value for the business if the business adopts the input.
In the C2B model, a reverse auction or demand collection model, enables buyers to name or demand their own price, which is often binding, for a specific good or service. Inside of a consumer to business market the roles involved in the transaction must be established and the consumer must offer something of value to the business.

Exam Probability: **Medium**

3. *Answer choices:*

(see index for correct answer)

- a. Consumer-to-business
- b. Bayesian inference in marketing
- c. elaboration likelihood
- d. Drug coupon

Guidance: level 1

:: Data management ::

In business, _____ is a method used to define and manage the critical data of an organization to provide, with data integration, a single point of reference. The data that is mastered may include reference data- the set of permissible values, and the analytical data that supports decision making.

4. *Answer choices:*

(see index for correct answer)

- a. Learning object metadata
- b. Data room
- c. Master data management
- d. Database server

Guidance: level 1

:: Management ::

A _____ describes the rationale of how an organization creates, delivers, and captures value, in economic, social, cultural or other contexts. The process of _____ construction and modification is also called _____ innovation and forms a part of business strategy.

Exam Probability: **High**

5. *Answer choices:*

(see index for correct answer)

- a. Knowledge Based Decision Making
- b. Sales outsourcing
- c. Commercial management

- d. Extended enterprise

Guidance: level 1

:: Computer access control protocols ::

An _____ is a type of computer communications protocol or cryptographic protocol specifically designed for transfer of authentication data between two entities. It allows the receiving entity to authenticate the connecting entity as well as authenticate itself to the connecting entity by declaring the type of information needed for authentication as well as syntax. It is the most important layer of protection needed for secure communication within computer networks.

Exam Probability: **High**

6. *Answer choices:*

(see index for correct answer)

- a. TACACS
- b. Authentication protocol
- c. Reflection attack
- d. RADIUS

Guidance: level 1

:: Google services ::

_____ is a time-management and scheduling calendar service developed by Google. It became available in beta release April 13, 2006, and in general release in July 2009, on the web and as mobile apps for the Android and iOS platforms.

Exam Probability: **High**

7. *Answer choices:*

(see index for correct answer)

- a. Google Current
- b. Google Calendar
- c. Google Friend Connect
- d. Google Web History

Guidance: level 1

:: Industrial design ::

In physics and mathematics, the _____ of a mathematical space is informally defined as the minimum number of coordinates needed to specify any point within it. Thus a line has a _____ of one because only one coordinate is needed to specify a point on it for example, the point at 5 on a number line. A surface such as a plane or the surface of a cylinder or sphere has a _____ of two because two coordinates are needed to specify a point on it for example, both a latitude and longitude are required to locate a point on the surface of a sphere. The inside of a cube, a cylinder or a sphere is three-_____ al because three coordinates are needed to locate a point within these spaces.

8. *Answer choices:*

(see index for correct answer)

- a. Dimension
- b. Constructal law
- c. Sports engineering
- d. Design Academy Eindhoven

Guidance: level 1

:: Computer networking ::

A backbone is a part of computer network that interconnects various pieces of network, providing a path for the exchange of information between different LANs or subnetworks. A backbone can tie together diverse networks in the same building, in different buildings in a campus environment, or over wide areas. Normally, the backbone's capacity is greater than the networks connected to it.

Exam Probability: **Medium**

9. *Answer choices:*

(see index for correct answer)

- a. RendezVous Routing Daemon
- b. Big Switch Networks

- c. Backbone network
- d. Application Session Controller

Guidance: level 1

:: Systems theory ::

A _____ is a group of interacting or interrelated entities that form a unified whole. A _____ is delineated by its spatial and temporal boundaries, surrounded and influenced by its environment, described by its structure and purpose and expressed in its functioning.

Exam Probability: **Medium**

10. *Answer choices:*

(see index for correct answer)

- a. System
- b. equifinality
- c. management system
- d. Viable System Model

Guidance: level 1

:: ::

The _____ , commonly known as the Web, is an information system where documents and other web resources are identified by Uniform Resource Locators , which may be interlinked by hypertext, and are accessible over the Internet. The resources of the WWW may be accessed by users by a software application called a web browser.

Exam Probability: **High**

11. *Answer choices:*

(see index for correct answer)

- a. Sarbanes-Oxley act of 2002
- b. World Wide Web
- c. hierarchical
- d. cultural

Guidance: level 1

:: Digital rights management ::

_____ tools or technological protection measures are a set of access control technologies for restricting the use of proprietary hardware and copyrighted works. DRM technologies try to control the use, modification, and distribution of copyrighted works , as well as systems within devices that enforce these policies.

Exam Probability: **High**

12. *Answer choices:*

(see index for correct answer)

- a. User operation prohibition
- b. Digital rights management
- c. Defective by Design
- d. NTSC-C

Guidance: level 1

:: Google services ::

Google Ads is an online advertising platform developed by Google, where advertisers pay to display brief advertisements, service offerings, product listings, video content, and generate mobile application installs within the Google ad network to web users.

Exam Probability: **Low**

13. *Answer choices:*

(see index for correct answer)

- a. WDYL
- b. Google Plugin for Eclipse
- c. Google Custom Search
- d. Zygote Body

:: Data management ::

A _____ , or metadata repository, as defined in the IBM Dictionary of Computing, is a "centralized repository of information about data such as meaning, relationships to other data, origin, usage, and format". Oracle defines it as a collection of tables with metadata. The term can have one of several closely related meanings pertaining to databases and database management systems .

Exam Probability: **High**

14. *Answer choices:*

(see index for correct answer)

- a. Data monetization
- b. Database-centric architecture
- c. Serializability
- d. Data dictionary

:: Consumer behaviour ::

_____ is the ratio of users who click on a specific link to the number of total users who view a page, email, or advertisement. It is commonly used to measure the success of an online advertising campaign for a particular website as well as the effectiveness of email campaigns.

Exam Probability: **Medium**

15. *Answer choices:*

(see index for correct answer)

- a. Center for a New American Dream
- b. Consumer ethnocentrism
- c. Social norms approach
- d. Click-through rate

Guidance: level 1

:: Information systems ::

A _____ is an information system that supports business or organizational decision-making activities. DSSs serve the management, operations and planning levels of an organization and help people make decisions about problems that may be rapidly changing and not easily specified in advance—i.e. unstructured and semi-structured decision problems. _____ s can be either fully computerized or human-powered, or a combination of both.

Exam Probability: **High**

16. *Answer choices:*

(see index for correct answer)

- a. Decision support system
- b. Shadow IT
- c. Association for Information Systems
- d. Proactive information delivery

Guidance: level 1

:: E-commerce ::

_____ is a type of performance-based marketing in which a business rewards one or more affiliates for each visitor or customer brought by the affiliate's own marketing efforts.

Exam Probability: **Low**

17. *Answer choices:*

(see index for correct answer)

- a. Freelance marketplace
- b. DVD-by-mail
- c. EBay API
- d. Affiliate marketing

Guidance: level 1

:: Network management ::

_____ is the process of administering and managing computer networks. Services provided by this discipline include fault analysis, performance management, provisioning of networks and maintaining the quality of service. Software that enables network administrators to perform their functions is called _____ software.

Exam Probability: **Low**

18. *Answer choices:*

(see index for correct answer)

- a. Java Management Extensions
- b. Network management
- c. OAMP
- d. Route Views

Guidance: level 1

:: Production economics ::

In microeconomics, _____ are the cost advantages that enterprises obtain due to their scale of operation , with cost per unit of output decreasing with increasing scale.

19. *Answer choices:*

(see index for correct answer)

- a. Economies of scale
- b. Productivity Alpha
- c. Learning-by-doing
- d. Cost-of-production theory of value

Guidance: level 1

:: Business process ::

A _____ or business method is a collection of related, structured activities or tasks by people or equipment which in a specific sequence produce a service or product for a particular customer or customers. _____ es occur at all organizational levels and may or may not be visible to the customers. A _____ may often be visualized as a flowchart of a sequence of activities with interleaving decision points or as a process matrix of a sequence of activities with relevance rules based on data in the process. The benefits of using _____ es include improved customer satisfaction and improved agility for reacting to rapid market change. Process-oriented organizations break down the barriers of structural departments and try to avoid functional silos.

20. *Answer choices:*

(see index for correct answer)

- a. Intention mining
- b. Closure by stealth
- c. Business Process Modeling Language
- d. Communication-enabled business process

Guidance: level 1

:: Help desk ::

Data center management is the collection of tasks performed by those responsible for managing ongoing operation of a data center This includes Business service management and planning for the future.

Exam Probability: **High**

21. *Answer choices:*
(see index for correct answer)

- a. Help desk
- b. HEAT
- c. Computer-aided maintenance
- d. Vitalyst

Guidance: level 1

:: Information systems ::

_____ s are information systems that are developed in response to corporate business initiative. They are intended to give competitive advantage to the organization. They may deliver a product or service that is at a lower cost, that is differentiated, that focuses on a particular market segment, or is innovative.

Exam Probability: **High**

22. *Answer choices:*

(see index for correct answer)

- a. VAT Information Exchange System
- b. Clinical decision support system
- c. Business informatics
- d. Electronic Case Filing System

Guidance: level 1

:: Information science ::

_____ has been defined as "the branch of ethics that focuses on the relationship between the creation, organization, dissemination, and use of information, and the ethical standards and moral codes governing human conduct in society". It examines the morality that comes from information as a resource, a product, or as a target. It provides a critical framework for considering moral issues concerning informational privacy, moral agency , new environmental issues , problems arising from the life-cycle of information .
It is very vital to understand that librarians, archivists, information professionals among others, really understand the importance of knowing how to disseminate proper information as well as being responsible with their actions when addressing information.

Exam Probability: **High**

23. *Answer choices:*

(see index for correct answer)

- a. Information architecture
- b. Scientific literature
- c. Information ethics
- d. Subject

Guidance: level 1

:: Market research ::

_____ is the action of defining, gathering, analyzing, and distributing intelligence about products, customers, competitors, and any aspect of the environment needed to support executives and managers in strategic decision making for an organization.

Exam Probability: **Medium**

24. *Answer choices:*

(see index for correct answer)

- a. GlobalWebIndex
- b. AQH Share
- c. Competitive intelligence
- d. INDEX

Guidance: level 1

:: ::

_____ is a set of documents provided on paper, or online, or on digital or analog media, such as audio tape or CDs. Examples are user guides, white papers, on-line help, quick-reference guides. It is becoming less common to see paper _____ . _____ is distributed via websites, software products, and other on-line applications.

Exam Probability: **Low**

25. *Answer choices:*

(see index for correct answer)

- a. interpersonal communication
- b. deep-level diversity
- c. Documentation
- d. surface-level diversity

Guidance: level 1

:: Management ::

In organizational studies, _____ is the efficient and effective development of an organization's resources when they are needed. Such resources may include financial resources, inventory, human skills, production resources, or information technology and natural resources.

Exam Probability: **Medium**

26. *Answer choices:*

(see index for correct answer)

- a. Productive efficiency
- b. Target operating model
- c. Risk management
- d. Resource management

:: Policy ::

A _____ is a statement or a legal document that discloses some or all of the ways a party gathers, uses, discloses, and manages a customer or client's data. It fulfills a legal requirement to protect a customer or client's privacy. Personal information can be anything that can be used to identify an individual, not limited to the person's name, address, date of birth, marital status, contact information, ID issue, and expiry date, financial records, credit information, medical history, where one travels, and intentions to acquire goods and services. In the case of a business it is often a statement that declares a party's policy on how it collects, stores, and releases personal information it collects. It informs the client what specific information is collected, and whether it is kept confidential, shared with partners, or sold to other firms or enterprises. Privacy policies typically represent a broader, more generalized treatment, as opposed to data use statements, which tend to be more detailed and specific.

Exam Probability: **Medium**

27. *Answer choices:*

(see index for correct answer)

- a. Privacy policy
- b. Overton window
- c. Veterinary Feed Directive
- d. Policy Monitoring

:: IT risk management ::

_____ involves a set of policies, tools and procedures to enable the recovery or continuation of vital technology infrastructure and systems following a natural or human-induced disaster. _____ focuses on the IT or technology systems supporting critical business functions, as opposed to business continuity, which involves keeping all essential aspects of a business functioning despite significant disruptive events. _____ can therefore be considered as a subset of business continuity.

Exam Probability: **Low**

28. *Answer choices:*

(see index for correct answer)

- a. Information assurance
- b. Incident response team
- c. Business continuity

Guidance: level 1

:: Strategic management ::

In marketing strategy, first-mover advantage is the advantage gained by the initial significant occupant of a market segment. First-mover advantage may be gained by technological leadership, or early purchase of resources.

29. *Answer choices:*

(see index for correct answer)

- a. Technology strategy
- b. First mover advantage
- c. Corporate group
- d. Complexity management

Guidance: level 1

:: Business process ::

Business process re-engineering is a business management strategy, originally pioneered in the early 1990s, focusing on the analysis and design of workflows and business processes within an organization. BPR aimed to help organizations fundamentally rethink how they do their work in order to improve customer service, cut operational costs, and become world-class competitors.

30. *Answer choices:*

(see index for correct answer)

- a. Business process reengineering
- b. Business process outsourcing to India

- c. ProcessEdge
- d. Outsourced document processing

Guidance: level 1

:: Network architecture ::

An _____ is a controlled private network that allows access to partners, vendors and suppliers or an authorized set of customers – normally to a subset of the information accessible from an organization's intranet. An _____ is similar to a DMZ in that it provides access to needed services for authorized parties, without granting access to an organization's entire network. An _____ is a private network organization.

Exam Probability: **High**

31. *Answer choices:*

(see index for correct answer)

- a. client-server
- b. Internetworking

Guidance: level 1

:: Data security ::

_____ are safeguards or countermeasures to avoid, detect, counteract, or minimize security risks to physical property, information, computer systems, or other assets.

Exam Probability: **Medium**

32. *Answer choices:*

(see index for correct answer)

- a. Virtual private database
- b. Common Criteria Evaluation and Validation Scheme
- c. Crypto cloud computing
- d. Doxing

Guidance: level 1

:: Computer memory ::

_____ is an electronic non-volatile computer storage medium that can be electrically erased and reprogrammed.

Exam Probability: **High**

33. *Answer choices:*

(see index for correct answer)

- a. Plated wire memory
- b. Word-addressable
- c. Sequential access memory
- d. Command Data Buffer

Guidance: level 1

:: Mereology ::

_____ , in the abstract, is what belongs to or with something, whether as an attribute or as a component of said thing. In the context of this article, it is one or more components , whether physical or incorporeal, of a person's estate; or so belonging to, as in being owned by, a person or jointly a group of people or a legal entity like a corporation or even a society. Depending on the nature of the _____ , an owner of _____ has the right to consume, alter, share, redefine, rent, mortgage, pawn, sell, exchange, transfer, give away or destroy it, or to exclude others from doing these things, as well as to perhaps abandon it; whereas regardless of the nature of the _____ , the owner thereof has the right to properly use it , or at the very least exclusively keep it.

Exam Probability: **Medium**

34. *Answer choices:*
(see index for correct answer)

- a. Property
- b. Mereological nihilism
- c. Mereology

- d. Mereological essentialism

Guidance: level 1

:: Service-oriented (business computing) ::

_____ is a style of software design where services are provided to the other components by application components, through a communication protocol over a network. The basic principles of _____ are independent of vendors, products and technologies.A service is a discrete unit of functionality that can be accessed remotely and acted upon and updated independently, such as retrieving a credit card statement online.

Exam Probability: **Low**

35. *Answer choices:*

(see index for correct answer)

- a. Net-Centric Enterprise Services
- b. Service-oriented architecture
- c. Mushroom Networks
- d. Service discovery

Guidance: level 1

:: World Wide Web Consortium standards ::

_____ is a markup language that defines a set of rules for encoding documents in a format that is both human-readable and machine-readable. The W3C's XML 1.0 Specification and several other related specifications—all of them free open standards—define XML.

Exam Probability: **Low**

36. *Answer choices:*

(see index for correct answer)

- a. Extensible Markup Language
- b. Hyper Text Markup Language

Guidance: level 1

:: Data collection ::

_____ is the application of data mining techniques to discover patterns from the World Wide Web. As the name proposes, this is information gathered by mining the web. It makes utilization of automated apparatuses to reveal and extricate data from servers and web2 reports, and it permits organizations to get to both organized and unstructured information from browser activities, server logs, website and link structure, page content and different sources.

Exam Probability: **High**

37. *Answer choices:*

(see index for correct answer)

- a. German General Social Survey
- b. Field recording
- c. BanxQuote
- d. Web mining

Guidance: level 1

:: Big data ::

_____ refers to the skills, technologies, practices for continuous iterative exploration and investigation of past business performance to gain insight and drive business planning. _____ focuses on developing new insights and understanding of business performance based on data and statistical methods. In contrast, business intelligence traditionally focuses on using a consistent set of metrics to both measure past performance and guide business planning, which is also based on data and statistical methods.

Exam Probability: **Medium**

38. *Answer choices:*

(see index for correct answer)

- a. SAP HANA
- b. Business analytics
- c. Hibari
- d. Ninja Metrics

:: Information technology management ::

_____ is a good-practice framework created by international professional association ISACA for information technology management and IT governance. _____ provides an implementable "set of controls over information technology and organizes them around a logical framework of IT-related processes and enablers."

Exam Probability: **High**

39. *Answer choices:*

(see index for correct answer)

- a. Corporate Governance of ICT
- b. COBIT
- c. Data warehouse appliance
- d. OMII-UK

:: Outsourcing ::

A service-level agreement is a commitment between a service provider and a client. Particular aspects of the service – quality, availability, responsibilities – are agreed between the service provider and the service user. The most common component of SLA is that the services should be provided to the customer as agreed upon in the contract. As an example, Internet service providers and telcos will commonly include _____ s within the terms of their contracts with customers to define the level of service being sold in plain language terms. In this case the SLA will typically have a technical definition in mean time between failures , mean time to repair or mean time to recovery ; identifying which party is responsible for reporting faults or paying fees; responsibility for various data rates; throughput; jitter; or similar measurable details.

Exam Probability: **Low**

40. *Answer choices:*

(see index for correct answer)

- a. Extengineering
- b. Service level agreement
- c. Service review
- d. Oregon Bridge Delivery Partners

Guidance: level 1

:: Data management ::

_____ involves combining data residing in different sources and providing users with a unified view of them. This process becomes significant in a variety of situations, which include both commercial and scientific domains. _____ appears with increasing frequency as the volume and the need to share existing data explodes. It has become the focus of extensive theoretical work, and numerous open problems remain unsolved. _____ encourages collaboration between internal as well as external users

Exam Probability: **High**

41. *Answer choices:*

- a. Inverted index
- b. Data integration
- c. Data steward
- d. Control break

Guidance: level 1

:: Data management ::

_____ , or IG, is the management of information at an organization. _____ balances the use and security of information. _____ helps with legal compliance, operational transparency, and reducing expenditures associated with legal discovery. An organization can establish a consistent and logical framework for employees to handle data through their _____ policies and procedures. These policies guide proper behavior regarding how organizations and their employees handle electronically stored information .

42. *Answer choices:*

(see index for correct answer)

- a. Tagsistant
- b. Information governance
- c. Cognos ReportNet
- d. Data architecture

Guidance: level 1

:: Costs ::

In economics, _____ is the total economic cost of production and is made up of variable cost, which varies according to the quantity of a good produced and includes inputs such as labour and raw materials, plus fixed cost, which is independent of the quantity of a good produced and includes inputs that cannot be varied in the short term: fixed costs such as buildings and machinery, including sunk costs if any. Since cost is measured per unit of time, it is a flow variable.

Exam Probability: **High**

43. *Answer choices:*

(see index for correct answer)

- a. Direct labor cost

- b. Travel and subsistence
- c. Total cost
- d. Explicit cost

Guidance: level 1

:: Data privacy ::

_____ is the relationship between the collection and dissemination of data, technology, the public expectation of privacy, legal and political issues surrounding them. It is also known as data privacy or data protection,

Exam Probability: **Low**

44. *Answer choices:*
(see index for correct answer)

- a. Information privacy
- b. Personal Information Protection and Electronic Documents Act
- c. Christopher Graham
- d. Federal Data Protection and Information Commissioner

Guidance: level 1

:: Payment systems ::

A _____ is any system used to settle financial transactions through the transfer of monetary value. This includes the institutions, instruments, people, rules, procedures, standards, and technologies that make it exchange possible. A common type of _____ is called an operational network that links bank accounts and provides for monetary exchange using bank deposits. Some _____ s also include credit mechanisms, which are essentially a different aspect of payment.

Exam Probability: **Low**

45. *Answer choices:*

(see index for correct answer)

- a. Payment system
- b. Check Clearing for the 21st Century Act
- c. Clinkle
- d. Payment processor

Guidance: level 1

:: Customer relationship management software ::

_____ Software Corporation is a Global Business Software company based in Austin, TX and was founded in 1972. Its products are aimed at the manufacturing, distribution, retail and services industries.

Exam Probability: **High**

46. *Answer choices:*

(see index for correct answer)

- a. VTECRM
- b. SmartFocus
- c. Epicor
- d. Selltis

Guidance: level 1

:: Asset ::

In financial accounting, an _____ is any resource owned by the business. Anything tangible or intangible that can be owned or controlled to produce value and that is held by a company to produce positive economic value is an _____ . Simply stated, _____ s represent value of ownership that can be converted into cash . The balance sheet of a firm records the monetary value of the _____ s owned by that firm. It covers money and other valuables belonging to an individual or to a business.

Exam Probability: **Low**

47. *Answer choices:*

(see index for correct answer)

- a. Asset
- b. Current asset

:: Information systems ::

An _____ , or a group of such silos, is an insular management system in which one information system or subsystem is incapable of reciprocal operation with others that are, or should be, related. Thus information is not adequately shared but rather remains sequestered within each system or subsystem, figuratively trapped within a container like grain is trapped within a silo: there may be a lot of it, and it may be stacked quite high and freely available within those limits, but it has no effect outside those limits. Such data silos are proving to be an obstacle for businesses wishing to use data mining to make productive use of their data.

Exam Probability: **Low**

48. *Answer choices:*

(see index for correct answer)

- a. Content management system
- b. Information Systems Journal
- c. Information filtering system
- d. Information silo

:: Network analyzers ::

A _____ , meaning "meat eater" , is an organism that derives its energy and nutrient requirements from a diet consisting mainly or exclusively of animal tissue, whether through predation or scavenging. Animals that depend solely on animal flesh for their nutrient requirements are called obligate _____ s while those that also consume non-animal food are called facultative _____ s. Omnivores also consume both animal and non-animal food, and, apart from the more general definition, there is no clearly defined ratio of plant to animal material that would distinguish a facultative _____ from an omnivore. A _____ at the top of the food chain, not preyed upon by other animals, is termed an apex predator.

Exam Probability: **High**

49. *Answer choices:*

(see index for correct answer)

- a. Carnivore
- b. Pirni
- c. Zx Sniffer
- d. AirSnort

Guidance: level 1

:: Data management ::

"_____" is a field that treats ways to analyze, systematically extract information from, or otherwise deal with data sets that are too large or complex to be dealt with by traditional data-processing application software. Data with many cases offer greater statistical power, while data with higher complexity may lead to a higher false discovery rate. _____ challenges include capturing data, data storage, data analysis, search, sharing, transfer, visualization, querying, updating, information privacy and data source.

_____ was originally associated with three key concepts: volume, variety, and velocity. Other concepts later attributed with _____ are veracity and value.

Exam Probability: **Low**

50. *Answer choices:*

(see index for correct answer)

- a. SQL injection
- b. Big data
- c. Storage block
- d. Consistency

Guidance: level 1

:: ::

Within the Internet, _____ s are formed by the rules and procedures of the _____ System. Any name registered in the DNS is a _____. _____ s are used in various networking contexts and for application-specific naming and addressing purposes. In general, a _____ represents an Internet Protocol resource, such as a personal computer used to access the Internet, a server computer hosting a web site, or the web site itself or any other service communicated via the Internet. In 2017, 330.6 million _____ s had been registered.

Exam Probability: **Low**

51. *Answer choices:*

(see index for correct answer)

- a. deep-level diversity
- b. hierarchical perspective
- c. Character
- d. imperative

Guidance: level 1

:: Automatic identification and data capture ::

_____ uses electromagnetic fields to automatically identify and track tags attached to objects. The tags contain electronically stored information. Passive tags collect energy from a nearby RFID reader's interrogating radio waves. Active tags have a local power source and may operate hundreds of meters from the RFID reader. Unlike a barcode, the tag need not be within the line of sight of the reader, so it may be embedded in the tracked object. RFID is one method of automatic identification and data capture .

Exam Probability: **Medium**

52. *Answer choices:*

(see index for correct answer)

- a. Chipless RFID
- b. Radio-frequency identification
- c. Retriever Communications
- d. Smart label

Guidance: level 1

:: Credit cards ::

A _____ is a payment card issued to users to enable the cardholder to pay a merchant for goods and services based on the cardholder's promise to the card issuer to pay them for the amounts plus the other agreed charges. The card issuer creates a revolving account and grants a line of credit to the cardholder, from which the cardholder can borrow money for payment to a merchant or as a cash advance.

53. *Answer choices:*

(see index for correct answer)

- a. CardLab
- b. Offshore credit card
- c. Credit card
- d. Payoneer

Guidance: level 1

:: User interfaces ::

_____ , keystroke biometrics, typing dynamics and lately typing biometrics, is the detailed timing information which describes exactly when each key was pressed and when it was released as a person is typing at a computer keyboard.

Exam Probability: **Low**

54. *Answer choices:*

(see index for correct answer)

- a. Login
- b. Keystroke dynamics
- c. Information design

- d. Rich user interaction

:: Information and communication technologies for development ::

_____ is a non-profit initiative established with the goal of transforming education for children around the world; this goal was to be achieved by creating and distributing educational devices for the developing world, and by creating software and content for those devices.

Exam Probability: **Medium**

55. *Answer choices:*
(see index for correct answer)

- a. Technical Centre for Agricultural and Rural Cooperation ACP-EU
- b. Open Knowledge Network
- c. Asia Source
- d. PlayPower

:: Satellite navigation systems ::

_____ Galilei was an Italian astronomer, physicist and engineer, sometimes described as a polymath. _____ has been called the "father of observational astronomy", the "father of modern physics", the "father of the scientific method", and the "father of modern science".

Exam Probability: **Medium**

56. *Answer choices:*

(see index for correct answer)

- a. NAVV
- b. Transit
- c. Galileo
- d. GIOVE Mission

Guidance: level 1

:: Product testing ::

_____ is a characteristic of a product or system, whose interfaces are completely understood, to work with other products or systems, at present or in the future, in either implementation or access, without any restrictions.

Exam Probability: **Medium**

57. *Answer choices:*

(see index for correct answer)

- a. Testing cosmetics on animals
- b. NIST stone test wall
- c. Defect tracking
- d. Interoperability

:: Industrial design ::

Across the many fields concerned with _____ , including information science, computer science, human-computer interaction, communication, and industrial design, there is little agreement over the meaning of the term " _____ ", although all are related to interaction with computers and other machines with a user interface.

Exam Probability: **Medium**

58. *Answer choices:*
(see index for correct answer)

- a. Solid Ground Curing
- b. World Design Capital
- c. Projection augmented model
- d. Interactivity

:: Google services ::

A blog is a discussion or informational website published on the World Wide Web consisting of discrete, often informal diary-style text entries . Posts are typically displayed in reverse chronological order, so that the most recent post appears first, at the top of the web page. Until 2009, blogs were usually the work of a single individual, occasionally of a small group, and often covered a single subject or topic. In the 2010s, "multi-author blogs" emerged, featuring the writing of multiple authors and sometimes professionally edited. MABs from newspapers, other media outlets, universities, think tanks, advocacy groups, and similar institutions account for an increasing quantity of blog traffic. The rise of Twitter and other "microblogging" systems helps integrate MABs and single-author blogs into the news media. Blog can also be used as a verb, meaning to maintain or add content to a blog.

Exam Probability: **High**

59. *Answer choices:*

(see index for correct answer)

- a. Picasa
- b. Google Audio Indexing
- c. Google Classroom
- d. Google Website Optimizer

Guidance: level 1

Marketing

Marketing is the study and management of exchange relationships. Marketing is the business process of creating relationships with and satisfying customers. With its focus on the customer, marketing is one of the premier components of business management.

Marketing is defined by the American Marketing Association as "the activity, set of institutions, and processes for creating, communicating, delivering, and exchanging offerings that have value for customers, clients, partners, and society at large."

:: Monopoly (economics) ::

A _____ exists when a specific person or enterprise is the only supplier of a particular commodity. This contrasts with a monopsony which relates to a single entity's control of a market to purchase a good or service, and with oligopoly which consists of a few sellers dominating a market. Monopolies are thus characterized by a lack of economic competition to produce the good or service, a lack of viable substitute goods, and the possibility of a high _____ price well above the seller's marginal cost that leads to a high _____ profit. The verb monopolise or monopolize refers to the process by which a company gains the ability to raise prices or exclude competitors. In economics, a _____ is a single seller. In law, a _____ is a business entity that has significant market power, that is, the power to charge overly high prices. Although monopolies may be big businesses, size is not a characteristic of a _____ . A small business may still have the power to raise prices in a small industry .

Exam Probability: **Low**

1. *Answer choices:*

(see index for correct answer)

- a. Herfindahl index
- b. Monopoly
- c. Statute of Monopolies
- d. Dominance

Guidance: level 1

:: Data management ::

_____ is a form of intellectual property that grants the creator of an original creative work an exclusive legal right to determine whether and under what conditions this original work may be copied and used by others, usually for a limited term of years. The exclusive rights are not absolute but limited by limitations and exceptions to _____ law, including fair use. A major limitation on _____ on ideas is that _____ protects only the original expression of ideas, and not the underlying ideas themselves.

Exam Probability: **Medium**

2. *Answer choices:*

(see index for correct answer)

- a. Electronically stored information
- b. Australian National Data Service
- c. Commit
- d. Copyright

Guidance: level 1

:: Cultural appropriation ::

_____ is a social and economic order that encourages the acquisition of goods and services in ever-increasing amounts. With the industrial revolution, but particularly in the 20th century, mass production led to an economic crisis: there was overproduction—the supply of goods would grow beyond consumer demand, and so manufacturers turned to planned obsolescence and advertising to manipulate consumer spending. In 1899, a book on _____ published by Thorstein Veblen, called The Theory of the Leisure Class, examined the widespread values and economic institutions emerging along with the widespread "leisure time" in the beginning of the 20th century. In it Veblen "views the activities and spending habits of this leisure class in terms of conspicuous and vicarious consumption and waste. Both are related to the display of status and not to functionality or usefulness."

Exam Probability: **Low**

3. *Answer choices:*

(see index for correct answer)

- a. National-Anarchism
- b. Koshare Indian Dancers
- c. Consumerism
- d. Washington Redskins Original Americans Foundation

Guidance: level 1

:: Market research ::

_____ is the action of defining, gathering, analyzing, and distributing intelligence about products, customers, competitors, and any aspect of the environment needed to support executives and managers in strategic decision making for an organization.

Exam Probability: **High**

4. *Answer choices:*

(see index for correct answer)

- a. Cogent Research
- b. Competitive intelligence
- c. Sectoral analysis
- d. AttentionTracking

Guidance: level 1

:: Advertising ::

A _____ is a large outdoor advertising structure , typically found in high-traffic areas such as alongside busy roads. _____ s present large advertisements to passing pedestrians and drivers. Typically showing witty slogans and distinctive visuals, _____ s are highly visible in the top designated market areas.

Exam Probability: **Low**

5. *Answer choices:*

- a. SocioBranding
- b. Billboard
- c. Frank Cannella
- d. Attention

Guidance: level 1

:: ::

_____ is the act of conveying meanings from one entity or group to another through the use of mutually understood signs, symbols, and semiotic rules.

Exam Probability: **Low**

6. *Answer choices:*

- a. deep-level diversity
- b. co-culture
- c. cultural
- d. Communication

Guidance: level 1

:: Marketing ::

_____ , sometimes called trigger-based or event-driven marketing, is a marketing strategy that uses two-way communication channels to allow consumers to connect with a company directly. Although this exchange can take place in person, in the last decade it has increasingly taken place almost exclusively online through email, social media, and blogs.

Exam Probability: **Medium**

7. *Answer choices:*

(see index for correct answer)

- a. Aftersales
- b. Profit chart
- c. Aspirational brand
- d. Interactive marketing

Guidance: level 1

:: Goods ::

In most contexts, the concept of _____ denotes the conduct that should be preferred when posed with a choice between possible actions. _____ is generally considered to be the opposite of evil, and is of interest in the study of morality, ethics, religion and philosophy. The specific meaning and etymology of the term and its associated translations among ancient and contemporary languages show substantial variation in its inflection and meaning depending on circumstances of place, history, religious, or philosophical context.

Exam Probability: **High**

8. *Answer choices:*

(see index for correct answer)

- a. Necessity good
- b. Good
- c. Search good
- d. Substitute good

Guidance: level 1

:: Decision theory ::

Within economics the concept of _____ is used to model worth or value, but its usage has evolved significantly over time. The term was introduced initially as a measure of pleasure or satisfaction within the theory of utilitarianism by moral philosophers such as Jeremy Bentham and John Stuart Mill. But the term has been adapted and reapplied within neoclassical economics, which dominates modern economic theory, as a _____ function that represents a consumer's preference ordering over a choice set. As such, it is devoid of its original interpretation as a measurement of the pleasure or satisfaction obtained by the consumer from that choice.

Exam Probability: **Low**

9. *Answer choices:*

(see index for correct answer)

- a. New Approach to Appraisal
- b. Rational Focal Point
- c. Risk compensation
- d. ERulemaking

Guidance: level 1

:: Data interchange standards ::

_____ is the concept of businesses electronically communicating information that was traditionally communicated on paper, such as purchase orders and invoices. Technical standards for EDI exist to facilitate parties transacting such instruments without having to make special arrangements.

10. *Answer choices:*

(see index for correct answer)

- a. Uniform Communication Standard
- b. Data Interchange Standards Association
- c. Electronic data interchange
- d. ASC X12

Guidance: level 1

:: Information technology ::

_____ is the use of computers to store, retrieve, transmit, and manipulate data, or information, often in the context of a business or other enterprise. IT is considered to be a subset of information and communications technology . An _____ system is generally an information system, a communications system or, more specifically speaking, a computer system – including all hardware, software and peripheral equipment – operated by a limited group of users.

Exam Probability: **Medium**

11. *Answer choices:*

(see index for correct answer)

- a. Information technology

- b. GroupLogic
- c. Information and communication technologies for environmental sustainability
- d. Open collaboration

Guidance: level 1

:: Business models ::

A _____ is "an autonomous association of persons united voluntarily to meet their common economic, social, and cultural needs and aspirations through a jointly-owned and democratically-controlled enterprise". _____ s may include.

Exam Probability: **Medium**

12. *Answer choices:*

(see index for correct answer)

- a. Revenue model
- b. Cooperative
- c. The India Way
- d. Professional open source

Guidance: level 1

_____ is the study and management of exchange relationships. _____ is the business process of creating relationships with and satisfying customers. With its focus on the customer, _____ is one of the premier components of business management.

Exam Probability: **Low**

13. *Answer choices:*

(see index for correct answer)

- a. Marketing
- b. surface-level diversity
- c. corporate values
- d. Sarbanes-Oxley act of 2002

Guidance: level 1

:: Business models ::

A _____ , _____ company or daughter company is a company that is owned or controlled by another company, which is called the parent company, parent, or holding company. The _____ can be a company, corporation, or limited liability company. In some cases it is a government or state-owned enterprise. In some cases, particularly in the music and book publishing industries, subsidiaries are referred to as imprints.

14. *Answer choices:*

(see index for correct answer)

- a. What if chart
- b. Cooperative
- c. Parent company
- d. Low-cost carrier

Guidance: level 1

:: Retailing ::

A _____ is a self-service shop offering a wide variety of food, beverages and household products, organized into sections and shelves. It is larger and has a wider selection than earlier grocery stores, but is smaller and more limited in the range of merchandise than a hypermarket or big-box market.

15. *Answer choices:*

(see index for correct answer)

- a. Consignment Store
- b. Supermarket

- c. Sbiten
- d. Warehouse store

Guidance: level 1

:: Stochastic processes ::

_____ in its modern meaning is a "new idea, creative thoughts, new imaginations in form of device or method". _____ is often also viewed as the application of better solutions that meet new requirements, unarticulated needs, or existing market needs. Such _____ takes place through the provision of more-effective products, processes, services, technologies, or business models that are made available to markets, governments and society. An _____ is something original and more effective and, as a consequence, new, that "breaks into" the market or society. _____ is related to, but not the same as, invention, as _____ is more apt to involve the practical implementation of an invention to make a meaningful impact in the market or society, and not all _____ s require an invention. _____ often manifests itself via the engineering process, when the problem being solved is of a technical or scientific nature. The opposite of _____ is exnovation.

Exam Probability: **Low**

16. *Answer choices:*

(see index for correct answer)

- a. Girsanov theorem
- b. Innovation
- c. Feller process
- d. Path space

:: Marketing by medium ::

_____ or viral advertising is a business strategy that uses existing social networks to promote a product. Its name refers to how consumers spread information about a product with other people in their social networks, much in the same way that a virus spreads from one person to another. It can be delivered by word of mouth or enhanced by the network effects of the Internet and mobile networks.

Exam Probability: **High**

17. *Answer choices:*

(see index for correct answer)

- a. Social video marketing
- b. Viral marketing
- c. Online advertising
- d. Direct Text Marketing

:: ::

Management is the administration of an organization, whether it is a business, a not-for-profit organization, or government body. Management includes the activities of setting the strategy of an organization and coordinating the efforts of its employees to accomplish its objectives through the application of available resources, such as financial, natural, technological, and human resources. The term "management" may also refer to those people who manage an organization.

Exam Probability: **High**

18. *Answer choices:*

(see index for correct answer)

- a. Sarbanes-Oxley act of 2002
- b. process perspective
- c. personal values
- d. Manager

Guidance: level 1

:: Commercial item transport and distribution ::

In commerce, supply-chain management , the management of the flow of goods and services, involves the movement and storage of raw materials, of work-in-process inventory, and of finished goods from point of origin to point of consumption. Interconnected or interlinked networks, channels and node businesses combine in the provision of products and services required by end customers in a supply chain. Supply-chain management has been defined as the "design, planning, execution, control, and monitoring of supply-chain activities with the objective of creating net value, building a competitive infrastructure, leveraging worldwide logistics, synchronizing supply with demand and measuring performance globally."SCM practice draws heavily from the areas of industrial engineering, systems engineering, operations management, logistics, procurement, information technology, and marketing and strives for an integrated approach. Marketing channels play an important role in supply-chain management. Current research in supply-chain management is concerned with topics related to sustainability and risk management, among others. Some suggest that the "people dimension" of SCM, ethical issues, internal integration, transparency/visibility, and human capital/talent management are topics that have, so far, been underrepresented on the research agenda.

Exam Probability: **Medium**

19. *Answer choices:*

(see index for correct answer)

- a. Freight terminal
- b. Truck
- c. Supply chain management
- d. Human mail

Guidance: level 1

:: ::

In law, a _____ is a coming together of parties to a dispute, to present information in a tribunal, a formal setting with the authority to adjudicate claims or disputes. One form of tribunal is a court. The tribunal, which may occur before a judge, jury, or other designated trier of fact, aims to achieve a resolution to their dispute.

Exam Probability: **Medium**

20. *Answer choices:*

(see index for correct answer)

- a. Trial
- b. open system
- c. cultural
- d. corporate values

Guidance: level 1

:: ::

An _____ is a systematic and independent examination of books, accounts, statutory records, documents and vouchers of an organization to ascertain how far the financial statements as well as non-financial disclosures present a true and fair view of the concern. It also attempts to ensure that the books of accounts are properly maintained by the concern as required by law. _____ ing has become such a ubiquitous phenomenon in the corporate and the public sector that academics started identifying an " _____ Society". The _____ or perceives and recognises the propositions before them for examination, obtains evidence, evaluates the same and formulates an opinion on the basis of his judgement which is communicated through their _____ ing report.

21. *Answer choices:*

(see index for correct answer)

- a. hierarchical
- b. interpersonal communication
- c. information systems assessment
- d. Audit

Guidance: level 1

:: Costs ::

In economics, _____ is the total economic cost of production and is made up of variable cost, which varies according to the quantity of a good produced and includes inputs such as labour and raw materials, plus fixed cost, which is independent of the quantity of a good produced and includes inputs that cannot be varied in the short term: fixed costs such as buildings and machinery, including sunk costs if any. Since cost is measured per unit of time, it is a flow variable.

Exam Probability: **High**

22. *Answer choices:*

(see index for correct answer)

- a. Total cost of acquisition
- b. Total cost
- c. Manufacturing cost
- d. Khozraschyot

Guidance: level 1

:: Health promotion ::

_____ , as defined by the World _____ Organization , is "a state of complete physical, mental and social well-being and not merely the absence of disease or infirmity." This definition has been subject to controversy, as it may have limited value for implementation. _____ may be defined as the ability to adapt and manage physical, mental and social challenges throughout life.

23. *Answer choices:*

(see index for correct answer)

- a. Breastfeeding promotion
- b. Black Report
- c. HealthEquity
- d. Health Promotion Practice

Guidance: level 1

:: Television commercials ::

_____ is a characteristic that distinguishes physical entities that have biological processes, such as signaling and self-sustaining processes, from those that do not, either because such functions have ceased , or because they never had such functions and are classified as inanimate. Various forms of _____ exist, such as plants, animals, fungi, protists, archaea, and bacteria. The criteria can at times be ambiguous and may or may not define viruses, viroids, or potential synthetic _____ as "living". Biology is the science concerned with the study of _____ .

Exam Probability: **Medium**

24. *Answer choices:*

(see index for correct answer)

- a. The Life
- b. Life
- c. Surfer
- d. Never Say No to Panda

Guidance: level 1

:: Marketing ::

_____ uses different marketing channels and tools in combination: Marketing communication channels focus on any way a business communicates a message to its desired market, or the market in general. A marketing communication tool can be anything from: advertising, personal selling, direct marketing, sponsorship, communication, and promotion to public relations.

Exam Probability: **Medium**

25. *Answer choices:*
(see index for correct answer)

- a. Accreditation in Public Relations
- b. Market share
- c. Marketing communications
- d. Presentation folder

Guidance: level 1

:: Data collection ::

A _____ is an utterance which typically functions as a request for information. _____ s can thus be understood as a kind of illocutionary act in the field of pragmatics or as special kinds of propositions in frameworks of formal semantics such as alternative semantics or inquisitive semantics. The information requested is expected to be provided in the form of an answer. _____ s are often conflated with interrogatives, which are the grammatical forms typically used to achieve them. Rhetorical _____ s, for example, are interrogative in form but may not be considered true _____ s as they are not expected to be answered. Conversely, non-interrogative grammatical structures may be considered _____ s as in the case of the imperative sentence "tell me your name".

Exam Probability: **Medium**

26. *Answer choices:*

(see index for correct answer)

- a. Guardian
- b. Global surveillance
- c. Data farming
- d. North Atlantic Population Project

Guidance: level 1

:: ::

_____ is both a research area and a practical skill encompassing the ability of an individual or organization to "lead" or guide other individuals, teams, or entire organizations. Specialist literature debates various viewpoints, contrasting Eastern and Western approaches to _____ , and also United States versus European approaches. U.S. academic environments define _____ as "a process of social influence in which a person can enlist the aid and support of others in the accomplishment of a common task".

Exam Probability: **Low**

27. *Answer choices:*

(see index for correct answer)

- a. functional perspective
- b. Leadership
- c. imperative
- d. open system

Guidance: level 1

:: Materials ::

A _____ , also known as a feedstock, unprocessed material, or primary commodity, is a basic material that is used to produce goods, finished products, energy, or intermediate materials which are feedstock for future finished products. As feedstock, the term connotes these materials are bottleneck assets and are highly important with regard to producing other products. An example of this is crude oil, which is a _____ and a feedstock used in the production of industrial chemicals, fuels, plastics, and pharmaceutical goods; lumber is a _____ used to produce a variety of products including all types of furniture. The term " _____ " denotes materials in minimally processed or unprocessed in states; e.g., raw latex, crude oil, cotton, coal, raw biomass, iron ore, air, logs, or water i.e. "...any product of agriculture, forestry, fishing and any other mineral that is in its natural form or which has undergone the transformation required to prepare it for internationally marketing in substantial volumes."

Exam Probability: **Low**

28. *Answer choices:*

(see index for correct answer)

- a. Raw material
- b. Orthotropic material
- c. Ice substitute
- d. Aerospace materials

Guidance: level 1

:: Commerce ::

_____ relates to "the exchange of goods and services, especially on a large scale". It includes legal, economic, political, social, cultural and technological systems that operate in a country or in international trade.

Exam Probability: **High**

29. *Answer choices:*

(see index for correct answer)

- a. Emerging Markets Index
- b. Grain trade
- c. Commerce
- d. Buy-side analyst

Guidance: level 1

:: ::

In the broadest sense, _____ is any practice which contributes to the sale of products to a retail consumer. At a retail in-store level, _____ refers to the variety of products available for sale and the display of those products in such a way that it stimulates interest and entices customers to make a purchase.

Exam Probability: **Medium**

30. *Answer choices:*

- a. interpersonal communication
- b. Merchandising
- c. co-culture
- d. surface-level diversity

Guidance: level 1

:: ::

_____ is a term frequently used in marketing. It is a measure of how products and services supplied by a company meet or surpass customer expectation. _____ is defined as "the number of customers, or percentage of total customers, whose reported experience with a firm, its products, or its services exceeds specified satisfaction goals."

Exam Probability: **Low**

31. *Answer choices:*

- a. co-culture
- b. functional perspective
- c. open system
- d. Customer satisfaction

:: Consumer behaviour ::

_____ is an activity in which a customer browses the available goods or services presented by one or more retailers with the potential intent to purchase a suitable selection of them. A typology of shopper types has been developed by scholars which identifies one group of shoppers as recreational shoppers, that is, those who enjoy _____ and view it as a leisure activity.

Exam Probability: **Medium**

32. *Answer choices:*

(see index for correct answer)

- a. Shopping
- b. Shopping while black
- c. Customer engagement
- d. Consumption smoothing

:: Stock market ::

_____ is freedom from, or resilience against, potential harm caused by others. Beneficiaries of _____ may be of persons and social groups, objects and institutions, ecosystems or any other entity or phenomenon vulnerable to unwanted change by its environment.

Exam Probability: **High**

33. *Answer choices:*

(see index for correct answer)

- a. Qualified institutional placement
- b. Security
- c. Rogue trader
- d. Stock promoter

Guidance: level 1

:: Information technology management ::

B2B is often contrasted with business-to-consumer . In B2B commerce, it is often the case that the parties to the relationship have comparable negotiating power, and even when they do not, each party typically involves professional staff and legal counsel in the negotiation of terms, whereas B2C is shaped to a far greater degree by economic implications of information asymmetry. However, within a B2B context, large companies may have many commercial, resource and information advantages over smaller businesses. The United Kingdom government, for example, created the post of Small Business Commissioner under the Enterprise Act 2016 to "enable small businesses to resolve disputes" and "consider complaints by small business suppliers about payment issues with larger businesses that they supply."

Exam Probability: **Low**

34. *Answer choices:*

(see index for correct answer)

- a. Business-to-business
- b. Device Management Forum
- c. Service Measurement Index
- d. Autonomic networking

Guidance: level 1

:: Marketing ::

A _____ is something that is necessary for an organism to live a healthy life. _____ s are distinguished from wants in that, in the case of a _____ , a deficiency causes a clear adverse outcome: a dysfunction or death. In other words, a _____ is something required for a safe, stable and healthy life while a want is a desire, wish or aspiration. When _____ s or wants are backed by purchasing power, they have the potential to become economic demands.

Exam Probability: **Medium**

35. *Answer choices:*

(see index for correct answer)

- a. Product proliferation
- b. Need
- c. Fourth screen
- d. Premium pricing

Guidance: level 1

:: ::

_____ or accountancy is the measurement, processing, and communication of financial information about economic entities such as businesses and corporations. The modern field was established by the Italian mathematician Luca Pacioli in 1494. _____ , which has been called the "language of business", measures the results of an organization's economic activities and conveys this information to a variety of users, including investors, creditors, management, and regulators. Practitioners of _____ are known as accountants. The terms " _____ " and "financial reporting" are often used as synonyms.

Exam Probability: **Low**

36. *Answer choices:*

(see index for correct answer)

- a. Accounting
- b. Sarbanes-Oxley act of 2002
- c. co-culture
- d. interpersonal communication

Guidance: level 1

:: Management ::

_____ is the process of thinking about the activities required to achieve a desired goal. It is the first and foremost activity to achieve desired results. It involves the creation and maintenance of a plan, such as psychological aspects that require conceptual skills. There are even a couple of tests to measure someone's capability of _____ well. As such, _____ is a fundamental property of intelligent behavior. An important further meaning, often just called " _____ " is the legal context of permitted building developments.

Exam Probability: **High**

37. *Answer choices:*

(see index for correct answer)

- a. Planning
- b. Critical path method
- c. Total Worker Health
- d. Smiling curve

Guidance: level 1

:: Commodities ::

In economics, a _____ is an economic good or service that has full or substantial fungibility: that is, the market treats instances of the good as equivalent or nearly so with no regard to who produced them. Most commodities are raw materials, basic resources, agricultural, or mining products, such as iron ore, sugar, or grains like rice and wheat. Commodities can also be mass-produced unspecialized products such as chemicals and computer memory.

38. *Answer choices:*

(see index for correct answer)

- a. Commoditization
- b. Commodity money
- c. Commodity
- d. Commodity pathway diversion

Guidance: level 1

:: Retailing ::

_____ is the process of selling consumer goods or services to customers through multiple channels of distribution to earn a profit. _____ ers satisfy demand identified through a supply chain. The term " _____ er" is typically applied where a service provider fills the small orders of a large number of individuals, who are end-users, rather than large orders of a small number of wholesale, corporate or government clientele. Shopping generally refers to the act of buying products. Sometimes this is done to obtain final goods, including necessities such as food and clothing; sometimes it takes place as a recreational activity. Recreational shopping often involves window shopping and browsing: it does not always result in a purchase.

39. *Answer choices:*

(see index for correct answer)

- a. Return fraud
- b. Video game store
- c. Convenience store
- d. Best before

Guidance: level 1

:: Marketing ::

_____ s are structured marketing strategies designed by merchants to encourage customers to continue to shop at or use the services of businesses associated with each program. These programs exist covering most types of commerce, each one having varying features and rewards-schemes.

Exam Probability: **Low**

40. *Answer choices:*

(see index for correct answer)

- a. Loyalty program
- b. Content creation
- c. Niche market
- d. Chaotics

Guidance: level 1

:: ::

According to the philosopher Piyush Mathur , "Tangibility is the property that a phenomenon exhibits if it has and/or transports mass and/or energy and/or momentum".

Exam Probability: **High**

41. *Answer choices:*

(see index for correct answer)

- a. deep-level diversity
- b. personal values
- c. Sarbanes-Oxley act of 2002
- d. similarity-attraction theory

Guidance: level 1

:: ::

_____ is the process of making predictions of the future based on past and present data and most commonly by analysis of trends. A commonplace example might be estimation of some variable of interest at some specified future date. Prediction is a similar, but more general term. Both might refer to formal statistical methods employing time series, cross-sectional or longitudinal data, or alternatively to less formal judgmental methods. Usage can differ between areas of application: for example, in hydrology the terms "forecast" and " _____ " are sometimes reserved for estimates of values at certain specific future times, while the term "prediction" is used for more general estimates, such as the number of times floods will occur over a long period.

Exam Probability: **High**

42. *Answer choices:*

(see index for correct answer)

- a. information systems assessment
- b. process perspective
- c. Forecasting
- d. empathy

Guidance: level 1

:: Supply chain management terms ::

In business and finance, _____ is a system of organizations, people, activities, information, and resources involved in moving a product or service from supplier to customer. _____ activities involve the transformation of natural resources, raw materials, and components into a finished product that is delivered to the end customer. In sophisticated _____ systems, used products may re-enter the _____ at any point where residual value is recyclable. _____ s link value chains.

Exam Probability: **Medium**

43. *Answer choices:*

(see index for correct answer)

- a. Capital spare
- b. Most valuable customers
- c. Supply-chain management
- d. Supply chain

Guidance: level 1

:: Types of marketing ::

_____ was first defined as a form of marketing developed from direct response marketing campaigns which emphasizes customer retention and satisfaction, rather than a focus on sales transactions.

Exam Probability: **Low**

44. *Answer choices:*

(see index for correct answer)

- a. Account planning
- b. Relationship marketing
- c. Shopper marketing
- d. Z-CARD

Guidance: level 1

:: Management ::

The term _____ refers to measures designed to increase the degree of autonomy and self-determination in people and in communities in order to enable them to represent their interests in a responsible and self-determined way, acting on their own authority. It is the process of becoming stronger and more confident, especially in controlling one`s life and claiming one`s rights.
_____ as action refers both to the process of self-_____ and to professional support of people, which enables them to overcome their sense of powerlessness and lack of influence, and to recognize and use their resources. To do work with power.

Exam Probability: **High**

45. *Answer choices:*

(see index for correct answer)

- a. Empowerment
- b. Design management

- c. Line manager
- d. Quality control

Guidance: level 1

:: Retailing ::

A _____ is a retail establishment offering a wide range of consumer goods in different product categories known as "departments". In modern major cities, the _____ made a dramatic appearance in the middle of the 19th century, and permanently reshaped shopping habits, and the definition of service and luxury. Similar developments were under way in London , in Paris and in New York .

Exam Probability: **High**

46. *Answer choices:*

(see index for correct answer)

- a. Brick and mortar
- b. Non-store retailing
- c. Department store
- d. Ticket resale

Guidance: level 1

:: Market research ::

_____ , an acronym for Information through Disguised Experimentation is an annual market research fair conducted by the students of IIM-Lucknow. Students create games and use various other simulated environments to capture consumers' subconscious thoughts. This innovative method of market research removes the sensitization effect that might bias peoples answers to questions. This ensures that the most truthful answers are captured to research questions. The games are designed in such a way that the observers can elicit all the required information just by observing and noting down the behaviour and the responses of the participants.

Exam Probability: **High**

47. *Answer choices:*

(see index for correct answer)

- a. Vehicle Dependability Study
- b. Australian Market and Social Research Society Limited
- c. TNS NIPO
- d. Computer-assisted telephone interviewing

Guidance: level 1

:: Sales ::

_____ is a business discipline which is focused on the practical application of sales techniques and the management of a firm's sales operations. It is an important business function as net sales through the sale of products and services and resulting profit drive most commercial business. These are also typically the goals and performance indicators of _____ .

48. *Answer choices:*

(see index for correct answer)

- a. Voice-based marketing automation
- b. Sales management
- c. Qualified prospect
- d. Leaseback

Guidance: level 1

:: Management ::

A _____ is an idea of the future or desired result that a person or a group of people envisions, plans and commits to achieve. People endeavor to reach _____ s within a finite time by setting deadlines.

Exam Probability: **Medium**

49. *Answer choices:*

(see index for correct answer)

- a. Planning
- b. Discovery-driven planning
- c. Goal
- d. Demand chain management

:: Marketing ::

_____ is a pricing strategy where the price of a product is initially set low to rapidly reach a wide fraction of the market and initiate word of mouth. The strategy works on the expectation that customers will switch to the new brand because of the lower price. _____ is most commonly associated with marketing objectives of enlarging market share and exploiting economies of scale or experience.

Exam Probability: **High**

50. *Answer choices:*

(see index for correct answer)

- a. Hype cycle
- b. Hakan Okay
- c. Engagement marketing
- d. Bricks and clicks

:: Product management ::

_____ or brand stretching is a marketing strategy in which a firm marketing a product with a well-developed image uses the same brand name in a different product category. The new product is called a spin-off. Organizations use this strategy to increase and leverage brand equity . An example of a _____ is Jello-gelatin creating Jello pudding pops. It increases awareness of the brand name and increases profitability from offerings in more than one product category.

Exam Probability: **Medium**

51. *Answer choices:*

(see index for correct answer)

- a. Pareto chart
- b. Diffusion of innovations
- c. Product manager
- d. Brand extension

Guidance: level 1

:: Internet privacy ::

An _____ is a private network accessible only to an organization's staff. Often, a wide range of information and services are available on an organization's internal _____ that are unavailable to the public, unlike the Internet. A company-wide _____ can constitute an important focal point of internal communication and collaboration, and provide a single starting point to access internal and external resources. In its simplest form, an _____ is established with the technologies for local area networks and wide area networks . Many modern _____ s have search engines, user profiles, blogs, mobile apps with notifications, and events planning within their infrastructure.

Exam Probability: **High**

52. *Answer choices:*

(see index for correct answer)

- a. Intranet
- b. Zombie cookie
- c. Web storage
- d. Email encryption

Guidance: level 1

:: Generally Accepted Accounting Principles ::

Expenditure is an outflow of money to another person or group to pay for an item or service, or for a category of costs. For a tenant, rent is an _____ . For students or parents, tuition is an _____ . Buying food, clothing, furniture or an automobile is often referred to as an _____ . An _____ is a cost that is "paid" or "remitted", usually in exchange for something of value. Something that seems to cost a great deal is "expensive". Something that seems to cost little is "inexpensive". " _____ s of the table" are _____ s of dining, refreshments, a feast, etc.

Exam Probability: **High**

53. *Answer choices:*

(see index for correct answer)

- a. Earnings before interest and taxes
- b. Fin 48
- c. Cash method of accounting
- d. Revenue

Guidance: level 1

:: Product management ::

A _____ is a professional role which is responsible for the development of products for an organization, known as the practice of product management. _____ s own the business strategy behind a product , specify its functional requirements and generally manage the launch of features. They coordinate work done by many other functions and are ultimately responsible for the business success of the product.

54. *Answer choices:*

(see index for correct answer)

- a. Electronic registration mark
- b. Product information management
- c. Product manager
- d. Consumer adoption of technological innovations

Guidance: level 1

:: Graphic design ::

An _____ is an artifact that depicts visual perception, such as a photograph or other two-dimensional picture, that resembles a subject—usually a physical object—and thus provides a depiction of it. In the context of signal processing, an _____ is a distributed amplitude of color.

Exam Probability: **Medium**

55. *Answer choices:*

(see index for correct answer)

- a. Graphic charter
- b. Image
- c. First Things First 2000 manifesto

- d. Colophon

Guidance: level 1

:: Stock market ::

The _____ of a corporation is all of the shares into which ownership of the corporation is divided. In American English, the shares are commonly known as " _____ s". A single share of the _____ represents fractional ownership of the corporation in proportion to the total number of shares. This typically entitles the _____ holder to that fraction of the company's earnings, proceeds from liquidation of assets , or voting power, often dividing these up in proportion to the amount of money each _____ holder has invested. Not all _____ is necessarily equal, as certain classes of _____ may be issued for example without voting rights, with enhanced voting rights, or with a certain priority to receive profits or liquidation proceeds before or after other classes of shareholders.

Exam Probability: **Low**

56. *Answer choices:*

(see index for correct answer)

- a. Purple chip
- b. Sell side
- c. Stock Catalyst
- d. Stock

Guidance: level 1

:: Marketing ::

_____ is the process of using surveys to evaluate consumer acceptance of a new product idea prior to the introduction of a product to the market. It is important not to confuse _____ with advertising testing, brand testing and packaging testing; as is sometimes done. _____ focuses on the basic product idea, without the embellishments and puffery inherent in advertising.

Exam Probability: **Medium**

57. *Answer choices:*
(see index for correct answer)

- a. Concept testing
- b. Bluetooth advertising
- c. Brand
- d. Adobe Experience Manager

Guidance: level 1

:: ::

_____ is change in the heritable characteristics of biological populations over successive generations. These characteristics are the expressions of genes that are passed on from parent to offspring during reproduction. Different characteristics tend to exist within any given population as a result of mutation, genetic recombination and other sources of genetic variation. _____ occurs when _____ ary processes such as natural selection and genetic drift act on this variation, resulting in certain characteristics becoming more common or rare within a population. It is this process of _____ that has given rise to biodiversity at every level of biological organisation, including the levels of species, individual organisms and molecules.

Exam Probability: **High**

58. *Answer choices:*

(see index for correct answer)

- a. Evolution
- b. co-culture
- c. deep-level diversity
- d. similarity-attraction theory

Guidance: level 1

:: ::

A _____ is a professional who provides expert advice in a particular area such as security , management, education, accountancy, law, human resources, marketing , finance, engineering, science or any of many other specialized fields.

Exam Probability: **Medium**

59. *Answer choices:*

(see index for correct answer)

- a. empathy
- b. hierarchical
- c. co-culture
- d. interpersonal communication

Guidance: level 1

Manufacturing

Manufacturing is the production of merchandise for use or sale using labor and machines, tools, chemical and biological processing, or formulation. The term may refer to a range of human activity, from handicraft to high tech, but is most commonly applied to industrial design , in which raw materials are transformed into finished goods on a large scale. Such finished goods may be sold to other manufacturers for the production of other, more complex products, such as aircraft, household appliances, furniture, sports equipment or automobiles, or sold to wholesalers, who in turn sell them to retailers, who then sell them to end users and consumers.

:: Quality ::

The _____ , formerly the _____ Control , is a knowledge-based global community of quality professionals, with nearly 80,000 members dedicated to promoting and advancing quality tools, principles, and practices in their workplaces and communities.

Exam Probability: **Low**

1. *Answer choices:*

(see index for correct answer)

- a. American Society for Quality
- b. Society for Software Quality
- c. Process architecture
- d. Japanese quality

Guidance: level 1

:: Management ::

_____ is a process by which entities review the quality of all factors involved in production. ISO 9000 defines _____ as "A part of quality management focused on fulfilling quality requirements".

Exam Probability: **High**

2. *Answer choices:*

(see index for correct answer)

- a. Intopia
- b. Business economics
- c. Managerial prerogative
- d. Information excellence

Guidance: level 1

:: Elementary mathematics ::

In mathematics, a _____ is an enumerated collection of objects in which repetitions are allowed. Like a set, it contains members . The number of elements is called the length of the _____ . Unlike a set, the same elements can appear multiple times at different positions in a _____ , and order matters. Formally, a _____ can be defined as a function whose domain is either the set of the natural numbers or the set of the first n natural numbers . The position of an element in a _____ is its rank or index; it is the natural number from which the element is the image. It depends on the context or a specific convention, if the first element has index 0 or 1. When a symbol has been chosen for denoting a _____ , the nth element of the _____ is denoted by this symbol with n as subscript; for example, the nth element of the Fibonacci _____ is generally denoted Fn.

Exam Probability: **High**

3. *Answer choices:*

(see index for correct answer)

- a. Abscissa

- b. Counting
- c. Integer
- d. Sequence

Guidance: level 1

:: Project management ::

Some scenarios associate "this kind of planning" with learning "life skills". _____ s are necessary, or at least useful, in situations where individuals need to know what time they must be at a specific location to receive a specific service, and where people need to accomplish a set of goals within a set time period.

Exam Probability: **Medium**

4. *Answer choices:*

(see index for correct answer)

- a. Project portfolio management
- b. Cost-benefit
- c. Aggregate planning
- d. Terms of reference

Guidance: level 1

:: Fault-tolerant computer systems ::

_____ decision-making is a group decision-making process in which group members develop, and agree to support a decision in the best interest of the whole group or common goal. _____ may be defined professionally as an acceptable resolution, one that can be supported, even if not the "favourite" of each individual. It has its origin in the Latin word consensus , which is from consentio meaning literally feel together. It is used to describe both the decision and the process of reaching a decision. _____ decision-making is thus concerned with the process of deliberating and finalizing a decision, and the social, economic, legal, environmental and political effects of applying this process.

Exam Probability: **High**

5. *Answer choices:*

(see index for correct answer)

- a. Processor array
- b. Server farm
- c. Self-stabilization
- d. RAID

Guidance: level 1

:: Gas technologies ::

A _____ is a rotary mechanical device that extracts energy from a fluid flow and converts it into useful work. The work produced by a _____ can be used for generating electrical power when combined with a generator. A _____ is a turbomachine with at least one moving part called a rotor assembly, which is a shaft or drum with blades attached. Moving fluid acts on the blades so that they move and impart rotational energy to the rotor. Early _____ examples are windmills and waterwheels.

Exam Probability: **High**

6. *Answer choices:*

(see index for correct answer)

- a. The Oval Gasholders
- b. Restrictive flow orifice
- c. Turbine
- d. Gas stove

Guidance: level 1

:: Project management ::

In economics and business decision-making, a sunk cost is a cost that has already been incurred and cannot be recovered.

Exam Probability: **High**

7. *Answer choices:*

(see index for correct answer)

- a. Sunk costs
- b. Theory X and Theory Y
- c. Bill of quantities
- d. Sustainable event management

Guidance: level 1

:: Inventory ::

The _____ is the level of inventory which triggers an action to replenish that particular inventory stock. It is a minimum amount of an item which a firm holds in stock, such that, when stock falls to this amount, the item must be reordered. It is normally calculated as the forecast usage during the replenishment lead time plus safety stock. In the EOQ model, it was assumed that there is no time lag between ordering and procuring of materials. Therefore the _____ for replenishing the stocks occurs at that level when the inventory level drops to zero and because instant delivery by suppliers, the stock level bounce back.

Exam Probability: **Low**

8. *Answer choices:*

(see index for correct answer)

- a. Specific identification
- b. Stock demands

- c. Reorder point
- d. Spare part

Guidance: level 1

:: Data management ::

_____ refers to a data-driven improvement cycle used for improving, optimizing and stabilizing business processes and designs. The _____ improvement cycle is the core tool used to drive Six Sigma projects. However, _____ is not exclusive to Six Sigma and can be used as the framework for other improvement applications.

Exam Probability: **High**

9. *Answer choices:*
(see index for correct answer)

- a. Online analytical processing
- b. DMAIC
- c. ADO.NET
- d. Distributed data store

Guidance: level 1

:: Alchemical processes ::

In chemistry, a _____ is a special type of homogeneous mixture composed of two or more substances. In such a mixture, a solute is a substance dissolved in another substance, known as a solvent. The mixing process of a _____ happens at a scale where the effects of chemical polarity are involved, resulting in interactions that are specific to solvation. The _____ assumes the phase of the solvent when the solvent is the larger fraction of the mixture, as is commonly the case. The concentration of a solute in a _____ is the mass of that solute expressed as a percentage of the mass of the whole _____ . The term aqueous _____ is when one of the solvents is water.

Exam Probability: **High**

10. *Answer choices:*

(see index for correct answer)

- a. Projection
- b. Fermentation in food processing
- c. Solution
- d. Corporification

Guidance: level 1

:: Management ::

_____ is a formal technique useful where many possible courses of action are competing for attention. In essence, the problem-solver estimates the benefit delivered by each action, then selects a number of the most effective actions that deliver a total benefit reasonably close to the maximal possible one.

11. *Answer choices:*

(see index for correct answer)

- a. Facilitator
- b. Hierarchical organization
- c. Middle management
- d. SimulTrain

Guidance: level 1

:: Business ::

The seller, or the provider of the goods or services, completes a sale in response to an acquisition, appropriation, requisition or a direct interaction with the buyer at the point of sale. There is a passing of title of the item, and the settlement of a price, in which agreement is reached on a price for which transfer of ownership of the item will occur. The seller, not the purchaser typically executes the sale and it may be completed prior to the obligation of payment. In the case of indirect interaction, a person who sells goods or service on behalf of the owner is known as a _____ man or _____ woman or _____ person, but this often refers to someone selling goods in a store/shop, in which case other terms are also common, including _____ clerk, shop assistant, and retail clerk.

Exam Probability: **Medium**

12. *Answer choices:*

(see index for correct answer)

- a. Joint employment
- b. Street marketing
- c. Growth platform
- d. Ametek

Guidance: level 1

:: Unit operations ::

_____ is the process of separating the components or substances from a liquid mixture by using selective boiling and condensation. _____ may result in essentially complete separation , or it may be a partial separation that increases the concentration of selected components in the mixture. In either case, the process exploits differences in the volatility of the mixture's components. In industrial chemistry, _____ is a unit operation of practically universal importance, but it is a physical separation process, not a chemical reaction.

Exam Probability: **Medium**

13. *Answer choices:*

(see index for correct answer)

- a. Heat transfer
- b. Settling
- c. Sedimentation coefficient

- d. Unit Operations of Chemical Engineering

Guidance: level 1

:: Procurement ::

Purchasing is the formal process of buying goods and services. The _____ can vary from one organization to another, but there are some common key elements.

Exam Probability: **Low**

14. *Answer choices:*

(see index for correct answer)

- a. Qualifications-Based Selection
- b. Request for quotation
- c. System Design Review
- d. Purchasing process

Guidance: level 1

:: Supply chain management ::

_____ is the process of finding and agreeing to terms, and acquiring goods, services, or works from an external source, often via a tendering or competitive bidding process. _____ is used to ensure the buyer receives goods, services, or works at the best possible price when aspects such as quality, quantity, time, and location are compared. Corporations and public bodies often define processes intended to promote fair and open competition for their business while minimizing risks such as exposure to fraud and collusion.

Exam Probability: **Medium**

15. *Answer choices:*

(see index for correct answer)

- a. Supply chain surplus
- b. Procurement
- c. ThoughtSpeed Corporation
- d. Suppliers and Parts database

Guidance: level 1

:: Procurement ::

A _____ is a standard business process whose purpose is to invite suppliers into a bidding process to bid on specific products or services. RfQ generally means the same thing as Call for bids and Invitation for bid .

Exam Probability: **Medium**

16. *Answer choices:*

(see index for correct answer)

- a. Procurement outsourcing
- b. Purchasing process
- c. Request price quotation
- d. Bulk purchasing

Guidance: level 1

:: ::

Catalysis is the process of increasing the rate of a chemical reaction by adding a substance known as a _____ , which is not consumed in the catalyzed reaction and can continue to act repeatedly. Because of this, only very small amounts of _____ are required to alter the reaction rate in principle.

Exam Probability: **Medium**

17. *Answer choices:*

(see index for correct answer)

- a. Catalyst
- b. hierarchical perspective
- c. process perspective
- d. interpersonal communication

:: Accounting source documents ::

A _____ is a commercial document and first official offer issued by a buyer to a seller indicating types, quantities, and agreed prices for products or services. It is used to control the purchasing of products and services from external suppliers. _____ s can be an essential part of enterprise resource planning system orders.

Exam Probability: **Medium**

18. *Answer choices:*

(see index for correct answer)

- a. Invoice
- b. Remittance advice
- c. Banknote
- d. Purchase order

:: Production and manufacturing ::

_____ is a theory of management that analyzes and synthesizes workflows. Its main objective is improving economic efficiency, especially labor productivity. It was one of the earliest attempts to apply science to the engineering of processes and to management. _____ is sometimes known as Taylorism after its founder, Frederick Winslow Taylor.

Exam Probability: **Low**

19. *Answer choices:*

(see index for correct answer)

- a. Scientific management
- b. Fab lab
- c. Digital materialization
- d. Foundation Fieldbus H1

Guidance: level 1

:: Production and manufacturing ::

_____ consists of organization-wide efforts to "install and make permanent climate where employees continuously improve their ability to provide on demand products and services that customers will find of particular value." "Total" emphasizes that departments in addition to production are obligated to improve their operations; "management" emphasizes that executives are obligated to actively manage quality through funding, training, staffing, and goal setting. While there is no widely agreed-upon approach, TQM efforts typically draw heavily on the previously developed tools and techniques of quality control. TQM enjoyed widespread attention during the late 1980s and early 1990s before being overshadowed by ISO 9000, Lean manufacturing, and Six Sigma.

Exam Probability: **Low**

20. *Answer choices:*

(see index for correct answer)

- a. Total quality management
- b. Computer-aided process planning
- c. Fab lab
- d. Workmanship

Guidance: level 1

:: Monopoly (economics) ::

_____ are "efficiencies formed by variety, not volume". For example, a gas station that sells gasoline can sell soda, milk, baked goods, etc through their customer service representatives and thus achieve gasoline companies _____ .

21. *Answer choices:*

- a. Practice of law
- b. Economies of scope
- c. De facto monopoly
- d. State monopoly capitalism

Guidance: level 1

:: Production and manufacturing ::

_____ is the production under license of technology developed elsewhere. It is an especially prominent commercial practice in developing nations, which often approach _____ as a starting point for indigenous industrial development.

22. *Answer choices:*

- a. Licensed production
- b. SynqNet
- c. Value-added agriculture

- d. Resource Breakdown

Guidance: level 1

:: Insulators ::

A _____ is a piece of soft cloth large enough either to cover or to enfold a great portion of the user's body, usually when sleeping or otherwise at rest, thereby trapping radiant bodily heat that otherwise would be lost through convection, and so keeping the body warm.

Exam Probability: **Low**

23. *Answer choices:*
(see index for correct answer)

- a. Thermal pad
- b. Draught excluder
- c. Blanket
- d. Mechanical insulation

Guidance: level 1

:: Commerce ::

A _____ is an employee within a company, business or other organization who is responsible at some level for buying or approving the acquisition of goods and services needed by the company. Responsible for buying the best quality products, goods and services for their company at the most competitive prices, _____ s work in a wide range of sectors for many different organizations. The position responsibilities may be the same as that of a buyer or purchasing agent, or may include wider supervisory or managerial responsibilities. A _____ may oversee the acquisition of materials needed for production, general supplies for offices and facilities, equipment, or construction contracts. A _____ often supervises purchasing agents and buyers, but in small companies the _____ may also be the purchasing agent or buyer. The _____ position may also carry the title "Procurement Manager" or in the public sector, "Procurement Officer". He or she can come from both an Engineering or Economics background.

Exam Probability: **High**

24. *Answer choices:*

(see index for correct answer)

- a. Electronic article surveillance
- b. Purchasing manager
- c. Hong Kong Mercantile Exchange
- d. Requisition

Guidance: level 1

:: Sampling (statistics) ::

_____ uses statistical sampling to determine whether to accept or reject a production lot of material. It has been a common quality control technique used in industry. It is usually done as products leaves the factory, or in some cases even within the factory. Most often a producer supplies a consumer a number of items and a decision to accept or reject the items is made by determining the number of defective items in a sample from the lot. The lot is accepted if the number of defects falls below where the acceptance number or otherwise the lot is rejected.

Exam Probability: **Low**

25. *Answer choices:*
(see index for correct answer)

- a. Imperfect induction
- b. Unmatched count
- c. Acceptance sampling
- d. Lot quality assurance sampling

Guidance: level 1

:: Project management ::

A _____ is a type of bar chart that illustrates a project schedule, named after its inventor, Henry Gantt , who designed such a chart around the years 1910–1915. Modern _____ s also show the dependency relationships between activities and current schedule status.

26. *Answer choices:*

(see index for correct answer)

- a. Gold plating
- b. Hammock activity
- c. Gantt chart
- d. Project governance

Guidance: level 1

:: Finance ::

_____ is a financial estimate intended to help buyers and owners determine the direct and indirect costs of a product or system. It is a management accounting concept that can be used in full cost accounting or even ecological economics where it includes social costs.

Exam Probability: **Medium**

27. *Answer choices:*

(see index for correct answer)

- a. Total cost of ownership
- b. Penalized present value
- c. Numbrs

- d. Regulatory News Service

Guidance: level 1

:: Information systems ::

_____ is the process of creating, sharing, using and managing the knowledge and information of an organisation. It refers to a multidisciplinary approach to achieving organisational objectives by making the best use of knowledge.

Exam Probability: **Low**

28. *Answer choices:*

(see index for correct answer)

- a. Knowledge management
- b. Personal knowledge management
- c. Student information system
- d. Clinical decision support system

Guidance: level 1

:: ::

The _____ is a project plan of how the production budget will be spent over a given timescale, for every phase of a business project.

Exam Probability: **High**

29. *Answer choices:*

(see index for correct answer)

- a. empathy
- b. functional perspective
- c. Production schedule
- d. hierarchical perspective

Guidance: level 1

:: Direct marketing ::

_____ Inc. is an American privately owned multi-level marketing company. According to Direct Selling News, _____ was the sixth largest network marketing company in the world in 2018, with a wholesale volume of US$3.25 billion. _____ is based in Addison, Texas, outside Dallas. The company was founded by _____ Ash in 1963. Richard Rogers, _____'s son, is the chairman, and David Holl is president and was named CEO in 2006.

Exam Probability: **Low**

30. *Answer choices:*

- a. Tupperware Brands
- b. Publishers Clearing House
- c. Mary Kay
- d. Direct marketing educational foundation

Guidance: level 1

:: Industrial engineering ::

_____ , in its contemporary conceptualisation, is a comparison of perceived expectations of a service with perceived performance , giving rise to the equation SQ=P-E. This conceptualistion of _____ has its origins in the expectancy-disconfirmation paradigm.

Exam Probability: **Low**

31. *Answer choices:*

- a. Worker-machine activity chart
- b. Activity relationship chart
- c. Industrial engineering and operations research
- d. Service quality

Guidance: level 1

A _____ is a covering that is applied to the surface of an object, usually referred to as the substrate. The purpose of applying the _____ may be decorative, functional, or both. The _____ itself may be an all-over _____ , completely covering the substrate, or it may only cover parts of the substrate. An example of all of these types of _____ is a product label on many drinks bottles- one side has an all-over functional _____ and the other side has one or more decorative _____ s in an appropriate pattern to form the words and images.

Exam Probability: **Medium**

32. *Answer choices:*

(see index for correct answer)

- a. Coating
- b. co-culture
- c. empathy
- d. surface-level diversity

Guidance: level 1

:: Industrial design ::

In physics and mathematics, the _____ of a mathematical space is informally defined as the minimum number of coordinates needed to specify any point within it. Thus a line has a _____ of one because only one coordinate is needed to specify a point on it for example, the point at 5 on a number line. A surface such as a plane or the surface of a cylinder or sphere has a _____ of two because two coordinates are needed to specify a point on it for example, both a latitude and longitude are required to locate a point on the surface of a sphere. The inside of a cube, a cylinder or a sphere is three-_____ al because three coordinates are needed to locate a point within these spaces.

Exam Probability: **High**

33. *Answer choices:*

(see index for correct answer)

- a. field study
- b. Objectified
- c. FOAK
- d. Chintz

Guidance: level 1

:: Computer memory companies ::

_____ Corporation is a Japanese multinational conglomerate headquartered in Tokyo, Japan. Its diversified products and services include information technology and communications equipment and systems, electronic components and materials, power systems, industrial and social infrastructure systems, consumer electronics, household appliances, medical equipment, office equipment, as well as lighting and logistics.

Exam Probability: **High**

34. *Answer choices:*

(see index for correct answer)

- a. Toshiba
- b. Elpida Memory
- c. Winbond
- d. UMAX Technologies

Guidance: level 1

:: Management ::

_____ is the process of thinking about the activities required to achieve a desired goal. It is the first and foremost activity to achieve desired results. It involves the creation and maintenance of a plan, such as psychological aspects that require conceptual skills. There are even a couple of tests to measure someone's capability of _____ well. As such, _____ is a fundamental property of intelligent behavior. An important further meaning, often just called " _____ " is the legal context of permitted building developments.

35. *Answer choices:*

(see index for correct answer)

- a. Functional management
- b. Systems analysis
- c. Local management board
- d. Planning

Guidance: level 1

:: ::

_____ is a kind of action that occur as two or more objects have an effect upon one another. The idea of a two-way effect is essential in the concept of _____ , as opposed to a one-way causal effect. A closely related term is interconnectivity, which deals with the _____ s of _____ s within systems: combinations of many simple _____ s can lead to surprising emergent phenomena. _____ has different tailored meanings in various sciences. Changes can also involve _____ .

36. *Answer choices:*

(see index for correct answer)

- a. interpersonal communication

- b. deep-level diversity
- c. Interaction
- d. process perspective

Guidance: level 1

:: Quality ::

_____ is a concept first outlined by quality expert Joseph M. Juran in publications, most notably Juran on _____ . Designing for quality and innovation is one of the three universal processes of the Juran Trilogy, in which Juran describes what is required to achieve breakthroughs in new products, services, and processes. Juran believed that quality could be planned, and that most quality crises and problems relate to the way in which quality was planned.

Exam Probability: **Low**

37. *Answer choices:*

(see index for correct answer)

- a. Society for Software Quality
- b. Diamond clarity
- c. Secure Stations Scheme
- d. Quality by Design

Guidance: level 1

:: Project management ::

_____ s can take many forms depending on the type of project being implemented and the nature of the organization. The _____ details the project deliverables and describes the major objectives. The objectives should include measurable success criteria for the project.

Exam Probability: **Low**

38. *Answer choices:*

(see index for correct answer)

- a. Project management 2.0
- b. Effective Development Group
- c. Scope statement
- d. The Transformation Project

Guidance: level 1

:: Quality assurance ::

Organizations that issue credentials or certify third parties against official standards are themselves formally accredited by _____ bodies ; hence they are sometimes known as "accredited certification bodies". The _____ process ensures that their certification practices are acceptable, typically meaning that they are competent to test and certify third parties, behave ethically and employ suitable quality assurance.

39. *Answer choices:*

(see index for correct answer)

- a. State Acceptance of Production
- b. Static testing
- c. National Certification Corporation
- d. Accreditation Commission for Health Care

Guidance: level 1

:: ::

_____ is the process of finding an estimate, or approximation, which is a value that is usable for some purpose even if input data may be incomplete, uncertain, or unstable. The value is nonetheless usable because it is derived from the best information available. Typically, _____ involves "using the value of a statistic derived from a sample to estimate the value of a corresponding population parameter". The sample provides information that can be projected, through various formal or informal processes, to determine a range most likely to describe the missing information. An estimate that turns out to be incorrect will be an overestimate if the estimate exceeded the actual result, and an underestimate if the estimate fell short of the actual result.

40. *Answer choices:*

(see index for correct answer)

- a. information systems assessment
- b. imperative
- c. Estimation
- d. functional perspective

Guidance: level 1

:: Management ::

_____ is a term used in business and Information Technology to describe the in-depth process of capturing customer's expectations, preferences and aversions. Specifically, the _____ is a market research technique that produces a detailed set of customer wants and needs, organized into a hierarchical structure, and then prioritized in terms of relative importance and satisfaction with current alternatives. _____ studies typically consist of both qualitative and quantitative research steps. They are generally conducted at the start of any new product, process, or service design initiative in order to better understand the customer's wants and needs, and as the key input for new product definition, Quality Function Deployment , and the setting of detailed design specifications.

Exam Probability: **High**

41. *Answer choices:*

(see index for correct answer)

- a. Event management
- b. Voice of the customer
- c. Communities of innovation

- d. Coworking

Guidance: level 1

:: Metals ::

A _____ is a material that, when freshly prepared, polished, or fractured, shows a lustrous appearance, and conducts electricity and heat relatively well. _____ s are typically malleable or ductile . A _____ may be a chemical element such as iron, or an alloy such as stainless steel.

Exam Probability: **Medium**

42. *Answer choices:*

(see index for correct answer)

- a. Tamahagane
- b. Telluric iron
- c. Refractory metals
- d. Metal

Guidance: level 1

:: ::

In production, research, retail, and accounting, a _____ is the value of money that has been used up to produce something or deliver a service, and hence is not available for use anymore. In business, the _____ may be one of acquisition, in which case the amount of money expended to acquire it is counted as _____ . In this case, money is the input that is gone in order to acquire the thing. This acquisition _____ may be the sum of the _____ of production as incurred by the original producer, and further _____ s of transaction as incurred by the acquirer over and above the price paid to the producer. Usually, the price also includes a mark-up for profit over the _____ of production.

Exam Probability: **Low**

43. *Answer choices:*

(see index for correct answer)

- a. levels of analysis
- b. deep-level diversity
- c. functional perspective
- d. hierarchical

Guidance: level 1

:: Packaging ::

In work place, _____ or job _____ means good ranking with the hypothesized conception of requirements of a role. There are two types of job _____ s: contextual and task. Task _____ is related to cognitive ability while contextual _____ is dependent upon personality. Task _____ are behavioral roles that are recognized in job descriptions and by remuneration systems, they are directly related to organizational _____, whereas, contextual _____ are value based and additional behavioral roles that are not recognized in job descriptions and covered by compensation; they are extra roles that are indirectly related to organizational _____ . Citizenship _____ like contextual _____ means a set of individual activity/contribution that supports the organizational culture.

Exam Probability: **Medium**

44. *Answer choices:*

(see index for correct answer)

- a. Record sleeve
- b. Modified atmosphere/modified humidity packaging
- c. Ifco tray
- d. Performance

Guidance: level 1

:: Industrial organization ::

In economics, specifically general equilibrium theory, a perfect market is defined by several idealizing conditions, collectively called _____ . In theoretical models where conditions of _____ hold, it has been theoretically demonstrated that a market will reach an equilibrium in which the quantity supplied for every product or service, including labor, equals the quantity demanded at the current price. This equilibrium would be a Pareto optimum.

Exam Probability: **High**

45. *Answer choices:*

(see index for correct answer)

- a. Perfect competition
- b. Williamson trade-off model
- c. Tapered integration
- d. Putting-out system

Guidance: level 1

:: Data management ::

_____ is an object-oriented program and library developed by CERN. It was originally designed for particle physics data analysis and contains several features specific to this field, but it is also used in other applications such as astronomy and data mining. The latest release is 6.16.00, as of 2018-11-14.

Exam Probability: **High**

46. *Answer choices:*

(see index for correct answer)

- a. Uniform data access
- b. ROOT
- c. Data warehouse
- d. Storage area network

Guidance: level 1

:: Management ::

_____ , also known as natural process limits, are horizontal lines drawn on a statistical process control chart, usually at a distance of ±3 standard deviations of the plotted statistic from the statistic's mean.

Exam Probability: **High**

47. *Answer choices:*

(see index for correct answer)

- a. Supervisory board
- b. Unified interoperability
- c. Smiling curve
- d. Control limits

Guidance: level 1

:: Process management ::

When used in the context of communication networks, such as Ethernet or packet radio, _____ or network _____ is the rate of successful message delivery over a communication channel. The data these messages belong to may be delivered over a physical or logical link, or it can pass through a certain network node. _____ is usually measured in bits per second , and sometimes in data packets per second or data packets per time slot.

Exam Probability: **Medium**

48. *Answer choices:*

(see index for correct answer)

- a. Process optimization
- b. Modular process skid
- c. Throughput
- d. Business process network

Guidance: level 1

:: Project management ::

_____ is a process of setting goals, planning and/or controlling the organizing and leading the execution of any type of activity, such as.

49. *Answer choices:*

(see index for correct answer)

- a. Value breakdown structure
- b. P3M3
- c. Project network
- d. Management process

Guidance: level 1

:: Metrics ::

_____ is a computer model developed by the University of Idaho, that uses Landsat satellite data to compute and map evapotranspiration . _____ calculates ET as a residual of the surface energy balance, where ET is estimated by keeping account of total net short wave and long wave radiation at the vegetation or soil surface, the amount of heat conducted into soil, and the amount of heat convected into the air above the surface. The difference in these three terms represents the amount of energy absorbed during the conversion of liquid water to vapor, which is ET. _____ expresses near-surface temperature gradients used in heat convection as indexed functions of radio _____ surface temperature, thereby eliminating the need for absolutely accurate surface temperature and the need for air-temperature measurements.

(see index for correct answer)

- a. METRIC
- b. Cleanroom suitability
- c. Accommodation index
- d. Software metric

Guidance: level 1

:: Supply chain management ::

_____ is a core supply chain function and includes supply chain planning and supply chain execution capabilities. Specifically, _____ is the capability firms use to plan total material requirements. The material requirements are communicated to procurement and other functions for sourcing. _____ is also responsible for determining the amount of material to be deployed at each stocking location across the supply chain, establishing material replenishment plans, determining inventory levels to hold for each type of inventory , and communicating information regarding material needs throughout the extended supply chain.

Exam Probability: **Medium**

51. *Answer choices:*

(see index for correct answer)

- a. Universal Product Code
- b. Supply chain surplus

- c. Capconn
- d. XIO Strategies

Guidance: level 1

:: Management ::

_____ is an iterative four-step management method used in business for the control and continuous improvement of processes and products. It is also known as the Deming circle/cycle/wheel, the Shewhart cycle, the control circle/cycle, or plan–do–study–act . Another version of this _____ cycle is O _____ . The added "O" stands for observation or as some versions say: "Observe the current condition." This emphasis on observation and current condition has currency with the literature on lean manufacturing and the Toyota Production System. The _____ cycle, with Ishikawa's changes, can be traced back to S. Mizuno of the Tokyo Institute of Technology in 1959.

Exam Probability: **Medium**

52. *Answer choices:*

(see index for correct answer)

- a. Six phases of a big project
- b. PDCA
- c. Downstream
- d. Target operating model

Guidance: level 1

:: Business process ::

_____ is the value to an enterprise which is derived from the
techniques, procedures, and programs that implement and enhance the delivery of
goods and services. _____ is one of the three components of structural
capital, itself a component of intellectual capital. _____ can be seen
as the value of processes to any entity, whether for profit or not-for profit,
but is most commonly used in reference to for-profit entities.

Exam Probability: **Medium**

53. *Answer choices:*

(see index for correct answer)

- a. Leverage-point modeling
- b. Process-centered design
- c. Process capital
- d. Real-time enterprise

Guidance: level 1

:: Production and manufacturing ::

A BOM can define products as they are designed , as they are ordered , as they are built , or as they are maintained . The different types of BOMs depend on the business need and use for which they are intended. In process industries, the BOM is also known as the formula, recipe, or ingredients list. The phrase "bill of material" is frequently used by engineers as an adjective to refer not to the literal bill, but to the current production configuration of a product, to distinguish it from modified or improved versions under study or in test.

Exam Probability: **High**

54. *Answer choices:*

(see index for correct answer)

- a. Zero Defects
- b. Low rate initial production
- c. Production engineering
- d. Bill of materials

Guidance: level 1

:: Supply chain management terms ::

In business and finance, _____ is a system of organizations, people, activities, information, and resources involved in moving a product or service from supplier to customer. _____ activities involve the transformation of natural resources, raw materials, and components into a finished product that is delivered to the end customer. In sophisticated _____ systems, used products may re-enter the _____ at any point where residual value is recyclable. _____ s link value chains.

Exam Probability: **Medium**

55. *Answer choices:*

(see index for correct answer)

- a. Supply chain
- b. Consumables
- c. Direct shipment
- d. Stockout

Guidance: level 1

:: Quality ::

A _____ is an initiating cause of either a condition or a causal chain that leads to an outcome or effect of interest. The term denotes the earliest, most basic, `deepest`, cause for a given behavior; most often a fault. The idea is that you can only see an error by its manifest signs. Those signs can be widespread, multitudinous, and convoluted, whereas the _____ leading to them often is a lot simpler.

56. *Answer choices:*

(see index for correct answer)

- a. Quality by Design
- b. Secure Stations Scheme
- c. Root cause
- d. Cleaning validation

Guidance: level 1

:: Natural resources ::

_____ s are resources that exist without actions of humankind. This includes all valued characteristics such as magnetic, gravitational, electrical properties and forces etc. On Earth it includes sunlight, atmosphere, water, land along with all vegetation, crops and animal life that naturally subsists upon or within the heretofore identified characteristics and substances.

Exam Probability: **High**

57. *Answer choices:*

(see index for correct answer)

- a. Natural resource
- b. Ecosystem Health

- c. Soil
- d. Dryland salinity

Guidance: level 1

:: Retailing ::

_____ is the process of selling consumer goods or services to customers through multiple channels of distribution to earn a profit. _____ ers satisfy demand identified through a supply chain. The term " _____ er" is typically applied where a service provider fills the small orders of a large number of individuals, who are end-users, rather than large orders of a small number of wholesale, corporate or government clientele. Shopping generally refers to the act of buying products. Sometimes this is done to obtain final goods, including necessities such as food and clothing; sometimes it takes place as a recreational activity. Recreational shopping often involves window shopping and browsing: it does not always result in a purchase.

Exam Probability: **High**

58. *Answer choices:*

(see index for correct answer)

- a. Retail
- b. Supermarket
- c. Outlet store
- d. Garage sale

Guidance: level 1

:: Project management ::

In general usage, a _____ is a comprehensive evaluation of an individual's current pay and future financial state by using current known variables to predict future income, asset values and withdrawal plans. This often includes a budget which organizes an individual's finances and sometimes includes a series of steps or specific goals for spending and saving in the future. This plan allocates future income to various types of expenses, such as rent or utilities, and also reserves some income for short-term and long-term savings. A _____ is sometimes referred to as an investment plan, but in personal finance a _____ can focus on other specific areas such as risk management, estates, college, or retirement.

Exam Probability: **Medium**

59. *Answer choices:*

(see index for correct answer)

- a. Direct changeover
- b. Project plan
- c. Financial plan
- d. project triangle

Guidance: level 1

Commerce

Commerce relates to "the exchange of goods and services, especially on a large scale." It includes legal, economic, political, social, cultural and technological systems that operate in any country or internationally.

:: Human resource management ::

An organizational chart is a diagram that shows the structure of an organization and the relationships and relative ranks of its parts and positions/jobs. The term is also used for similar diagrams, for example ones showing the different elements of a field of knowledge or a group of languages.

Exam Probability: **Low**

1. *Answer choices:*

(see index for correct answer)

- a. ABC Consultants
- b. Administrative services organization
- c. Organization chart
- d. Skill mix

Guidance: level 1

:: ::

A _____ is a professional who provides expert advice in a particular area such as security , management, education, accountancy, law, human resources, marketing , finance, engineering, science or any of many other specialized fields.

Exam Probability: **Low**

2. *Answer choices:*

(see index for correct answer)

- a. cultural
- b. Consultant
- c. Sarbanes-Oxley act of 2002
- d. similarity-attraction theory

:: ::

Employment is a relationship between two parties, usually based on a contract where work is paid for, where one party, which may be a corporation, for profit, not-for-profit organization, co-operative or other entity is the employer and the other is the employee. Employees work in return for payment, which may be in the form of an hourly wage, by piecework or an annual salary, depending on the type of work an employee does or which sector she or he is working in. Employees in some fields or sectors may receive gratuities, bonus payment or stock options. In some types of employment, employees may receive benefits in addition to payment. Benefits can include health insurance, housing, disability insurance or use of a gym. Employment is typically governed by employment laws, regulations or legal contracts.

Exam Probability: **Medium**

3. *Answer choices:*

(see index for correct answer)

- a. empathy
- b. Personnel
- c. process perspective
- d. hierarchical perspective

:: Economics terminology ::

_____ is the total receipts a seller can obtain from selling goods or services to buyers. It can be written as P × Q, which is the price of the goods multiplied by the quantity of the sold goods.

Exam Probability: **High**

4. *Answer choices:*

(see index for correct answer)

- a. spillover effect
- b. Physical capital
- c. Profit motive
- d. Total revenue

Guidance: level 1

:: Commercial item transport and distribution ::

A _____ in common law countries is a person or company that transports goods or people for any person or company and that is responsible for any possible loss of the goods during transport. A _____ offers its services to the general public under license or authority provided by a regulatory body. The regulatory body has usually been granted "ministerial authority" by the legislation that created it. The regulatory body may create, interpret, and enforce its regulations upon the _____ with independence and finality, as long as it acts within the bounds of the enabling legislation.

5. *Answer choices:*

(see index for correct answer)

- a. Dock
- b. Common carrier
- c. Half tide dock
- d. Trade facilitation

Guidance: level 1

:: Confidence tricks ::

_____ is the fraudulent attempt to obtain sensitive information such as usernames, passwords and credit card details by disguising oneself as a trustworthy entity in an electronic communication. Typically carried out by email spoofing or instant messaging, it often directs users to enter personal information at a fake website which matches the look and feel of the legitimate site.

Exam Probability: **Medium**

6. *Answer choices:*

(see index for correct answer)

- a. Phishing
- b. Hustling

- c. Bogus escrow
- d. White van speaker scam

Guidance: level 1

:: Management ::

The term _____ refers to measures designed to increase the degree of autonomy and self-determination in people and in communities in order to enable them to represent their interests in a responsible and self-determined way, acting on their own authority. It is the process of becoming stronger and more confident, especially in controlling one's life and claiming one's rights. _____ as action refers both to the process of self- _____ and to professional support of people, which enables them to overcome their sense of powerlessness and lack of influence, and to recognize and use their resources. To do work with power.

Exam Probability: **Medium**

7. *Answer choices:*
(see index for correct answer)

- a. Empowerment
- b. Hierarchical organization
- c. Quick response manufacturing
- d. Middle management

Guidance: level 1

:: Hospitality industry ::

_____ refers to the relationship between a guest and a host, wherein the host receives the guest with goodwill, including the reception and entertainment of guests, visitors, or strangers. Louis, chevalier de Jaucourt describes _____ in the Encyclopédie as the virtue of a great soul that cares for the whole universe through the ties of humanity.

Exam Probability: **Low**

8. *Answer choices:*

(see index for correct answer)

- a. Cover charge
- b. Restaurant rating
- c. Hospitality industry
- d. Hospitality

Guidance: level 1

:: Summary statistics ::

_____ is the number of occurrences of a repeating event per unit of time. It is also referred to as temporal _____ , which emphasizes the contrast to spatial _____ and angular _____ . The period is the duration of time of one cycle in a repeating event, so the period is the reciprocal of the _____ . For example: if a newborn baby's heart beats at a _____ of 120 times a minute, its period—the time interval between beats—is half a second . _____ is an important parameter used in science and engineering to specify the rate of oscillatory and vibratory phenomena, such as mechanical vibrations, audio signals , radio waves, and light.

Exam Probability: **High**

9. *Answer choices:*

(see index for correct answer)

- a. Percentile
- b. Frequency distribution
- c. Frequency
- d. Five-number summary

Guidance: level 1

:: Insolvency ::

_____ is a legal process through which people or other entities who cannot repay debts to creditors may seek relief from some or all of their debts. In most jurisdictions, _____ is imposed by a court order, often initiated by the debtor.

10. *Answer choices:*

(see index for correct answer)

- a. Liquidation
- b. George Samuel Ford
- c. Bankruptcy
- d. Financial distress

Guidance: level 1

:: ::

_____ is an American restaurant chain and international franchise which was founded in 1958 by Dan and Frank Carney. The company is known for its Italian-American cuisine menu, including pizza and pasta, as well as side dishes and desserts. _____ has 18,431 restaurants worldwide as of December 31, 2018, making it the world's largest pizza chain in terms of locations. It is a subsidiary of Yum! Brands, Inc., one of the world's largest restaurant companies.

Exam Probability: **Medium**

11. *Answer choices:*

(see index for correct answer)

- a. hierarchical perspective

- b. Pizza Hut
- c. corporate values
- d. levels of analysis

Guidance: level 1

:: ::

Senior management, executive management, upper management, or a _____ is generally a team of individuals at the highest level of management of an organization who have the day-to-day tasks of managing that organization — sometimes a company or a corporation.

Exam Probability: **High**

12. *Answer choices:*

(see index for correct answer)

- a. surface-level diversity
- b. information systems assessment
- c. empathy
- d. Management team

Guidance: level 1

:: ::

_____ is "property consisting of land and the buildings on it, along with its natural resources such as crops, minerals or water; immovable property of this nature; an interest vested in this an item of real property, buildings or housing in general. Also: the business of _____ ; the profession of buying, selling, or renting land, buildings, or housing." It is a legal term used in jurisdictions whose legal system is derived from English common law, such as India, England, Wales, Northern Ireland, United States, Canada, Pakistan, Australia, and New Zealand.

Exam Probability: **Low**

13. *Answer choices:*

(see index for correct answer)

- a. hierarchical
- b. similarity-attraction theory
- c. Real estate
- d. open system

Guidance: level 1

:: E-commerce ::

_____ is the business-to-business or business-to-consumer or business-to-government purchase and sale of supplies, work, and services through the Internet as well as other information and networking systems, such as electronic data interchange and enterprise resource planning.

14. *Answer choices:*

(see index for correct answer)

- a. E-procurement
- b. Tor
- c. Public key certificate
- d. Shopping directory

Guidance: level 1

:: ::

Advertising is a marketing communication that employs an openly sponsored, non-personal message to promote or sell a product, service or idea. Sponsors of advertising are typically businesses wishing to promote their products or services. Advertising is differentiated from public relations in that an advertiser pays for and has control over the message. It differs from personal selling in that the message is non-personal, i.e., not directed to a particular individual.Advertising is communicated through various mass media, including traditional media such as newspapers, magazines, television, radio, outdoor advertising or direct mail; and new media such as search results, blogs, social media, websites or text messages. The actual presentation of the message in a medium is referred to as an _____ , or "ad" or advert for short.

Exam Probability: **Medium**

15. *Answer choices:*

(see index for correct answer)

- a. process perspective
- b. Character
- c. similarity-attraction theory
- d. imperative

Guidance: level 1

:: Commercial item transport and distribution ::

A _____ , forwarder, or forwarding agent, also known as a non-vessel operating common carrier , is a person or company that organizes shipments for individuals or corporations to get goods from the manufacturer or producer to a market, customer or final point of distribution. Forwarders contract with a carrier or often multiple carriers to move the goods. A forwarder does not move the goods but acts as an expert in the logistics network. These carriers can use a variety of shipping modes, including ships, airplanes, trucks, and railroads, and often do utilize multiple modes for a single shipment. For example, the _____ may arrange to have cargo moved from a plant to an airport by truck, flown to the destination city, then moved from the airport to a customer`s building by another truck.

Exam Probability: **Medium**

16. *Answer choices:*
(see index for correct answer)

- a. SAP EWM

- b. Hydrogen pipeline transport
- c. Freight forwarder
- d. Standard Carrier Alpha Code

Guidance: level 1

:: Price fixing convictions ::

_____ is the flag carrier airline of the United Kingdom, headquartered at Waterside, Harmondsworth. It is the second largest airline in the United Kingdom, based on fleet size and passengers carried, behind easyJet. The airline is based in Waterside near its main hub at London Heathrow Airport. In January 2011 BA merged with Iberia, creating the International Airlines Group , a holding company registered in Madrid, Spain. IAG is the world's third-largest airline group in terms of annual revenue and the second-largest in Europe. It is listed on the London Stock Exchange and in the FTSE 100 Index. _____ is the first passenger airline to have generated more than $1 billion on a single air route in a year .

Exam Probability: **Medium**

17. *Answer choices:*

(see index for correct answer)

- a. Siemens
- b. SK Foods
- c. Danish Christmas Tree Growers Association
- d. British Airways

:: Computer access control ::

_____ is the act of confirming the truth of an attribute of a single piece of data claimed true by an entity. In contrast with identification, which refers to the act of stating or otherwise indicating a claim purportedly attesting to a person or thing's identity, _____ is the process of actually confirming that identity. It might involve confirming the identity of a person by validating their identity documents, verifying the authenticity of a website with a digital certificate, determining the age of an artifact by carbon dating, or ensuring that a product is what its packaging and labeling claim to be. In other words, _____ often involves verifying the validity of at least one form of identification.

Exam Probability: **Low**

18. *Answer choices:*

(see index for correct answer)

- a. Authentication
- b. Copy protection
- c. Security token
- d. Location-based authentication

:: Generally Accepted Accounting Principles ::

In accounting, _____ is the income that a business have from its normal business activities, usually from the sale of goods and services to customers. _____ is also referred to as sales or turnover. Some companies receive _____ from interest, royalties, or other fees. _____ may refer to business income in general, or it may refer to the amount, in a monetary unit, earned during a period of time, as in "Last year, Company X had _____ of $42 million". Profits or net income generally imply total _____ minus total expenses in a given period. In accounting, in the balance statement it is a subsection of the Equity section and _____ increases equity, it is often referred to as the "top line" due to its position on the income statement at the very top. This is to be contrasted with the "bottom line" which denotes net income .

Exam Probability: **High**

19. *Answer choices:*

(see index for correct answer)

- a. Chinese accounting standards
- b. Revenue
- c. Pro forma
- d. Treasury stock

Guidance: level 1

:: ::

A _____ is a person or firm who arranges transactions between a buyer and a seller for a commission when the deal is executed. A _____ who also acts as a seller or as a buyer becomes a principal party to the deal. Neither role should be confused with that of an agent—one who acts on behalf of a principal party in a deal.

Exam Probability: **High**

20. *Answer choices:*

(see index for correct answer)

- a. surface-level diversity
- b. hierarchical
- c. Broker
- d. imperative

Guidance: level 1

:: Stochastic processes ::

_____ in its modern meaning is a "new idea, creative thoughts, new imaginations in form of device or method". _____ is often also viewed as the application of better solutions that meet new requirements, unarticulated needs, or existing market needs. Such _____ takes place through the provision of more-effective products, processes, services, technologies, or business models that are made available to markets, governments and society. An _____ is something original and more effective and, as a consequence, new, that "breaks into" the market or society. _____ is related to, but not the same as, invention, as _____ is more apt to involve the practical implementation of an invention to make a meaningful impact in the market or society, and not all _____ s require an invention. _____ often manifests itself via the engineering process, when the problem being solved is of a technical or scientific nature. The opposite of _____ is exnovation.

Exam Probability: **High**

21. *Answer choices:*

(see index for correct answer)

- a. BCMP network
- b. Brownian tree
- c. Innovation
- d. Fractional Poisson process

Guidance: level 1

:: Commerce ::

A _____ is an employee within a company, business or other organization who is responsible at some level for buying or approving the acquisition of goods and services needed by the company. Responsible for buying the best quality products, goods and services for their company at the most competitive prices, _____ s work in a wide range of sectors for many different organizations. The position responsibilities may be the same as that of a buyer or purchasing agent, or may include wider supervisory or managerial responsibilities. A _____ may oversee the acquisition of materials needed for production, general supplies for offices and facilities, equipment, or construction contracts. A _____ often supervises purchasing agents and buyers, but in small companies the _____ may also be the purchasing agent or buyer. The _____ position may also carry the title "Procurement Manager" or in the public sector, "Procurement Officer". He or she can come from both an Engineering or Economics background.

Exam Probability: **High**

22. *Answer choices:*

(see index for correct answer)

- a. Kiosk
- b. White Elephant Sale
- c. Issuing bank
- d. Video rental shop

Guidance: level 1

:: ::

_____ is a type of government support for the citizens of that society. _____ may be provided to people of any income level, as with social security , but it is usually intended to ensure that the poor can meet their basic human needs such as food and shelter. _____ attempts to provide poor people with a minimal level of well-being, usually either a free- or a subsidized-supply of certain goods and social services, such as healthcare, education, and vocational training.

Exam Probability: **Medium**

23. *Answer choices:*

(see index for correct answer)

- a. open system
- b. Welfare
- c. deep-level diversity
- d. process perspective

Guidance: level 1

:: Marketing techniques ::

_____ is the activity of dividing a broad consumer or business market, normally consisting of existing and potential customers, into sub-groups of consumers based on some type of shared characteristics. In dividing or segmenting markets, researchers typically look for common characteristics such as shared needs, common interests, similar lifestyles or even similar demographic profiles. The overall aim of segmentation is to identify high yield segments – that is, those segments that are likely to be the most profitable or that have growth potential – so that these can be selected for special attention .

Exam Probability: **Medium**

24. *Answer choices:*

(see index for correct answer)

- a. Geodemographic segmentation
- b. Elevator pitch
- c. Stunt casting
- d. Market segmentation

Guidance: level 1

:: E-commerce ::

_____ is a method of e-commerce where shoppers' friends become involved in the shopping experience. _____ attempts to use technology to mimic the social interactions found in physical malls and stores. With the rise of mobile devices, _____ is now extending beyond the online world and into the offline world of shopping.

25. *Answer choices:*

(see index for correct answer)

- a. Social shopping
- b. Infomediary
- c. Lyoness
- d. Transactional Link

Guidance: level 1

:: Payment systems ::

_____ s are part of a payment system issued by financial institutions, such as a bank, to a customer that enables its owner to access the funds in the customer`s designated bank accounts, or through a credit account and make payments by electronic funds transfer and access automated teller machines . Such cards are known by a variety of names including bank cards, ATM cards, MAC , client cards, key cards or cash cards.

Exam Probability: **Medium**

26. *Answer choices:*

(see index for correct answer)

- a. WorldPay
- b. FreshBooks

- c. Payment card
- d. ChargeSmart

Guidance: level 1

:: ::

Business Model Canvas is a strategic management and lean startup template for developing new or documenting existing business models. It is a visual chart with elements describing a firm's or product's value proposition, infrastructure, customers, and finances. It assists firms in aligning their activities by illustrating potential trade-offs.

Exam Probability: **High**

27. *Answer choices:*

(see index for correct answer)

- a. levels of analysis
- b. surface-level diversity
- c. Cost structure
- d. interpersonal communication

Guidance: level 1

:: Management ::

_____ is a process by which entities review the quality of all factors involved in production. ISO 9000 defines _____ as "A part of quality management focused on fulfilling quality requirements".

Exam Probability: **Medium**

28. *Answer choices:*

(see index for correct answer)

- a. Dynamic enterprise modeling
- b. Quality control
- c. Value proposition
- d. Real property administrator

Guidance: level 1

:: Production economics ::

In economics and related disciplines, a _____ is a cost in making any economic trade when participating in a market.

Exam Probability: **Medium**

29. *Answer choices:*

(see index for correct answer)

- a. Division of work
- b. Multifactor productivity
- c. Economic batch quantity
- d. Transaction cost

Guidance: level 1

:: Auctioneering ::

An _____ is a process of buying and selling goods or services by offering them up for bid, taking bids, and then selling the item to the highest bidder. The open ascending price _____ is arguably the most common form of _____ in use today. Participants bid openly against one another, with each subsequent bid required to be higher than the previous bid. An _____ eer may announce prices, bidders may call out their bids themselves , or bids may be submitted electronically with the highest current bid publicly displayed. In a Dutch _____ , the _____ eer begins with a high asking price for some quantity of like items; the price is lowered until a participant is willing to accept the _____ eer's price for some quantity of the goods in the lot or until the seller's reserve price is met. While _____ s are most associated in the public imagination with the sale of antiques, paintings, rare collectibles and expensive wines, _____ s are also used for commodities, livestock, radio spectrum and used cars. In economic theory, an _____ may refer to any mechanism or set of trading rules for exchange.

Exam Probability: **Medium**

30. *Answer choices:*

(see index for correct answer)

- a. Auction
- b. Demsetz auction
- c. Virginity auction
- d. Public auction

Guidance: level 1

:: Production economics ::

In economics, _____ is the change in the total cost that arises when the quantity produced is incremented by one unit; that is, it is the cost of producing one more unit of a good. Intuitively, _____ at each level of production includes the cost of any additional inputs required to produce the next unit. At each level of production and time period being considered, _____ s include all costs that vary with the level of production, whereas other costs that do not vary with production are fixed and thus have no _____ . For example, the _____ of producing an automobile will generally include the costs of labor and parts needed for the additional automobile but not the fixed costs of the factory that have already been incurred. In practice, marginal analysis is segregated into short and long-run cases, so that, over the long run, all costs become marginal. Where there are economies of scale, prices set at _____ will fail to cover total costs, thus requiring a subsidy. _____ pricing is not a matter of merely lowering the general level of prices with the aid of a subsidy; with or without subsidy it calls for a drastic restructuring of pricing practices, with opportunities for very substantial improvements in efficiency at critical points.

Exam Probability: **Medium**

31. *Answer choices:*

- a. Capacity utilization
- b. Marginal cost
- c. Marginal cost of capital schedule
- d. Diseconomies of scale

Guidance: level 1

:: ::

A _____ is a fund into which a sum of money is added during an employee's employment years, and from which payments are drawn to support the person's retirement from work in the form of periodic payments. A _____ may be a "defined benefit plan" where a fixed sum is paid regularly to a person, or a "defined contribution plan" under which a fixed sum is invested and then becomes available at retirement age. _____ s should not be confused with severance pay; the former is usually paid in regular installments for life after retirement, while the latter is typically paid as a fixed amount after involuntary termination of employment prior to retirement.

Exam Probability: **Low**

32. *Answer choices:*

- a. surface-level diversity
- b. Pension
- c. levels of analysis

- d. co-culture

Guidance: level 1

:: Business law ::

A _____ is a contractual arrangement calling for the lessee to pay the lessor for use of an asset. Property, buildings and vehicles are common assets that are _____ d. Industrial or business equipment is also _____ d.

Exam Probability: **Low**

33. *Answer choices:*

(see index for correct answer)

- a. Installment sale
- b. United Kingdom commercial law
- c. Lease
- d. Unfair business practices

Guidance: level 1

:: ::

_____ is a concept of English common law and is a necessity for simple contracts but not for special contracts . The concept has been adopted by other common law jurisdictions, including the US.

Exam Probability: **High**

34. *Answer choices:*

(see index for correct answer)

- a. co-culture
- b. empathy
- c. Consideration
- d. surface-level diversity

Guidance: level 1

:: ::

_____ is the principled guide to action taken by the administrative executive branches of the state with regard to a class of issues, in a manner consistent with law and institutional customs.

Exam Probability: **Medium**

35. *Answer choices:*

(see index for correct answer)

- a. Sarbanes-Oxley act of 2002
- b. Public policy
- c. imperative
- d. open system

Guidance: level 1

:: Materials ::

A _____ , also known as a feedstock, unprocessed material, or primary commodity, is a basic material that is used to produce goods, finished products, energy, or intermediate materials which are feedstock for future finished products. As feedstock, the term connotes these materials are bottleneck assets and are highly important with regard to producing other products. An example of this is crude oil, which is a _____ and a feedstock used in the production of industrial chemicals, fuels, plastics, and pharmaceutical goods; lumber is a _____ used to produce a variety of products including all types of furniture. The term "_____" denotes materials in minimally processed or unprocessed in states; e.g., raw latex, crude oil, cotton, coal, raw biomass, iron ore, air, logs, or water i.e. "...any product of agriculture, forestry, fishing and any other mineral that is in its natural form or which has undergone the transformation required to prepare it for internationally marketing in substantial volumes."

Exam Probability: **Low**

36. *Answer choices:*

(see index for correct answer)

- a. Raw material

- b. Monocrystalline whisker
- c. Porous medium
- d. Putty

Guidance: level 1

:: Real property law ::

A _____ is the grant of authority or rights, stating that the granter formally recognizes the prerogative of the recipient to exercise the rights specified. It is implicit that the granter retains superiority , and that the recipient admits a limited status within the relationship, and it is within that sense that _____ s were historically granted, and that sense is retained in modern usage of the term.

Exam Probability: **Low**

37. *Answer choices:*

(see index for correct answer)

- a. Allodial title
- b. Claim club
- c. Deed
- d. Charter

Guidance: level 1

_____ refers to a business or organization attempting to acquire goods or services to accomplish its goals. Although there are several organizations that attempt to set standards in the _____ process, processes can vary greatly between organizations. Typically the word " _____ " is not used interchangeably with the word "procurement", since procurement typically includes expediting, supplier quality, and transportation and logistics in addition to _____ .

Exam Probability: **Low**

38. *Answer choices:*

(see index for correct answer)

- a. surface-level diversity
- b. open system
- c. levels of analysis
- d. Purchasing

Guidance: level 1

_____ is the extraction of valuable minerals or other geological materials from the earth, usually from an ore body, lode, vein, seam, reef or placer deposit. These deposits form a mineralized package that is of economic interest to the miner.

39. *Answer choices:*

(see index for correct answer)

- a. open system
- b. Mining
- c. personal values
- d. co-culture

Guidance: level 1

:: ::

_____ , also referred to as orthostasis, is a human position in which the body is held in an upright position and supported only by the feet.

40. *Answer choices:*

(see index for correct answer)

- a. functional perspective
- b. empathy
- c. deep-level diversity
- d. Character

:: Evaluation ::

_____ is a way of preventing mistakes and defects in manufactured products and avoiding problems when delivering products or services to customers; which ISO 9000 defines as "part of quality management focused on providing confidence that quality requirements will be fulfilled". This defect prevention in _____ differs subtly from defect detection and rejection in quality control and has been referred to as a shift left since it focuses on quality earlier in the process .

Exam Probability: **High**

41. *Answer choices:*

(see index for correct answer)

- a. Integrity
- b. Cryptographic Module Testing Laboratory
- c. Impact assessment
- d. Quality assurance

:: Business terms ::

_____ ning is an organization's process of defining its strategy, or direction, and making decisions on allocating its resources to pursue this strategy. It may also extend to control mechanisms for guiding the implementation of the strategy. _____ ning became prominent in corporations during the 1960s and remains an important aspect of strategic management. It is executed by _____ ners or strategists, who involve many parties and research sources in their analysis of the organization and its relationship to the environment in which it competes.

Exam Probability: **Low**

42. *Answer choices:*

(see index for correct answer)

- a. Owner Controlled Insurance Program
- b. back office
- c. operating cost
- d. Strategic plan

Guidance: level 1

:: E-commerce ::

A _____ is a financial transaction involving a very small sum of money and usually one that occurs online. A number of _____ systems were proposed and developed in the mid-to-late 1990s, all of which were ultimately unsuccessful. A second generation of _____ systems emerged in the 2010s.

43. *Answer choices:*

(see index for correct answer)

- a. Electronic Payment Services
- b. Micropayment
- c. PapiNet
- d. RSA

Guidance: level 1

:: ::

In Christian denominations that practice infant baptism, confirmation is seen as the sealing of Christianity created in baptism. Those being _____ are known as confirmands. In some denominations, such as the Anglican Communion and Methodist Churches, confirmation bestows full membership in a local congregation upon the recipient. In others, such as the Roman Catholic Church, Confirmation "renders the bond with the Church more perfect", because, while a baptized person is already a member, "reception of the sacrament of Confirmation is necessary for the completion of baptismal grace".

Exam Probability: **High**

44. *Answer choices:*

(see index for correct answer)

- a. hierarchical perspective
- b. corporate values
- c. Confirmed
- d. cultural

Guidance: level 1

:: Generally Accepted Accounting Principles ::

Expenditure is an outflow of money to another person or group to pay for an item or service, or for a category of costs. For a tenant, rent is an _____ . For students or parents, tuition is an _____ . Buying food, clothing, furniture or an automobile is often referred to as an _____ . An _____ is a cost that is "paid" or "remitted", usually in exchange for something of value. Something that seems to cost a great deal is "expensive". Something that seems to cost little is "inexpensive". " _____ s of the table" are _____ s of dining, refreshments, a feast, etc.

Exam Probability: **Medium**

45. *Answer choices:*

(see index for correct answer)

- a. Gross sales
- b. Earnings before interest and taxes
- c. Expense
- d. AICPA Statements of Position

:: Production economics ::

In economics long run is a theoretical concept where all markets are in equilibrium, and all prices and quantities have fully adjusted and are in equilibrium. The long run contrasts with the _____ where there are some constraints and markets are not fully in equilibrium.

Exam Probability: **Medium**

46. *Answer choices:*

(see index for correct answer)

- a. Split-off point
- b. Short run
- c. Specialization
- d. Producer's risk

:: ::

A _____ is a person who trades in commodities produced by other people. Historically, a _____ is anyone who is involved in business or trade. _____ s have operated for as long as industry, commerce, and trade have existed. During the 16th-century, in Europe, two different terms for _____ s emerged: One term, meerseniers, described local traders such as bakers, grocers, etc.; while a new term, koopman (Dutch: koopman, described _____ s who operated on a global stage, importing and exporting goods over vast distances, and offering added-value services such as credit and finance.

Exam Probability: **High**

47. *Answer choices:*

(see index for correct answer)

- a. imperative
- b. levels of analysis
- c. similarity-attraction theory
- d. hierarchical perspective

Guidance: level 1

:: ::

Walter Elias Disney was an American entrepreneur, animator, voice actor and film producer. A pioneer of the American animation industry, he introduced several developments in the production of cartoons. As a film producer, Disney holds the record for most Academy Awards earned by an individual, having won 22 Oscars from 59 nominations. He was presented with two Golden Globe Special Achievement Awards and an Emmy Award, among other honors. Several of his films are included in the National Film Registry by the Library of Congress.

Exam Probability: **High**

48. *Answer choices:*

(see index for correct answer)

- a. Walt Disney
- b. interpersonal communication
- c. open system
- d. Character

Guidance: level 1

:: ::

_____ is a qualitative measure used to relate the quality of motor vehicle traffic service. LOS is used to analyze roadways and intersections by categorizing traffic flow and assigning quality levels of traffic based on performance measure like vehicle speed, density, congestion, etc.

Exam Probability: **Medium**

49. *Answer choices:*

(see index for correct answer)

- a. similarity-attraction theory
- b. corporate values
- c. Level of service
- d. levels of analysis

Guidance: level 1

:: Insolvency ::

_____ is the process in accounting by which a company is brought to an end in the United Kingdom, Republic of Ireland and United States. The assets and property of the company are redistributed. _____ is also sometimes referred to as winding-up or dissolution, although dissolution technically refers to the last stage of _____. The process of _____ also arises when customs, an authority or agency in a country responsible for collecting and safeguarding customs duties, determines the final computation or ascertainment of the duties or drawback accruing on an entry.

Exam Probability: **High**

50. *Answer choices:*

(see index for correct answer)

- a. Preferential creditor
- b. Bankruptcy

- c. Liquidation
- d. Financial distress

Guidance: level 1

:: Industry ::

_____ , also known as flow production or continuous production, is the production of large amounts of standardized products, including and especially on assembly lines. Together with job production and batch production, it is one of the three main production methods.

Exam Probability: **High**

51. *Answer choices:*

(see index for correct answer)

- a. Industrial robot
- b. Sunset industry
- c. Mass production
- d. Wedge based mechanical exfoliation

Guidance: level 1

:: ::

In legal terminology, a _____ is any formal legal document that sets out the facts and legal reasons that the filing party or parties believes are sufficient to support a claim against the party or parties against whom the claim is brought that entitles the plaintiff to a remedy. For example, the Federal Rules of Civil Procedure that govern civil litigation in United States courts provide that a civil action is commenced with the filing or service of a pleading called a _____. Civil court rules in states that have incorporated the Federal Rules of Civil Procedure use the same term for the same pleading.

Exam Probability: **Low**

52. *Answer choices:*

(see index for correct answer)

- a. functional perspective
- b. interpersonal communication
- c. similarity-attraction theory
- d. Complaint

Guidance: level 1

:: ::

_____ is the social science that studies the production, distribution, and consumption of goods and services.

Exam Probability: **High**

53. *Answer choices:*

(see index for correct answer)

- a. Economics
- b. Sarbanes-Oxley act of 2002
- c. Character
- d. personal values

Guidance: level 1

:: Marketing analytics ::

_____ is a long-term, forward-looking approach to planning with the fundamental goal of achieving a sustainable competitive advantage. Strategic planning involves an analysis of the company's strategic initial situation prior to the formulation, evaluation and selection of market-oriented competitive position that contributes to the company's goals and marketing objectives.

Exam Probability: **Medium**

54. *Answer choices:*

(see index for correct answer)

- a. Marketing strategy
- b. Marketing operations management
- c. Advertising adstock
- d. marketing dashboard

:: ::

The _____ or just chief executive , is the most senior corporate, executive, or administrative officer in charge of managing an organization especially an independent legal entity such as a company or nonprofit institution. CEOs lead a range of organizations, including public and private corporations, non-profit organizations and even some government organizations . The CEO of a corporation or company typically reports to the board of directors and is charged with maximizing the value of the entity, which may include maximizing the share price, market share, revenues or another element. In the non-profit and government sector, CEOs typically aim at achieving outcomes related to the organization's mission, such as reducing poverty, increasing literacy, etc.

Exam Probability: **Medium**

55. *Answer choices:*

(see index for correct answer)

- a. hierarchical
- b. cultural
- c. information systems assessment
- d. Chief executive officer

:: Banking ::

A _____ is a financial institution that accepts deposits from the public and creates credit. Lending activities can be performed either directly or indirectly through capital markets. Due to their importance in the financial stability of a country, _____ s are highly regulated in most countries. Most nations have institutionalized a system known as fractional reserve _____ ing under which _____ s hold liquid assets equal to only a portion of their current liabilities. In addition to other regulations intended to ensure liquidity, _____ s are generally subject to minimum capital requirements based on an international set of capital standards, known as the Basel Accords.

Exam Probability: **Medium**

56. *Answer choices:*

(see index for correct answer)

- a. Zombie bank
- b. Highly confident letter
- c. Retail banking
- d. Bank

Guidance: level 1

:: Business terms ::

The _____ or reception is an area where visitors arrive and first encounter a staff at a place of business. _____ staff will deal with whatever question the visitor has and put them in contact with a relevant person at the company. Broadly speaking, the _____ includes roles that affect the revenues of the business. The term _____ is in contrast to the term back office which refers to a company's operations, personnel, accounting, payroll and financial departments which do not interact directly with customers.

Exam Probability: **High**

57. *Answer choices:*

(see index for correct answer)

- a. Owner Controlled Insurance Program
- b. operating cost
- c. churn rate
- d. Personal selling

Guidance: level 1

:: Business law ::

The _____ , first published in 1952, is one of a number of Uniform Acts that have been established as law with the goal of harmonizing the laws of sales and other commercial transactions across the United States of America through UCC adoption by all 50 states, the District of Columbia, and the Territories of the United States.

58. *Answer choices:*

(see index for correct answer)

- a. Business valuation
- b. Limited liability company
- c. Contract failure
- d. Uniform Commercial Code

Guidance: level 1

:: Marketing ::

_____ comes from the Latin neg and otsia referring to businessmen who, unlike the patricians, had no leisure time in their industriousness; it held the meaning of business until the 17th century when it took on the diplomatic connotation as a dialogue between two or more people or parties intended to reach a beneficial outcome over one or more issues where a conflict exists with respect to at least one of these issues. Thus, _____ is a process of combining divergent positions into a joint agreement under a decision rule of unanimity.

Exam Probability: **High**

59. *Answer choices:*

(see index for correct answer)

- a. societal marketing
- b. Aspirational brand
- c. Negotiation
- d. Price war

Guidance: level 1

Business ethics

   Business ethics (also known as corporate ethics) is a form of applied ethics
or professional ethics, that examines ethical principles and moral or ethical
problems that can arise in a business environment. It applies to all aspects of
business conduct and is relevant to the conduct of individuals and entire
organizations. These ethics originate from individuals, organizational
statements or from the legal system. These norms, values, ethical, and
unethical practices are what is used to guide business. They help those
businesses maintain a better connection with their stakeholders.

:: ::

_____ generally refers to a focus on the needs or desires of one's self. A number of philosophical, psychological, and economic theories examine the role of _____ in motivating human action.

Exam Probability: **Low**

1. *Answer choices:*

(see index for correct answer)

- a. corporate values
- b. imperative
- c. Self-interest
- d. empathy

Guidance: level 1

:: Parental leave ::

_____ , or family leave, is an employee benefit available in almost all countries. The term " _____ " may include maternity, paternity, and adoption leave; or may be used distinctively from "maternity leave" and "paternity leave" to describe separate family leave available to either parent to care for small children. In some countries and jurisdictions, "family leave" also includes leave provided to care for ill family members. Often, the minimum benefits and eligibility requirements are stipulated by law.

Exam Probability: **Low**

2. *Answer choices:*

(see index for correct answer)

- a. Parental leave
- b. Additional Paternity Leave Regulations 2010
- c. Cleveland Board of Education v. LaFleur
- d. Geduldig v. Aiello

Guidance: level 1

:: Types of marketing ::

_____ is an advertisement strategy in which a company uses surprise and/or unconventional interactions in order to promote a product or service. It is a type of publicity. The term was popularized by Jay Conrad Levinson's 1984 book _____ .

Exam Probability: **Medium**

3. *Answer choices:*

(see index for correct answer)

- a. Global marketing
- b. Guerrilla Marketing
- c. Association of Publishing Agencies
- d. Secret brand

:: ::

Oriental Nicety, formerly _____ , Exxon Mediterranean, SeaRiver Mediterranean, S/R Mediterranean, Mediterranean, and Dong Fang Ocean, was an oil tanker that gained notoriety after running aground in Prince William Sound spilling hundreds of thousands of barrels of crude oil in Alaska. On March 24, 1989, while owned by the former Exxon Shipping Company, and captained by Joseph Hazelwood and First Mate James Kunkel bound for Long Beach, California, the vessel ran aground on the Bligh Reef resulting in the second largest oil spill in United States history. The size of the spill is estimated to have been 40,900 to 120,000 m3 , or 257,000 to 750,000 barrels. In 1989, the _____ oil spill was listed as the 54th largest spill in history.

Exam Probability: **Low**

4. *Answer choices:*

(see index for correct answer)

- a. information systems assessment
- b. hierarchical
- c. Exxon Valdez
- d. Sarbanes-Oxley act of 2002

:: ::

A _____ is the ability to carry out a task with determined results often within a given amount of time, energy, or both. _____ s can often be divided into domain-general and domain-specific _____ s. For example, in the domain of work, some general _____ s would include time management, teamwork and leadership, self-motivation and others, whereas domain-specific _____ s would be used only for a certain job. _____ usually requires certain environmental stimuli and situations to assess the level of _____ being shown and used.

Exam Probability: **Low**

5. *Answer choices:*

(see index for correct answer)

- a. Skill
- b. Character
- c. interpersonal communication
- d. empathy

Guidance: level 1

:: Hazard analysis ::

Broadly speaking, a _____ is the combined effort of 1. identifying and analyzing potential events that may negatively impact individuals, assets, and/or the environment ; and 2. making judgments "on the tolerability of the risk on the basis of a risk analysis" while considering influencing factors . Put in simpler terms, a _____ analyzes what can go wrong, how likely it is to happen, what the potential consequences are, and how tolerable the identified risk is. As part of this process, the resulting determination of risk may be expressed in a quantitative or qualitative fashion. The _____ is an inherent part of an overall risk management strategy, which attempts to, after a _____ , "introduce control measures to eliminate or reduce" any potential risk-related consequences.

Exam Probability: **Low**

6. *Answer choices:*

(see index for correct answer)

- a. Hazardous Materials Identification System
- b. Swiss cheese model
- c. Risk assessment

Guidance: level 1

:: ::

In regulatory jurisdictions that provide for it , _____ is a group of laws and organizations designed to ensure the rights of consumers as well as fair trade, competition and accurate information in the marketplace. The laws are designed to prevent the businesses that engage in fraud or specified unfair practices from gaining an advantage over competitors. They may also provides additional protection for those most vulnerable in society. _____ laws are a form of government regulation that aim to protect the rights of consumers. For example, a government may require businesses to disclose detailed information about products—particularly in areas where safety or public health is an issue, such as food.

Exam Probability: **High**

7. *Answer choices:*

(see index for correct answer)

- a. Consumer Protection
- b. deep-level diversity
- c. Character
- d. functional perspective

Guidance: level 1

:: Majority–minority relations ::

It was established as axiomatic in anthropological research by Franz Boas in the first few decades of the 20th century and later popularized by his students. Boas first articulated the idea in 1887: "civilization is not something absolute, but ... is relative, and ... our ideas and conceptions are true only so far as our civilization goes". However, Boas did not coin the term.

8. *Answer choices:*

(see index for correct answer)

- a. positive discrimination
- b. Affirmative action
- c. Cultural relativism

Guidance: level 1

:: Electronic waste ::

_____ or e-waste describes discarded electrical or electronic devices. Used electronics which are destined for refurbishment, reuse, resale, salvage, recycling through material recovery, or disposal are also considered e-waste. Informal processing of e-waste in developing countries can lead to adverse human health effects and environmental pollution.

9. *Answer choices:*

(see index for correct answer)

- a. ReGlobe
- b. Computer liquidator
- c. Digger gold
- d. Electronic waste

Guidance: level 1

:: Culture ::

_____ is a society which is characterized by individualism, which is the prioritization or emphasis, of the individual over the entire group. _____ s are oriented around the self, being independent instead of identifying with a group mentality. They see each other as only loosely linked, and value personal goals over group interests. _____ s tend to have a more diverse population and are characterized with emphasis on personal achievements, and a rational assessment of both the beneficial and detrimental aspects of relationships with others. _____ s have such unique aspects of communication as being a low power-distance culture and having a low-context communication style. The United States, Australia, Great Britain, Canada, the Netherlands, and New Zealand have been identified as highly _____ s.

Exam Probability: **Low**

10. *Answer choices:*

(see index for correct answer)

- a. cultural framework
- b. High-context
- c. Low-context culture
- d. Individualistic culture

Guidance: level 1

:: Private equity ::

In finance, a high-yield bond is a bond that is rated below investment grade. These bonds have a higher risk of default or other adverse credit events, but typically pay higher yields than better quality bonds in order to make them attractive to investors.

Exam Probability: **Medium**

11. *Answer choices:*

(see index for correct answer)

- a. Earnout
- b. Junk bond
- c. World Business Angels Association
- d. Private money investing

Guidance: level 1

The _____ is an agency of the United States Department of Labor. Congress established the agency under the Occupational Safety and Health Act , which President Richard M. Nixon signed into law on December 29, 1970. OSHA`s mission is to "assure safe and healthy working conditions for working men and women by setting and enforcing standards and by providing training, outreach, education and assistance". The agency is also charged with enforcing a variety of whistleblower statutes and regulations. OSHA is currently headed by Acting Assistant Secretary of Labor Loren Sweatt. OSHA`s workplace safety inspections have been shown to reduce injury rates and injury costs without adverse effects to employment, sales, credit ratings, or firm survival.

Exam Probability: **Medium**

12. *Answer choices:*

(see index for correct answer)

- a. interpersonal communication
- b. empathy
- c. Occupational Safety and Health Administration
- d. similarity-attraction theory

Guidance: level 1

The _____ is an institution of the European Union, responsible for proposing legislation, implementing decisions, upholding the EU treaties and managing the day-to-day business of the EU. Commissioners swear an oath at the European Court of Justice in Luxembourg City, pledging to respect the treaties and to be completely independent in carrying out their duties during their mandate. Unlike in the Council of the European Union, where members are directly and indirectly elected, and the European Parliament, where members are directly elected, the Commissioners are proposed by the Council of the European Union, on the basis of suggestions made by the national governments, and then appointed by the European Council after the approval of the European Parliament.

Exam Probability: **Low**

13. *Answer choices:*

(see index for correct answer)

- a. process perspective
- b. Character
- c. levels of analysis
- d. hierarchical perspective

Guidance: level 1

:: Corporate crime ::

_____ LLP, based in Chicago, was an American holding company. Formerly one of the "Big Five" accounting firms , the firm had provided auditing, tax, and consulting services to large corporations. By 2001, it had become one of the world's largest multinational companies.

Exam Probability: **Low**

14. *Answer choices:*

(see index for correct answer)

- a. Arthur Andersen
- b. Arthur Andersen LLP v. United States
- c. Corporate Manslaughter and Corporate Homicide Act 2007
- d. backdating

Guidance: level 1

:: ::

_____ in the United States is a federal and state program that helps with medical costs for some people with limited income and resources. _____ also offers benefits not normally covered by Medicare, including nursing home care and personal care services. The Health Insurance Association of America describes _____ as "a government insurance program for persons of all ages whose income and resources are insufficient to pay for health care." _____ is the largest source of funding for medical and health-related services for people with low income in the United States, providing free health insurance to 74 million low-income and disabled people as of 2017. It is a means-tested program that is jointly funded by the state and federal governments and managed by the states, with each state currently having broad leeway to determine who is eligible for its implementation of the program. States are not required to participate in the program, although all have since 1982. _____ recipients must be U.S. citizens or qualified non-citizens, and may include low-income adults, their children, and people with certain disabilities. Poverty alone does not necessarily qualify someone for _____ .

Exam Probability: **High**

15. *Answer choices:*

(see index for correct answer)

- a. corporate values
- b. similarity-attraction theory
- c. Medicaid
- d. deep-level diversity

Guidance: level 1

:: Agricultural labor ::

The _____ of America, or more commonly just _____, is a labor union for farmworkers in the United States. It originated from the merger of two workers' rights organizations, the Agricultural Workers Organizing Committee led by organizer Larry Itliong, and the National Farm Workers Association led by César Chávez and Dolores Huerta. They became allied and transformed from workers' rights organizations into a union as a result of a series of strikes in 1965, when the mostly Filipino farmworkers of the AWOC in Delano, California initiated a grape strike, and the NFWA went on strike in support. As a result of the commonality in goals and methods, the NFWA and the AWOC formed the _____ Organizing Committee on August 22, 1966. This organization was accepted into the AFL-CIO in 1972 and changed its name to the _____ Union.

Exam Probability: **Medium**

16. *Answer choices:*

(see index for correct answer)

- a. Collective farming
- b. United Farm Workers
- c. Harvest excursion
- d. California Agricultural Labor Relations Act

Guidance: level 1

:: Business ethics ::

A _____ is a person who exposes any kind of information or activity that is deemed illegal, unethical, or not correct within an organization that is either private or public. The information of alleged wrongdoing can be classified in many ways: violation of company policy/rules, law, regulation, or threat to public interest/national security, as well as fraud, and corruption. Those who become _____ s can choose to bring information or allegations to surface either internally or externally. Internally, a _____ can bring his/her accusations to the attention of other people within the accused organization such as an immediate supervisor. Externally, a _____ can bring allegations to light by contacting a third party outside of an accused organization such as the media, government, law enforcement, or those who are concerned. _____ s, however, take the risk of facing stiff reprisal and retaliation from those who are accused or alleged of wrongdoing.

Exam Probability: **Low**

17. *Answer choices:*

(see index for correct answer)

- a. Corporate Knights
- b. Workplace bullying
- c. Burson-Marsteller
- d. Whistleblower

Guidance: level 1

:: Financial markets ::

The _____ is a United States federal government organization, established by Title I of the Dodd–Frank Wall Street Reform and Consumer Protection Act, which was signed into law by President Barack Obama on July 21, 2010. The Office of Financial Research is intended to provide support to the council.

Exam Probability: **Medium**

18. *Answer choices:*

(see index for correct answer)

- a. dark pool
- b. Convergence trade
- c. Financial Stability Oversight Council
- d. Payment for order flow

Guidance: level 1

:: Labour relations ::

_____ is a field of study that can have different meanings depending on the context in which it is used. In an international context, it is a subfield of labor history that studies the human relations with regard to work – in its broadest sense – and how this connects to questions of social inequality. It explicitly encompasses unregulated, historical, and non-Western forms of labor. Here, _____ define "for or with whom one works and under what rules. These rules determine the type of work, type and amount of remuneration, working hours, degrees of physical and psychological strain, as well as the degree of freedom and autonomy associated with the work."

19. *Answer choices:*

(see index for correct answer)

- a. Association of German Chambers of Industry and Commerce
- b. Inflatable rat
- c. United Students Against Sweatshops
- d. Labor relations

Guidance: level 1

:: ::

Competition law is a law that promotes or seeks to maintain market competition by regulating anti-competitive conduct by companies. Competition law is implemented through public and private enforcement. Competition law is known as " _____ law" in the United States for historical reasons, and as "anti-monopoly law" in China and Russia. In previous years it has been known as trade practices law in the United Kingdom and Australia. In the European Union, it is referred to as both _____ and competition law.

Exam Probability: **Medium**

20. *Answer choices:*

(see index for correct answer)

- a. deep-level diversity

- b. personal values
- c. Antitrust
- d. co-culture

Guidance: level 1

:: Social enterprise ::

Corporate social responsibility   is a type of international private business self-regulation. While once it was possible to describe CSR as an internal organisational policy or a corporate ethic strategy, that time has passed as various international laws have been developed and various organisations have used their authority to push it beyond individual or even industry-wide initiatives. While it has been considered a form of corporate self-regulation for some time, over the last decade or so it has moved considerably from voluntary decisions at the level of individual organisations, to mandatory schemes at regional, national and even transnational levels.

Exam Probability: **High**

21. *Answer choices:*

(see index for correct answer)

- a. Social enterprise
- b. Social venture

Guidance: level 1

The Ethics & Compliance Initiative was formed in 2015 and consists of three nonprofit organizations: the Ethics Research Center, the Ethics & Compliance Association, and the Ethics & Compliance Certification Institute. Based in Arlington, Virginia, United States, ECI is devoted to the advancement of high ethical standards and practices in public and private institutions, and provides research about ethical standards, workplace integrity, and compliance practices and processes.

Exam Probability: **Medium**

22. *Answer choices:*

(see index for correct answer)

- a. Ethics Resource Center
- b. Character
- c. interpersonal communication
- d. functional perspective

Guidance: level 1

:: Organizational structure ::

An _____ defines how activities such as task allocation, coordination, and supervision are directed toward the achievement of organizational aims.

23. *Answer choices:*

(see index for correct answer)

- a. Unorganisation
- b. Automated Bureaucracy
- c. Followership
- d. Blessed Unrest

Guidance: level 1

:: Price fixing convictions ::

_____ AG is a German multinational conglomerate company headquartered in Berlin and Munich and the largest industrial manufacturing company in Europe with branch offices abroad.

Exam Probability: **Medium**

24. *Answer choices:*

(see index for correct answer)

- a. Siemens
- b. Danish Christmas Tree Growers Association
- c. United States v. Archer Daniels Midland Co.
- d. Asahi Glass Co.

:: Product certification ::

_____ is food produced by methods that comply with the standards of organic farming. Standards vary worldwide, but organic farming features practices that cycle resources, promote ecological balance, and conserve biodiversity. Organizations regulating organic products may restrict the use of certain pesticides and fertilizers in the farming methods used to produce such products. _____ s typically are not processed using irradiation, industrial solvents, or synthetic food additives.

Exam Probability: **Medium**

25. *Answer choices:*
(see index for correct answer)

- a. Listing and approval use and compliance
- b. Organic food
- c. B Corporation
- d. Organic Crop Improvement Association

:: Socialism ::

_____ is a label used to define the first currents of modern socialist thought as exemplified by the work of Henri de Saint-Simon, Charles Fourier, Étienne Cabet and Robert Owen.

Exam Probability: **Low**

26. *Answer choices:*

(see index for correct answer)

- a. Mutualization
- b. Red-baiting
- c. The Ragged-Trousered Philanthropists
- d. Utopian socialism

Guidance: level 1

:: Water law ::

The _____ is the primary federal law in the United States governing water pollution. Its objective is to restore and maintain the chemical, physical, and biological integrity of the nation's waters; recognizing the responsibilities of the states in addressing pollution and providing assistance to states to do so, including funding for publicly owned treatment works for the improvement of wastewater treatment; and maintaining the integrity of wetlands. It is one of the United States' first and most influential modern environmental laws. As with many other major U.S. federal environmental statutes, it is administered by the U.S. Environmental Protection Agency , in coordination with state governments. Its implementing regulations are codified at 40 C.F.R. Subchapters D, N, and O .

27. *Answer choices:*

(see index for correct answer)

- a. Clean Water Act
- b. Water law
- c. Berlin Rules on Water Resources
- d. Correlative rights doctrine

Guidance: level 1

:: Management ::

The term _____ refers to measures designed to increase the degree of autonomy and self-determination in people and in communities in order to enable them to represent their interests in a responsible and self-determined way, acting on their own authority. It is the process of becoming stronger and more confident, especially in controlling one's life and claiming one's rights. _____ as action refers both to the process of self- _____ and to professional support of people, which enables them to overcome their sense of powerlessness and lack of influence, and to recognize and use their resources. To do work with power.

Exam Probability: **High**

28. *Answer choices:*

(see index for correct answer)

- a. Supplier performance management
- b. Quick response manufacturing
- c. Supplier relationship management
- d. Capability management

Guidance: level 1

:: Anti-capitalism ::

_____ is a range of economic and social systems characterised by social ownership of the means of production and workers' self-management, as well as the political theories and movements associated with them. Social ownership can be public, collective or cooperative ownership, or citizen ownership of equity. There are many varieties of _____ and there is no single definition encapsulating all of them, with social ownership being the common element shared by its various forms.

Exam Probability: **Low**

29. *Answer choices:*

(see index for correct answer)

- a. Communalism
- b. The Anti-Capitalistic Mentality
- c. Anarchism
- d. Socialism

Guidance: level 1

:: Business ethics ::

_____ is a type of international private business self-regulation. While once it was possible to describe CSR as an internal organisational policy or a corporate ethic strategy, that time has passed as various international laws have been developed and various organisations have used their authority to push it beyond individual or even industry-wide initiatives. While it has been considered a form of corporate self-regulation for some time, over the last decade or so it has moved considerably from voluntary decisions at the level of individual organisations, to mandatory schemes at regional, national and even transnational levels.

Exam Probability: **Low**

30. *Answer choices:*

(see index for correct answer)

- a. Cost the limit of price
- b. Corporate social responsibility
- c. Being Globally Responsible Conference
- d. Journal of Business Ethics Education

Guidance: level 1

:: Office work ::

_____ is the process and behavior in human interactions involving power and authority. It is also a tool to assess the operational capacity and to balance diverse views of interested parties. It is also known as office politics and organizational politics.It is the use of power and social networking within an organization to achieve changes that benefit the organization or individuals within it. Influence by individuals may serve personal interests without regard to their effect on the organization itself. Some of the personal advantages may include access to tangible assets, or intangible benefits such as status or pseudo-authority that influences the behavior of others. On the other hand, organizational politics can increase efficiency, form interpersonal relationships, expedite change, and profit the organization and its members simultaneously.Both individuals and groups may engage in office politics which can be highly destructive, as people focus on personal gains at the expense of the organization. "Self-serving political actions can negatively influence our social groupings, cooperation, information sharing, and many other organizational functions." Thus, it is vital to pay attention to organizational politics and create the right political landscape. "Politics is the lubricant that oils your organization`s internal gears." Office politics has also been described as "simply how power gets worked out on a practical, day-to-day basis."

Exam Probability: **High**

31. *Answer choices:*

(see index for correct answer)

- a. Workplace politics
- b. Salaryman
- c. Service bureau
- d. Small office/home office

Guidance: level 1

:: Minimum wage ::

The _____ are working people whose incomes fall below a given poverty line due to lack of work hours and/or low wages.Largely because they are earning such low wages, the _____ face numerous obstacles that make it difficult for many of them to find and keep a job, save up money, and maintain a sense of self-worth.

Exam Probability: **Medium**

32. *Answer choices:*

(see index for correct answer)

- a. Minimum Wage Fairness Act
- b. Minimum wage in Taiwan
- c. Minimum wage in the United States
- d. National Anti-Sweating League

Guidance: level 1

:: Cultural appropriation ::

_____ is a social and economic order that encourages the acquisition of goods and services in ever-increasing amounts. With the industrial revolution, but particularly in the 20th century, mass production led to an economic crisis: there was overproduction—the supply of goods would grow beyond consumer demand, and so manufacturers turned to planned obsolescence and advertising to manipulate consumer spending. In 1899, a book on _____ published by Thorstein Veblen, called The Theory of the Leisure Class, examined the widespread values and economic institutions emerging along with the widespread "leisure time" in the beginning of the 20th century. In it Veblen "views the activities and spending habits of this leisure class in terms of conspicuous and vicarious consumption and waste. Both are related to the display of status and not to functionality or usefulness."

Exam Probability: **High**

33. *Answer choices:*

(see index for correct answer)

- a. Representation of African Americans in media
- b. Atlanta Braves
- c. Plastic Paddy
- d. Washington Redskins

Guidance: level 1

:: Real estate ::

_____ s serve several societal needs – primarily as shelter from weather, security, living space, privacy, to store belongings, and to comfortably live and work. A _____ as a shelter represents a physical division of the human habitat and the outside .

Exam Probability: **High**

34. *Answer choices:*

(see index for correct answer)

- a. Letting agent
- b. Real estate economics
- c. Association law
- d. Building

Guidance: level 1

:: ::

The _____ , founded in 1912, is a private, nonprofit organization whose self-described mission is to focus on advancing marketplace trust, consisting of 106 independently incorporated local BBB organizations in the United States and Canada, coordinated under the Council of _____ s in Arlington, Virginia.

Exam Probability: **High**

35. *Answer choices:*

(see index for correct answer)

- a. surface-level diversity
- b. imperative
- c. open system
- d. co-culture

Guidance: level 1

:: Majority–minority relations ::

_____ , also known as reservation in India and Nepal, positive discrimination / action in the United Kingdom, and employment equity in Canada and South Africa, is the policy of promoting the education and employment of members of groups that are known to have previously suffered from discrimination. Historically and internationally, support for _____ has sought to achieve goals such as bridging inequalities in employment and pay, increasing access to education, promoting diversity, and redressing apparent past wrongs, harms, or hindrances.

Exam Probability: **Medium**

36. *Answer choices:*

(see index for correct answer)

- a. cultural Relativism
- b. positive discrimination

- c. Affirmative action

Guidance: level 1

:: Corporations law ::

A normal _____ consists of various departments that contribute to the company's overall mission and goals. Common departments include Marketing, [Finance, [[Operations managementOperations, Human Resource, and IT. These five divisions represent the major departments within a publicly traded company, though there are often smaller departments within autonomous firms. There is typically a CEO, and Board of Directors composed of the directors of each department. There are also company presidents, vice presidents, and CFOs. There is a great diversity in corporate forms as enterprises may range from single company to multi-corporate conglomerate. The four main _____ s are Functional, Divisional, Geographic, and the Matrix. Realistically, most corporations tend to have a "hybrid" structure, which is a combination of different models with one dominant strategy.

Exam Probability: **High**

37. *Answer choices:*

(see index for correct answer)

- a. Direct debit dividend contributions
- b. Companies Office
- c. Quasi-foreign corporation
- d. Corporate structure

Guidance: level 1

_____ Corporation was an American energy, commodities, and services company based in Houston, Texas. It was founded in 1985 as a merger between Houston Natural Gas and InterNorth, both relatively small regional companies. Before its bankruptcy on December 3, 2001, _____ employed approximately 29,000 staff and was a major electricity, natural gas, communications and pulp and paper company, with claimed revenues of nearly $101 billion during 2000. Fortune named _____ "America's Most Innovative Company" for six consecutive years.

Exam Probability: **Medium**

38. *Answer choices:*

(see index for correct answer)

- a. levels of analysis
- b. process perspective
- c. Enron
- d. personal values

Guidance: level 1

:: Human resource management ::

_____ encompasses values and behaviors that contribute to the unique social and psychological environment of a business. The _____ influences the way people interact, the context within which knowledge is created, the resistance they will have towards certain changes, and ultimately the way they share knowledge. _____ represents the collective values, beliefs and principles of organizational members and is a product of factors such as history, product, market, technology, strategy, type of employees, management style, and national culture; culture includes the organization's vision, values, norms, systems, symbols, language, assumptions, environment, location, beliefs and habits.

Exam Probability: **High**

39. *Answer choices:*

(see index for correct answer)

- a. Organizational culture
- b. ABC Consultants
- c. Public service motivation
- d. Leadership development

Guidance: level 1

:: Waste ::

_____ is any unwanted material in all forms that can cause harm . Many of today's household products such as televisions, computers and phones contain toxic chemicals that can pollute the air and contaminate soil and water. Disposing of such waste is a major public health issue.

40. *Answer choices:*

(see index for correct answer)

- a. Toxic waste
- b. Marine debris
- c. Commercial waste
- d. The Clean Oceans Project

Guidance: level 1

:: Decentralization ::

_____ or sub _____ mainly refers to the unrestricted growth in many urban areas of housing, commercial development, and roads over large expanses of land, with little concern for urban planning. In addition to describing a particular form of urbanization, the term also relates to the social and environmental consequences associated with this development. In Continental Europe the term "peri-urbanisation" is often used to denote similar dynamics and phenomena, although the term _____ is currently being used by the European Environment Agency. There is widespread disagreement about what constitutes sprawl and how to quantify it. For example, some commentators measure sprawl only with the average number of residential units per acre in a given area. But others associate it with decentralization , discontinuity , segregation of uses, and so forth.

41. *Answer choices:*

(see index for correct answer)

- a. Industrial deconcentration
- b. Urban sprawl
- c. Reform Party of Canada
- d. Devolution

Guidance: level 1

:: Renewable energy ::

A _____ is a fuel that is produced through contemporary biological processes, such as agriculture and anaerobic digestion, rather than a fuel produced by geological processes such as those involved in the formation of fossil fuels, such as coal and petroleum, from prehistoric biological matter. If the source biomatter can regrow quickly, the resulting fuel is said to be a form of renewable energy.

Exam Probability: **Low**

42. *Answer choices:*

(see index for correct answer)

- a. Biofuel
- b. Solar water heating
- c. Biomass briquettes
- d. Solar cooker

:: ::

The _____ , the Calvinist work ethic or the Puritan work ethic is a work ethic concept in theology, sociology, economics and history that emphasizes that hard work, discipline and frugality are a result of a person's subscription to the values espoused by the Protestant faith, particularly Calvinism. The phrase was initially coined in 1904–1905 by Max Weber in his book The Protestant Ethic and the Spirit of Capitalism.

Exam Probability: **Low**

43. *Answer choices:*

(see index for correct answer)

- a. corporate values
- b. process perspective
- c. functional perspective
- d. Protestant work ethic

:: Toxicology ::

_____ or lead-based paint is paint containing lead. As pigment, lead chromate , Lead oxide, , and lead carbonate are the most common forms. Lead is added to paint to accelerate drying, increase durability, maintain a fresh appearance, and resist moisture that causes corrosion. It is one of the main health and environmental hazards associated with paint. In some countries, lead continues to be added to paint intended for domestic use, whereas countries such as the U.S. and the UK have regulations prohibiting this, although _____ may still be found in older properties painted prior to the introduction of such regulations. Although lead has been banned from household paints in the United States since 1978, paint used in road markings may still contain it. Alternatives such as water-based, lead-free traffic paint are readily available, and many states and federal agencies have changed their purchasing contracts to buy these instead.

Exam Probability: **Low**

44. *Answer choices:*

(see index for correct answer)

- a. Tarantism
- b. Palm Island mystery disease
- c. Tolerable daily intake
- d. CIOMS/RUCAM scale

Guidance: level 1

:: Human resource management ::

_____ is the ethics of an organization, and it is how an organization responds to an internal or external stimulus. _____ is interdependent with the organizational culture. Although it is akin to both organizational behavior and industrial and organizational psychology as well as business ethics on the micro and macro levels, _____ is neither OB or I/O psychology, nor is it solely business ethics . _____ express the values of an organization to its employees and/or other entities irrespective of governmental and/or regulatory laws.

Exam Probability: **Low**

45. *Answer choices:*

(see index for correct answer)

- a. Organizational ethics
- b. Corporate Equality Index
- c. ABC Consultants
- d. Restructuring

Guidance: level 1

:: Power (social and political) ::

_____ is a form of reverence gained by a leader who has strong interpersonal relationship skills. _____ , as an aspect of personal power, becomes particularly important as organizational leadership becomes increasingly about collaboration and influence, rather than command and control.

Exam Probability: **Medium**

46. *Answer choices:*

(see index for correct answer)

- a. need for power
- b. Referent power
- c. Expert power

Guidance: level 1

:: Patent law ::

A _________ is generally any statement intended to specify or delimit the scope of rights and obligations that may be exercised and enforced by parties in a legally recognized relationship. In contrast to other terms for legally operative language, the term _________ usually implies situations that involve some level of uncertainty, waiver, or risk.

Exam Probability: **Low**

47. *Answer choices:*

(see index for correct answer)

- a. Reverse payment patent settlement
- b. SCRIPDB
- c. Internet as a source of prior art

- d. Utility model

:: Industry ::

_____ is the manner in which a given entity has decided to address issues of energy development including energy production, distribution and consumption. The attributes of _____ may include legislation, international treaties, incentives to investment, guidelines for energy conservation, taxation and other public policy techniques. Energy is a core component of modern economies. A functioning economy requires not only labor and capital but also energy, for manufacturing processes, transportation, communication, agriculture, and more.

Exam Probability: **Low**

48. *Answer choices:*

(see index for correct answer)

- a. Standard Industrial Classification
- b. Industrial symbiosis
- c. Energy policy
- d. Sexual division of labour

:: Offshoring ::

A _____ is the temporary suspension or permanent termination of employment of an employee or, more commonly, a group of employees for business reasons, such as personnel management or downsizing an organization. Originally, _____ referred exclusively to a temporary interruption in work, or employment but this has evolved to a permanent elimination of a position in both British and US English, requiring the addition of "temporary" to specify the original meaning of the word. A _____ is not to be confused with wrongful termination. Laid off workers or displaced workers are workers who have lost or left their jobs because their employer has closed or moved, there was insufficient work for them to do, or their position or shift was abolished . Downsizing in a company is defined to involve the reduction of employees in a workforce. Downsizing in companies became a popular practice in the 1980s and early 1990s as it was seen as a way to deliver better shareholder value as it helps to reduce the costs of employers . Indeed, recent research on downsizing in the U.S., UK, and Japan suggests that downsizing is being regarded by management as one of the preferred routes to help declining organizations, cutting unnecessary costs, and improve organizational performance. Usually a _____ occurs as a cost cutting measure.

Exam Probability: **Medium**

49. *Answer choices:*

(see index for correct answer)

- a. Flag of convenience
- b. Layoff
- c. Offshore company
- d. Body shopping

Guidance: level 1

:: Criminal law ::

_____ is the body of law that relates to crime. It proscribes conduct perceived as threatening, harmful, or otherwise endangering to the property, health, safety, and moral welfare of people inclusive of one's self. Most _____ is established by statute, which is to say that the laws are enacted by a legislature. _____ includes the punishment and rehabilitation of people who violate such laws. _____ varies according to jurisdiction, and differs from civil law, where emphasis is more on dispute resolution and victim compensation, rather than on punishment or rehabilitation. Criminal procedure is a formalized official activity that authenticates the fact of commission of a crime and authorizes punitive or rehabilitative treatment of the offender.

Exam Probability: **Medium**

50. *Answer choices:*

(see index for correct answer)

- a. Self-incrimination
- b. complicit
- c. Criminal law
- d. Mala in se

Guidance: level 1

:: Labour law ::

An _____ is special or specified circumstances that partially or fully exempt a person or organization from performance of a legal obligation so as to avoid an unreasonable or disproportionate burden or obstacle.

Exam Probability: **Medium**

51. *Answer choices:*

(see index for correct answer)

- a. Undue hardship
- b. Work permit
- c. Danish Vacation Law
- d. Maximum medical improvement

Guidance: level 1

:: Fraud ::

In law, _____ is intentional deception to secure unfair or unlawful gain, or to deprive a victim of a legal right. _____ can violate civil law , a criminal law , or it may cause no loss of money, property or legal right but still be an element of another civil or criminal wrong. The purpose of _____ may be monetary gain or other benefits, for example by obtaining a passport, travel document, or driver`s license, or mortgage _____ , where the perpetrator may attempt to qualify for a mortgage by way of false statements.

Exam Probability: **High**

52. *Answer choices:*

(see index for correct answer)

- a. Essay mill
- b. Fraud
- c. Fraud Squad
- d. Credit card kiting

Guidance: level 1

:: Business law ::

A _____ is an arrangement where parties, known as partners, agree to cooperate to advance their mutual interests. The partners in a _____ may be individuals, businesses, interest-based organizations, schools, governments or combinations. Organizations may partner to increase the likelihood of each achieving their mission and to amplify their reach. A _____ may result in issuing and holding equity or may be only governed by a contract.

Exam Probability: **High**

53. *Answer choices:*

(see index for correct answer)

- a. Single business enterprise
- b. Equity of redemption
- c. WIPO Copyright Treaty
- d. Limited liability

:: Production and manufacturing ::

_____ is a set of techniques and tools for process improvement. Though as a shortened form it may be found written as 6S, it should not be confused with the methodology known as 6S .

Exam Probability: **Low**

54. *Answer choices:*

(see index for correct answer)

- a. Managed services
- b. Six Sigma
- c. Expediting
- d. Time to market

:: Business ethics ::

The _____ are the names of two corporate codes of conduct, developed by the African-American preacher Rev. Leon Sullivan, promoting corporate social responsibility.

55. *Answer choices:*

(see index for correct answer)

- a. Symantec
- b. Sullivan principles
- c. United Nations Global Compact
- d. MBA Oath

Guidance: level 1

:: Fraud ::

In the United States, _____ is the claiming of Medicare health care reimbursement to which the claimant is not entitled. There are many different types of _____ , all of which have the same goal: to collect money from the Medicare program illegitimately.

Exam Probability: **High**

56. *Answer choices:*

(see index for correct answer)

- a. Medicare fraud
- b. Voice phishing
- c. 2010 Medicaid fraud

- d. Lip-synching in music

Guidance: level 1

:: Management ::

A _____ describes the rationale of how an organization creates, delivers, and captures value, in economic, social, cultural or other contexts. The process of _____ construction and modification is also called _____ innovation and forms a part of business strategy.

Exam Probability: **Medium**

57. *Answer choices:*

(see index for correct answer)

- a. Business model
- b. Cross ownership
- c. Reval
- d. Supervisory board

Guidance: level 1

:: False advertising law ::

The Lanham Act is the primary federal trademark statute of law in the United States. The Act prohibits a number of activities, including trademark infringement, trademark dilution, and false advertising.

Exam Probability: **Low**

58. *Answer choices:*

(see index for correct answer)

- a. Rebecca Tushnet
- b. Lanham Act

Guidance: level 1

:: United States federal defense and national security legislation ::

The USA _____ is an Act of the U.S. Congress that was signed into law by President George W. Bush on October 26, 2001. The title of the Act is a contrived three letter initialism preceding a seven letter acronym , which in combination stand for Uniting and Strengthening America by Providing Appropriate Tools Required to Intercept and Obstruct Terrorism Act of 2001. The acronym was created by a 23 year old Congressional staffer, Chris Kyle.

Exam Probability: **Low**

59. *Answer choices:*

(see index for correct answer)

- a. Patriot Act
- b. USA PATRIOT Act

Guidance: level 1

Accounting

Accounting or accountancy is the measurement, processing, and communication of financial information about economic entities such as businesses and corporations. The modern field was established by the Italian mathematician Luca Pacioli in 1494. Accounting, which has been called the "language of business", measures the results of an organization's economic activities and conveys this information to a variety of users, including investors, creditors, management, and regulators.

:: Financial ratios ::

The _____ shows the percentage of how profitable a company's assets are in generating revenue.

Exam Probability: **Low**

1. *Answer choices:*

(see index for correct answer)

- a. Days sales outstanding
- b. Sortino ratio
- c. Social return on investment
- d. Return on assets

Guidance: level 1

:: Free accounting software ::

A _____ is the principal book or computer file for recording and totaling economic transactions measured in terms of a monetary unit of account by account type, with debits and credits in separate columns and a beginning monetary balance and ending monetary balance for each account.

Exam Probability: **Low**

2. *Answer choices:*

(see index for correct answer)

- a. GnuCash
- b. Frontaccounting
- c. Ledger
- d. HomeBank

Guidance: level 1

:: Management ::

The _____ is a strategy performance management tool – a semi-standard structured report, that can be used by managers to keep track of the execution of activities by the staff within their control and to monitor the consequences arising from these actions.

Exam Probability: **Medium**

3. *Answer choices:*

(see index for correct answer)

- a. Staff management
- b. Dominant design
- c. Balanced scorecard
- d. Planning

Guidance: level 1

:: Internal Revenue Code ::

The _____ , formally the _____ of 1986, is the domestic portion of federal statutory tax law in the United States, published in various volumes of the United States Statutes at Large, and separately as Title 26 of the United States Code . It is organized topically, into subtitles and sections, covering income tax , payroll taxes, estate taxes, gift taxes, and excise taxes; as well as procedure and administration. Its implementing agency is the Internal Revenue Service.

Exam Probability: **Low**

4. *Answer choices:*

(see index for correct answer)

- a. 527 organization
- b. Casualty loss
- c. 475 fund
- d. Johnson Amendment

Guidance: level 1

:: ::

Accounts _____ is a legally enforceable claim for payment held by a business for goods supplied and/or services rendered that customers/clients have ordered but not paid for. These are generally in the form of invoices raised by a business and delivered to the customer for payment within an agreed time frame. Accounts _____ is shown in a balance sheet as an asset. It is one of a series of accounting transactions dealing with the billing of a customer for goods and services that the customer has ordered. These may be distinguished from notes _____, which are debts created through formal legal instruments called promissory notes.

Exam Probability: **Medium**

5. *Answer choices:*

(see index for correct answer)

- a. hierarchical
- b. Character
- c. corporate values
- d. Receivable

Guidance: level 1

:: Generally Accepted Accounting Principles ::

A _____ or reacquired stock is stock which is bought back by the issuing company, reducing the amount of outstanding stock on the open market .

Exam Probability: **Low**

6. *Answer choices:*

(see index for correct answer)

- a. Generally Accepted Accounting Practice
- b. Treasury stock
- c. Statement of recommended practice
- d. Normal balance

Guidance: level 1

:: ::

_____ is a means of protection from financial loss. It is a form of risk management, primarily used to hedge against the risk of a contingent or uncertain loss

Exam Probability: **High**

7. *Answer choices:*

(see index for correct answer)

- a. Insurance
- b. open system
- c. personal values
- d. hierarchical perspective

Guidance: level 1

:: Accounting in the United States ::

Founded in 1887, the _____ is the national professional organization of Certified Public Accountants in the United States, with more than 418,000 members in 143 countries in business and industry, public practice, government, education, student affiliates and international associates. It sets ethical standards for the profession and U.S. auditing standards for audits of private companies, non-profit organizations, federal, state and local governments. It also develops and grades the Uniform CPA Examination. The AICPA maintains offices in New York City; Washington, DC; Durham, NC; and Ewing, NJ. The AICPA celebrated the 125th anniversary of its founding in 2012.

Exam Probability: **High**

8. *Answer choices:*

(see index for correct answer)

- a. International Qualification Examination
- b. Positive assurance
- c. American Institute of Certified Public Accountants
- d. Accounting Research Bulletins

Guidance: level 1

:: United States Generally Accepted Accounting Principles ::

In the United States, the _____ , Subpart F of the OMB Uniform Guidance, is a rigorous, organization-wide audit or examination of an entity that expends $750,000 or more of federal assistance received for its operations. Usually performed annually, the _____ 's objective is to provide assurance to the US federal government as to the management and use of such funds by recipients such as states, cities, universities, non-profit organizations, and Indian Tribes. The audit is typically performed by an independent certified public accountant and encompasses both financial and compliance components. The _____ s must be submitted to the Federal Audit Clearinghouse along with a data collection form, Form SF-SAC.

Exam Probability: **Medium**

9. *Answer choices:*

(see index for correct answer)

- a. Cost segregation study
- b. Working Group on Financial Markets
- c. Single Audit
- d. GASB 45

Guidance: level 1

:: Classification systems ::

_____ is the practice of comparing business processes and performance metrics to industry bests and best practices from other companies. Dimensions typically measured are quality, time and cost.

Exam Probability: **High**

10. *Answer choices:*

(see index for correct answer)

- a. Parataxonomy
- b. Benchmarking
- c. PANOSE
- d. RosettaNet

Guidance: level 1

:: Business law ::

A _____ is a form of partnership similar to a general partnership except that while a general partnership must have at least two general partners , a _____ must have at least one GP and at least one limited partner.

Exam Probability: **Low**

11. *Answer choices:*

(see index for correct answer)

- a. Apparent authority
- b. Lex mercatoria
- c. Complex structured finance transactions
- d. Limited partnership

:: Taxation in the United States ::

The Modified Accelerated Cost Recovery System is the current tax depreciation system in the United States. Under this system, the capitalized cost of tangible property is recovered over a specified life by annual deductions for depreciation. The lives are specified broadly in the Internal Revenue Code. The Internal Revenue Service publishes detailed tables of lives by classes of assets. The deduction for depreciation is computed under one of two methods at the election of the taxpayer, with limitations. See IRS Publication 946 for a 120-page guide to _____ .

Exam Probability: **Medium**

12. *Answer choices:*

(see index for correct answer)

- a. Car donation
- b. Above-the-line deduction
- c. MACRS
- d. Amount realized

:: Competition (economics) ::

In taxation and accounting, _____ refers to the rules and methods for pricing transactions within and between enterprises under common ownership or control. Because of the potential for cross-border controlled transactions to distort taxable income, tax authorities in many countries can adjust intragroup transfer prices that differ from what would have been charged by unrelated enterprises dealing at arm's length . The OECD and World Bank recommend intragroup pricing rules based on the arm's-length principle, and 19 of the 20 members of the G20 have adopted similar measures through bilateral treaties and domestic legislation, regulations, or administrative practice. Countries with _____ legislation generally follow the OECD _____ Guidelines for Multinational Enterprises and Tax Administrations in most respects, although their rules can differ on some important details.

Exam Probability: **Low**

13. *Answer choices:*

(see index for correct answer)

- a. Category killer
- b. Currency competition
- c. Self-competition
- d. School choice

Guidance: level 1

:: ::

From an accounting perspective, _____ is crucial because _____ and _____ taxes considerably affect the net income of most companies and because they are subject to laws and regulations .

Exam Probability: **Medium**

14. *Answer choices:*

(see index for correct answer)

- a. imperative
- b. Payroll
- c. empathy
- d. surface-level diversity

Guidance: level 1

:: Supply chain management terms ::

In business and finance, _____ is a system of organizations, people, activities, information, and resources involved in moving a product or service from supplier to customer. _____ activities involve the transformation of natural resources, raw materials, and components into a finished product that is delivered to the end customer. In sophisticated _____ systems, used products may re-enter the _____ at any point where residual value is recyclable. _____ s link value chains.

Exam Probability: **High**

15. *Answer choices:*

(see index for correct answer)

- a. Consumables
- b. Last mile
- c. Direct shipment
- d. Supply chain

Guidance: level 1

:: Financial accounting ::

In macroeconomics and international finance, the _____ is one of two primary components of the balance of payments, the other being the current account. Whereas the current account reflects a nation's net income, the _____ reflects net change in ownership of national assets.

Exam Probability: **Medium**

16. *Answer choices:*

(see index for correct answer)

- a. Convenience translation
- b. Capital account
- c. Financial Condition Report
- d. Money measurement concept

:: Accounting systems ::

In accounting, the controlling account is an account in the general ledger for which a corresponding subsidiary ledger has been created. The subsidiary ledger allows for tracking transactions within the controlling account in more detail. Individual transactions are posted both to the controlling account and the corresponding subsidiary ledger, and the totals for both are compared when preparing a trial balance to ensure accuracy.

Exam Probability: **Low**

17. *Answer choices:*

(see index for correct answer)

- a. Open-book accounting
- b. Confidence accounting
- c. Controlling account
- d. Control account

:: Payment systems ::

An _____ is an electronic telecommunications device that enables customers of financial institutions to perform financial transactions, such as cash withdrawals, deposits, transfer funds, or obtaining account information, at any time and without the need for direct interaction with bank staff.

Exam Probability: **Medium**

18. *Answer choices:*

(see index for correct answer)

- a. Cheque truncation
- b. ACI Worldwide
- c. Honesty box
- d. 1LINK

Guidance: level 1

:: Expense ::

_____ relates to the cost of borrowing money. It is the price that a lender charges a borrower for the use of the lender's money. On the income statement, _____ can represent the cost of borrowing money from banks, bond investors, and other sources. _____ is different from operating expense and CAPEX, for it relates to the capital structure of a company, and it is usually tax-deductible.

Exam Probability: **Medium**

19. *Answer choices:*

(see index for correct answer)

- a. Accretion expense
- b. Tax expense
- c. Interest expense
- d. Expense account

Guidance: level 1

:: Employment classifications ::

Generally, tax authorities will view a person as self-employed if the person chooses to be recognized as such, or is generating income such that the person is required to file a tax return under legislation in the relevant jurisdiction. In the real world, the critical issue for the taxing authorities is not that the person is trading but is whether the person is profitable and hence potentially taxable. In other words, the activity of trading is likely to be ignored if no profit is present, so occasional and hobby- or enthusiast-based economic activity is generally ignored by authorities.

Exam Probability: **Low**

20. *Answer choices:*

(see index for correct answer)

- a. Temporary work
- b. Gainful employment

- c. Responsible position
- d. Self-employment

Guidance: level 1

:: ::

_____ is the process of making predictions of the future based on past and present data and most commonly by analysis of trends. A commonplace example might be estimation of some variable of interest at some specified future date. Prediction is a similar, but more general term. Both might refer to formal statistical methods employing time series, cross-sectional or longitudinal data, or alternatively to less formal judgmental methods. Usage can differ between areas of application: for example, in hydrology the terms "forecast" and "_____" are sometimes reserved for estimates of values at certain specific future times, while the term "prediction" is used for more general estimates, such as the number of times floods will occur over a long period.

Exam Probability: **High**

21. *Answer choices:*

(see index for correct answer)

- a. empathy
- b. deep-level diversity
- c. Forecasting
- d. similarity-attraction theory

Guidance: level 1

:: Business law ::

A _____ is a business entity created by two or more parties, generally characterized by shared ownership, shared returns and risks, and shared governance. Companies typically pursue _____ s for one of four reasons: to access a new market, particularly emerging markets; to gain scale efficiencies by combining assets and operations; to share risk for major investments or projects; or to access skills and capabilities.

Exam Probability: **Medium**

22. *Answer choices:*

(see index for correct answer)

- a. Joint venture
- b. Novation
- c. Examinership
- d. Independent contractor

Guidance: level 1

:: Macroeconomics ::

_____ is a change in a price of a good or product, or especially of a currency, in which case it is specifically an official rise of the value of the currency in relation to a foreign currency in a fixed exchange rate system. Under floating exchange rates, by contrast, a rise in a currency's value is an appreciation. Altering the face value of a currency without changing its purchasing power is a redenomination, not a _____ .

23. *Answer choices:*

(see index for correct answer)

- a. Ex-ante
- b. Consumer spending
- c. Revaluation
- d. Factor shares

Guidance: level 1

:: Stock market ::

A _____ , equity market or share market is the aggregation of buyers and sellers of stocks , which represent ownership claims on businesses; these may include securities listed on a public stock exchange, as well as stock that is only traded privately. Examples of the latter include shares of private companies which are sold to investors through equity crowdfunding platforms. Stock exchanges list shares of common equity as well as other security types, e.g. corporate bonds and convertible bonds.

24. *Answer choices:*

(see index for correct answer)

- a. Cross listing
- b. Stock Market
- c. Slippage
- d. Earnings call

Guidance: level 1

:: Options (finance) ::

A _____ bond is a type of bond that allows the issuer of the bond to retain the privilege of redeeming the bond at some point before the bond reaches its date of maturity. In other words, on the call date, the issuer has the right, but not the obligation, to buy back the bonds from the bond holders at a defined call price. Technically speaking, the bonds are not really bought and held by the issuer but are instead cancelled immediately.

Exam Probability: **Medium**

25. *Answer choices:*

(see index for correct answer)

- a. Interest rate guarantee
- b. Rainbow option

- c. Credit default option
- d. Callable

Guidance: level 1

:: ::

A _____ , in the word's original meaning, is a sheet of paper on which one performs work. They come in many forms, most commonly associated with children's school work assignments, tax forms, and accounting or other business environments. Software is increasingly taking over the paper-based _____ .

Exam Probability: **Low**

26. *Answer choices:*

(see index for correct answer)

- a. information systems assessment
- b. cultural
- c. deep-level diversity
- d. Worksheet

Guidance: level 1

:: Business law ::

An _____ is a natural person, business, or corporation that provides goods or services to another entity under terms specified in a contract or within a verbal agreement. Unlike an employee, an _____ does not work regularly for an employer but works as and when required, during which time they may be subject to law of agency. _____ s are usually paid on a freelance basis. Contractors often work through a limited company or franchise, which they themselves own, or may work through an umbrella company.

Exam Probability: **Low**

27. *Answer choices:*

(see index for correct answer)

- a. Fraudulent trading
- b. Independent contractor
- c. OHADA
- d. Voidable floating charge

Guidance: level 1

:: Legal terms ::

An _____ is an action which is inaccurate or incorrect. In some usages, an _____ is synonymous with a mistake. In statistics, "_____ " refers to the difference between the value which has been computed and the correct value. An _____ could result in failure or in a deviation from the intended performance or behaviour.

28. *Answer choices:*

(see index for correct answer)

- a. Error
- b. Europeanisation of law
- c. Comparative negligence
- d. Good cause

Guidance: level 1

:: Password authentication ::

A _____ , or sometimes redundantly a PIN number, is a numeric or alpha-numeric password used in the process of authenticating a user accessing a system.

29. *Answer choices:*

(see index for correct answer)

- a. Password length parameter
- b. OTPW
- c. Cognitive password
- d. Personal identification number

:: Generally Accepted Accounting Principles ::

A _____ is a reduction of the recognized value of something. In accounting, this is a recognition of the reduced or zero value of an asset. In income tax statements, this is a reduction of taxable income, as a recognition of certain expenses required to produce the income.

Exam Probability: **High**

30. *Answer choices:*

(see index for correct answer)

- a. Long-term liabilities
- b. Write-off
- c. Deferred income
- d. Contributed capital

:: Organizational behavior ::

_____ is the state or fact of exclusive rights and control over property, which may be an object, land/real estate or intellectual property. _____ involves multiple rights, collectively referred to as title, which may be separated and held by different parties.

Exam Probability: **High**

31. *Answer choices:*

(see index for correct answer)

- a. Ownership
- b. Conformity
- c. Positive organizational behavior
- d. Counterproductive norms

Guidance: level 1

:: Information systems ::

_____ are formal, sociotechnical, organizational systems designed to collect, process, store, and distribute information. In a sociotechnical perspective, _____ are composed by four components: task, people, structure , and technology.

Exam Probability: **Medium**

32. *Answer choices:*

(see index for correct answer)

- a. Self-service software
- b. STARLIMS
- c. Ocean Biogeographic Information System
- d. Information systems

Guidance: level 1

:: ::

An _____ is a comprehensive report on a company's activities throughout the preceding year. _____ s are intended to give shareholders and other interested people information about the company's activities and financial performance. They may be considered as grey literature. Most jurisdictions require companies to prepare and disclose _____ s, and many require the _____ to be filed at the company's registry. Companies listed on a stock exchange are also required to report at more frequent intervals .

Exam Probability: **Low**

33. *Answer choices:*

(see index for correct answer)

- a. hierarchical
- b. process perspective
- c. Annual report
- d. information systems assessment

:: Accounting ::

_____ are key sources of information and evidence used to prepare, verify and/or audit the financial statements. They also include documentation to prove asset ownership for creation of liabilities and proof of monetary and non monetary transactions.

Exam Probability: **High**

34. *Answer choices:*

(see index for correct answer)

- a. Bookkeeping
- b. Financing cost
- c. KashFlow
- d. Teeming and lading

:: Financial regulatory authorities of the United States ::

The _____ is the revenue service of the United States federal government. The government agency is a bureau of the Department of the Treasury, and is under the immediate direction of the Commissioner of Internal Revenue, who is appointed to a five-year term by the President of the United States. The IRS is responsible for collecting taxes and administering the Internal Revenue Code, the main body of federal statutory tax law of the United States. The duties of the IRS include providing tax assistance to taxpayers and pursuing and resolving instances of erroneous or fraudulent tax filings. The IRS has also overseen various benefits programs, and enforces portions of the Affordable Care Act.

Exam Probability: **Low**

35. *Answer choices:*

(see index for correct answer)

- a. Office of the Comptroller of the Currency
- b. Farm Credit Administration
- c. Federal Deposit Insurance Corporation
- d. Office of Thrift Supervision

Guidance: level 1

:: Auditing ::

An _____ is a security-relevant chronological record, set of records, and/or destination and source of records that provide documentary evidence of the sequence of activities that have affected at any time a specific operation, procedure, or event. Audit records typically result from activities such as financial transactions, scientific research and health care data transactions, or communications by individual people, systems, accounts, or other entities.

Exam Probability: **Medium**

36. *Answer choices:*

(see index for correct answer)

- a. BPA Worldwide
- b. Recovery Auditing
- c. Audit trail
- d. International Federation of Audit Bureaux of Circulations

Guidance: level 1

:: Business ::

The seller, or the provider of the goods or services, completes a sale in response to an acquisition, appropriation, requisition or a direct interaction with the buyer at the point of sale. There is a passing of title of the item, and the settlement of a price, in which agreement is reached on a price for which transfer of ownership of the item will occur. The seller, not the purchaser typically executes the sale and it may be completed prior to the obligation of payment. In the case of indirect interaction, a person who sells goods or service on behalf of the owner is known as a _____ man or _____ woman or _____ person, but this often refers to someone selling goods in a store/shop, in which case other terms are also common, including _____ clerk, shop assistant, and retail clerk.

Exam Probability: **Medium**

37. *Answer choices:*

(see index for correct answer)

- a. Disadvantaged business enterprise
- b. Cost externalizing
- c. Sales
- d. American Environmental Assessment and Solutions Inc.

Guidance: level 1

:: Financial ratios ::

_____ or asset turns is a financial ratio that measures the efficiency of a company`s use of its assets in generating sales revenue or sales income to the company.

38. *Answer choices:*

(see index for correct answer)

- a. Return on capital
- b. Cash flow return on investment
- c. Return on capital employed
- d. Asset turnover

Guidance: level 1

:: ::

_____ is a process whereby a person assumes the parenting of another, usually a child, from that person's biological or legal parent or parents.
Legal _____ s permanently transfers all rights and responsibilities, along with filiation, from the biological parent or parents.

Exam Probability: **Medium**

39. *Answer choices:*

(see index for correct answer)

- a. levels of analysis
- b. Character
- c. cultural

- d. Adoption

Guidance: level 1

:: Real property law ::

A _____ or millage rate is an ad valorem tax on the value of a property, usually levied on real estate. The tax is levied by the governing authority of the jurisdiction in which the property is located. This can be a national government, a federated state, a county or geographical region or a municipality. Multiple jurisdictions may tax the same property. This tax can be contrasted to a rent tax which is based on rental income or imputed rent, and a land value tax, which is a levy on the value of land, excluding the value of buildings and other improvements.

Exam Probability: **Medium**

40. *Answer choices:*

(see index for correct answer)

- a. Trespass
- b. Catasto
- c. Adverse possession
- d. Property tax

Guidance: level 1

:: Corporations law ::

_____ , also referred to as the certificate of incorporation or the corporate charter, are a document or charter that establishes the existence of a corporation in the United States and Canada. They generally are filed with the Secretary of State or other company registrar.

Exam Probability: **High**

41. *Answer choices:*

(see index for correct answer)

- a. Non-stock corporation
- b. Piercing the corporate veil
- c. Corporate law
- d. Articles of incorporation

Guidance: level 1

:: Financial statements ::

In financial accounting, a _____ or statement of financial position or statement of financial condition is a summary of the financial balances of an individual or organization, whether it be a sole proprietorship, a business partnership, a corporation, private limited company or other organization such as Government or not-for-profit entity. Assets, liabilities and ownership equity are listed as of a specific date, such as the end of its financial year. A _____ is often described as a "snapshot of a company's financial condition". Of the four basic financial statements, the _____ is the only statement which applies to a single point in time of a business' calendar year.

Exam Probability: **Low**

42. *Answer choices:*

(see index for correct answer)

- a. Balance sheet
- b. Statements on auditing standards
- c. Statement on Auditing Standards No. 55
- d. Financial statement

Guidance: level 1

:: Loans ::

In finance, a _____ is the lending of money by one or more individuals, organizations, or other entities to other individuals, organizations etc. The recipient incurs a debt, and is usually liable to pay interest on that debt until it is repaid, and also to repay the principal amount borrowed.

43. *Answer choices:*

(see index for correct answer)

- a. Soft loan
- b. Loan
- c. Concessionary loan
- d. Refund anticipation loan

Guidance: level 1

:: ::

The _____ of 1934 is a law governing the secondary trading of securities in the United States of America. A landmark of wide-ranging legislation, the Act of '34 and related statutes form the basis of regulation of the financial markets and their participants in the United States. The 1934 Act also established the Securities and Exchange Commission , the agency primarily responsible for enforcement of United States federal securities law.

44. *Answer choices:*

(see index for correct answer)

- a. co-culture
- b. information systems assessment

- c. corporate values
- d. Securities Exchange Act

Guidance: level 1

:: Investment ::

In economics, _____ is spending which increases the availability of fixed capital goods or means of production and goods inventories. It is the total spending on newly produced physical capital and on inventories —that is, gross investment—minus replacement investment, which simply replaces depreciated capital goods. It is productive capital formation plus net additions to the stock of housing and the stock of inventories.

Exam Probability: **Medium**

45. *Answer choices:*

(see index for correct answer)

- a. China International Fair for Investment and Trade
- b. Net investment
- c. Shock absorber fee
- d. Buy to let

Guidance: level 1

:: International taxation ::

_____ is the levying of tax by two or more jurisdictions on the same declared income , asset , or financial transaction . Double liability is mitigated in a number of ways, for example.

Exam Probability: **High**

46. *Answer choices:*

(see index for correct answer)

- a. Currency transaction tax
- b. Arm's-length transaction
- c. Double taxation
- d. Tax information exchange agreement

Guidance: level 1

:: Corporate taxation in the United States ::

A _____ , under United States federal income tax law, refers to any corporation that is taxed separately from its owners. A _____ is distinguished from an S corporation, which generally is not taxed separately. Most major companies are treated as _____ s for U.S. federal income tax purposes. _____ s and S corporations both enjoy limited liability, but only _____ s are subject to corporate income taxation.

Exam Probability: **Medium**

47. *Answer choices:*

(see index for correct answer)

- a. C corporation
- b. Taxation of cooperative corporations in the United States
- c. Low-profit limited liability company
- d. Excess profits tax

Guidance: level 1

:: Accounting ::

_____ is a process of providing relief to shared service organization's cost centers that provide a product or service. In turn, the associated expense is assigned to internal clients' cost centers that consume the products and services. For example, the CIO may provide all IT services within the company and assign the costs back to the business units that consume each offering.

Exam Probability: **High**

48. *Answer choices:*

(see index for correct answer)

- a. Cost allocation
- b. Trading statement
- c. Efficiency Based Absorption Costing
- d. Earnings surprise

:: Generally Accepted Accounting Principles ::

_____ is a measure of a fixed or current asset's worth when held in inventory, in the field of accounting. NRV is part of the Generally Accepted Accounting Principles and International Financial Reporting Standards that apply to valuing inventory, so as to not overstate or understate the value of inventory goods. _____ is generally equal to the selling price of the inventory goods less the selling costs . Therefore, it is expected sales price less selling costs . NRV prevents overstating or understating of an assets value. NRV is the price cap when using the Lower of Cost or Market Rule.

Exam Probability: **High**

49. *Answer choices:*

(see index for correct answer)

- a. Gross sales
- b. AICPA Statements of Position
- c. Deferral
- d. Consolidation

:: ::

_____ is the income that is gained by governments through taxation. Taxation is the primary source of income for a state. Revenue may be extracted from sources such as individuals, public enterprises, trade, royalties on natural resources and/or foreign aid. An inefficient collection of taxes is greater in countries characterized by poverty, a large agricultural sector and large amounts of foreign aid.

Exam Probability: **Low**

50. *Answer choices:*

(see index for correct answer)

- a. similarity-attraction theory
- b. imperative
- c. deep-level diversity
- d. Tax revenue

Guidance: level 1

:: Generally Accepted Accounting Principles ::

In accounting, an economic item's _____ is the original nominal monetary value of that item. _____ accounting involves reporting assets and liabilities at their _____ s, which are not updated for changes in the items' values. Consequently, the amounts reported for these balance sheet items often differ from their current economic or market values.

Exam Probability: **Medium**

51. *Answer choices:*

(see index for correct answer)

- a. Historical cost
- b. Profit
- c. Net income
- d. Net profit

Guidance: level 1

:: Business economics ::

_____ is one of the constituents of a leasing calculus or operation. It describes the future value of a good in terms of absolute value in monetary terms and it is sometimes abbreviated into a percentage of the initial price when the item was new.

Exam Probability: **Low**

52. *Answer choices:*

(see index for correct answer)

- a. Corporate ecosystem
- b. Gross operating surplus
- c. Residual value
- d. Units of transportation measurement

:: Generally Accepted Accounting Principles ::

The first published description of the process is found in Luca Pacioli`s 1494 work Summa de arithmetica, in the section titled Particularis de Computis et Scripturis. Although he did not use the term, he essentially prescribed a technique similar to a post-closing _____ .

Exam Probability: **Medium**

53. *Answer choices:*

(see index for correct answer)

- a. Consolidation
- b. Insurance asset management
- c. Vendor-specific objective evidence
- d. Trial balance

:: Management accounting ::

"_____ s are the structural determinants of the cost of an activity, reflecting any linkages or interrelationships that affect it". Therefore we could assume that the _____ s determine the cost behavior within the activities, reflecting the links that these have with other activities and relationships that affect them.

Exam Probability: **Low**

54. *Answer choices:*

(see index for correct answer)

- a. Construction accounting
- b. Variable cost
- c. Cost driver
- d. Certified Management Accountants of Canada

Guidance: level 1

:: Legal terms ::

_____ is a state of prolonged public dispute or debate, usually concerning a matter of conflicting opinion or point of view. The word was coined from the Latin controversia, as a composite of controversus – "turned in an opposite direction," from contra – "against" – and vertere – to turn, or versus , hence, "to turn against."

Exam Probability: **Low**

55. *Answer choices:*

- a. Controversy
- b. Prayer for relief
- c. Material fact
- d. Good conduct time

Guidance: level 1

:: Cash flow ::

In corporate finance, _____ or _____ to firm is a way of looking at a business's cash flow to see what is available for distribution among all the securities holders of a corporate entity. This may be useful to parties such as equity holders, debt holders, preferred stock holders, and convertible security holders when they want to see how much cash can be extracted from a company without causing issues to its operations.

Exam Probability: **Low**

56. *Answer choices:*

- a. Cash flow hedge
- b. First Chicago Method
- c. Cash flow loan
- d. Discounted cash flow

:: Notes (finance) ::

A _____ , sometimes referred to as a note payable, is a legal instrument , in which one party promises in writing to pay a determinate sum of money to the other , either at a fixed or determinable future time or on demand of the payee, under specific terms.

Exam Probability: **Low**

57. *Answer choices:*

(see index for correct answer)

- a. Promissory note
- b. Surplus note
- c. Large-sized note
- d. Capital note

:: Stock market ::

_____ is a form of stock which may have any combination of features not possessed by common stock including properties of both an equity and a debt instrument, and is generally considered a hybrid instrument. _____ s are senior to common stock, but subordinate to bonds in terms of claim and may have priority over common stock in the payment of dividends and upon liquidation. Terms of the _____ are described in the issuing company's articles of association or articles of incorporation.

Exam Probability: **Low**

58. *Answer choices:*

(see index for correct answer)

- a. Control premium
- b. Preferred stock
- c. Stock market bubble
- d. Stock market index

Guidance: level 1

:: Real property law ::

_____ is the judicial process whereby a will is "proved" in a court of law and accepted as a valid public document that is the true last testament of the deceased, or whereby the estate is settled according to the laws of intestacy in the state of residence [or real property] of the deceased at time of death in the absence of a legal will.

59. *Answer choices:*

(see index for correct answer)

- a. Probate
- b. Pronoia
- c. Gavelkind
- d. Latent defect

Guidance: level 1

INDEX: Correct Answers

Foundations of Business

1. d: Mission statement

2. c: Sustainability

3. b: Schedule

4. b: Regulation

5. c: Duty

6. c: Economic Development

7. : Free trade

8. a: Marketing research

9. d: Competitive advantage

10. b: Security

11. d: Present value

12. c: Cooperation

13. b: Authority

14. d: Quality management

15. c: Market share

16. c: Competition

17. : Specification

18. b: Globalization

19. : Crisis

20. d: Best practice

21. : Business process

22. a: Document

23. d: Consumer Protection

24. c: Fraud

25. d: Balanced scorecard

26. : Industry

27. a: Dimension

28. a: Information technology

29. d: Board of directors

30. : Patent

31. b: Meeting

32. b: Shareholders

33. b: Performance

34. a: Resource

35. d: Arthur Andersen

36. c: Accounting

37. c: Tariff

38. d: Organizational structure

39. b: System

40. c: Project

41. d: Description

42. a: Ownership

43. c: Arbitration

44. a: Brainstorming

45. d: Franchising

46. a: Goal

47. d: Stock exchange

48. : Fixed cost

49. d: Strategic alliance

50. c: Dividend

51. b: Scheduling

52. d: Office

53. d: Joint venture

54. d: Internal control

55. d: Stock

56. b: Perception

57. a: Partnership

58. b: Human resources

59. a: Raw material

Management

1. b: Authority

2. d: Forecasting

3. a: Gantt chart

4. b: Feedback

5. d: Facilitator

6. b: Property

7. b: Continuous improvement

8. c: Balanced scorecard

9. c: Supply chain

10. c: Linear programming

11. d: Bounded rationality

12. c: Autonomy

13. d: Trade

14. d: Inspection

15. b: Benchmarking

16. : Globalization

17. d: Dimension

18. d: Market share

19. : Bargaining

20. c: Sharing

21. : Job satisfaction

22. c: Span of control

23. d: Resource allocation

24. d: Overtime

25. b: Description

26. c: Employee stock

27. c: Bureaucracy

28. d: Entrepreneurship

29. b: Theory X

30. d: Halo effect

31. a: Cross-functional team

32. a: Human resources

33. a: Offshoring

34. b: Utility

35. c: Business process

36. d: Socialization

37. a: American Express

38. b: Protection

39. : Problem

40. a: Stereotype

41. c: Research and development

42. c: Statistic

43. a: Telecommuting

44. a: Performance appraisal

45. c: Creativity

46. b: Individualism

47. b: Strategic planning

48. a: Quality control

49. b: Committee

50. c: Organization chart

51. c: Mass customization

52. a: Customer

53. d: 360-degree feedback

54. : Industrial Revolution

55. c: Incentive

56. : Performance measurement

57. a: Consultant

58. : Choice

59. d: Operations management

Business law

1. a: False imprisonment

2. a: Respondeat superior

3. : Offeree

4. d: Security interest

5. b: Breach of contract

6. d: Enron

7. c: World Trade Organization

8. b: Summary judgment

9. : Technology

10. d: Welfare

11. a: Certiorari

12. b: Estoppel

13. c: Constitutional law

14. : Service mark

15. d: Commerce Clause

16. b: Warehouse receipt

17. : Corporation

18. : Misdemeanor

19. a: Economic espionage

20. : Arbitration

21. a: Constitution

22. d: Delegation

23. c: Condition precedent

24. b: Shares

25. a: Common carrier

26. b: Limited liability

27. a: Investment

28. c: Securities and Exchange Commission

29. b: Garnishment

30. b: Duty

31. c: Implied warranty

32. a: Bankruptcy

33. b: Competitor

34. : Personal property

35. a: Consumer protection

36. c: Fair use

37. : Disclaimer

38. c: Anticipatory repudiation

39. c: Treaty

40. d: Specific performance

41. b: Negotiable instrument

42. : Preference

43. b: Labor relations

44. c: Liquidated damages

45. d: Perfect tender

46. d: Negligence

47. a: Uniform Electronic Transactions Act

48. c: First Amendment

49. c: Amendment

50. a: Procedural law

51. : Pregnancy discrimination

52. b: Private law

53. c: Employment law

54. a: Environmental Protection

55. b: Damages

56. a: Due diligence

57. d: Presumption

58. a: Securities Act

59. : Manufacturing

Finance

1. : Financial risk

2. b: Current asset

3. : Property

4. : Patent

5. d: Capital budgeting

6. b: Bad debt

7. a: Fixed asset

8. d: Stock price

9. d: Raw material

10. b: Dividend yield

11. d: Derivative

12. c: Risk assessment

13. a: Marketing

14. a: Interest

15. c: Put option

16. d: Volume

17. a: Payroll

18. a: Restructuring

19. b: Normal balance

20. c: Limited liability

21. b: Accrued liabilities

22. c: Net present value

23. a: Free cash flow

24. a: Bond market

25. c: Coupon

26. : Historical cost

27. c: Value Line

28. a: Price

29. a: Contribution margin

30. a: Schedule

31. a: Incentive

32. : Debenture

33. c: Exercise

34. c: Promissory note

35. d: Forward contract

36. b: Amortization

37. a: Bank reconciliation

38. a: Financial market

39. : Asset management

40. b: Generally accepted accounting principles

41. c: Goldman Sachs

42. : Capital asset pricing model

43. d: Economy

44. a: Aging

45. c: Board of directors

46. d: Fair value

47. : Financial analysis

48. a: Return on investment

49. c: Intangible asset

50. c: Adjusting entries

51. d: Long-term liabilities

52. : Time value of money

53. a: Trial balance

54. a: Liquidity

55. a: Revenue

56. a: Creditor

57. d: Equity method

58. a: Total cost

59. b: Preferred stock

Human resource management

1. : Executive search

2. : Physician

3. d: Interdependence

4. d: Drug test

5. c: Needs assessment

6. d: Job enrichment

7. d: Criterion validity

8. d: International Brotherhood of Teamsters

9. : Job rotation

10. c: Cross-training

11. : Employee stock ownership plan

12. a: Public administration

13. d: Human resources

14. d: E-learning

15. b: Organizational socialization

16. d: Enforcement

17. b: Training and development

18. a: Coaching

19. c: Ingratiation

20. : Decentralization

21. b: Meritor Savings Bank v. Vinson

22. : Innovation

23. c: Expatriate

24. a: Management

25. c: Labor relations

26. b: Sexual orientation

27. : Human resource management

28. c: Six Sigma

29. b: Cost of living

30. d: Union shop

31. : Ownership

32. a: Stock appreciation right

33. b: Social contract

34. b: Best practice

35. a: Unemployment insurance

36. b: American Federation of Government Employees

37. c: Reinforcement

38. b: McDonnell Douglas Corp. v. Green

39. b: Asset

40. c: Officer

41. a: Local union

42. b: Balance sheet

43. : Onboarding

44. c: Information overload

45. c: Employee referral

46. b: Unfair labor practice

47. d: Control group

48. a: Mediation

49. c: Fair Labor Standards Act

50. c: Social network

51. a: Recruitment

52. d: Person Analysis

53. a: Overlearning

54. b: Nearshoring

55. c: Structured interview

56. b: Job description

57. c: Workplace bullying

58. b: Just cause

59. a: Talent management

Information systems

1. c: Microprocessor

2. b: Information literacy

3. a: Consumer-to-business

4. c: Master data management

5. : Business model

6. b: Authentication protocol

7. b: Google Calendar

8. a: Dimension

9. c: Backbone network

10. a: System

11. b: World Wide Web

12. b: Digital rights management

13. : AdWords

14. d: Data dictionary

15. d: Click-through rate

16. a: Decision support system

17. d: Affiliate marketing

18. b: Network management

19. a: Economies of scale

20. : Business process

21. a: Help desk

22. : Strategic information system

23. c: Information ethics

24. c: Competitive intelligence

25. c: Documentation

26. d: Resource management

27. a: Privacy policy

28. d: Disaster recovery

29. b: First mover advantage

30. a: Business process reengineering

31. c: Extranet

32. : Security controls

33. : Flash memory

34. a: Property

35. b: Service-oriented architecture

36. a: Extensible Markup Language

37. d: Web mining

38. b: Business analytics

39. b: COBIT

40. b: Service level agreement

41. b: Data integration

42. b: Information governance

43. c: Total cost

44. a: Information privacy

45. a: Payment system

46. c: Epicor

47. a: Asset

48. d: Information silo

49. a: Carnivore

50. b: Big data

51. : Domain name

52. b: Radio-frequency identification

53. c: Credit card

54. b: Keystroke dynamics

55. : One Laptop per Child

56. c: Galileo

57. d: Interoperability

58. d: Interactivity

59. : Blogger

Marketing

1. b: Monopoly

2. d: Copyright

3. c: Consumerism

4. b: Competitive intelligence

5. b: Billboard

6. d: Communication

7. d: Interactive marketing

8. b: Good

9. : Utility

10. c: Electronic data interchange

11. a: Information technology

12. b: Cooperative

13. a: Marketing

14. : Subsidiary

15. b: Supermarket

16. b: Innovation

17. b: Viral marketing

18. d: Manager

19. c: Supply chain management

20. a: Trial

21. d: Audit

22. b: Total cost

23. : Health

24. b: Life

25. c: Marketing communications

26. : Question

27. b: Leadership

28. a: Raw material

29. c: Commerce

30. b: Merchandising

31. d: Customer satisfaction

32. a: Shopping

33. b: Security

34. a: Business-to-business

35. b: Need

36. a: Accounting

37. a: Planning

38. c: Commodity

39. : Retail

40. a: Loyalty program

41. : Tangible

42. c: Forecasting

43. d: Supply chain

44. b: Relationship marketing

45. a: Empowerment

46. c: Department store

47. : INDEX

48. b: Sales management

49. c: Goal

50. : Penetration pricing

51. d: Brand extension

52. a: Intranet

53. : Expense

54. c: Product manager

55. b: Image

56. d: Stock

57. a: Concept testing

58. a: Evolution

59. : Consultant

Manufacturing

1. a: American Society for Quality

2. : Quality control

3. d: Sequence

4. : Schedule

5. : Consensus

6. c: Turbine

7. a: Sunk costs

8. c: Reorder point

9. b: DMAIC

10. c: Solution

11. : Pareto analysis

12. : Sales

13. : Distillation

14. d: Purchasing process

15. b: Procurement

16. : Request for quotation

17. a: Catalyst

18. d: Purchase order

19. a: Scientific management

20. a: Total quality management

21. b: Economies of scope

22. a: Licensed production

23. c: Blanket

24. b: Purchasing manager

25. c: Acceptance sampling

26. c: Gantt chart

27. a: Total cost of ownership

28. a: Knowledge management

29. c: Production schedule

30. c: Mary Kay

31. d: Service quality

32. a: Coating

33. : Dimension

34. a: Toshiba

35. d: Planning

36. c: Interaction

37. d: Quality by Design

38. c: Scope statement

39. : Accreditation

40. c: Estimation

41. b: Voice of the customer

42. d: Metal

43. : Cost

44. d: Performance

45. a: Perfect competition

46. b: ROOT

47. d: Control limits

48. c: Throughput

49. d: Management process

50. a: METRIC

51. : Materials management

52. b: PDCA

53. c: Process capital

54. d: Bill of materials

55. a: Supply chain

56. c: Root cause

57. a: Natural resource

58. a: Retail

59. c: Financial plan

Commerce

1. c: Organization chart

2. b: Consultant

3. b: Personnel

4. d: Total revenue

5. b: Common carrier

6. a: Phishing

7. a: Empowerment

8. d: Hospitality

9. c: Frequency

10. c: Bankruptcy

11. b: Pizza Hut

12. d: Management team

13. c: Real estate

14. a: E-procurement

15. : Advertisement

16. c: Freight forwarder

17. d: British Airways

18. a: Authentication

19. b: Revenue

20. c: Broker

21. c: Innovation

22. : Purchasing manager

23. b: Welfare

24. d: Market segmentation

25. a: Social shopping

26. c: Payment card

27. c: Cost structure

28. b: Quality control

29. d: Transaction cost

30. a: Auction

31. b: Marginal cost

32. b: Pension

33. c: Lease

34. c: Consideration

35. b: Public policy

36. a: Raw material

37. d: Charter

38. d: Purchasing

39. b: Mining

40. : Standing

41. d: Quality assurance

42. d: Strategic plan

43. b: Micropayment

44. c: Confirmed

45. c: Expense

46. b: Short run

47. : Merchant

48. a: Walt Disney

49. c: Level of service

50. c: Liquidation

51. c: Mass production

52. d: Complaint

53. a: Economics

54. a: Marketing strategy

55. d: Chief executive officer

56. d: Bank

57. : Front office

58. d: Uniform Commercial Code

59. c: Negotiation

Business ethics

1. c: Self-interest

2. a: Parental leave

3. b: Guerrilla Marketing

4. c: Exxon Valdez

5. a: Skill

6. c: Risk assessment

7. a: Consumer Protection

8. c: Cultural relativism

9. d: Electronic waste

10. d: Individualistic culture

11. b: Junk bond

12. c: Occupational Safety and Health Administration

13. : European Commission

14. a: Arthur Andersen

15. c: Medicaid

16. b: United Farm Workers

17. d: Whistleblower

18. c: Financial Stability Oversight Council

19. d: Labor relations

20. c: Antitrust

21. c: Corporate citizenship

22. a: Ethics Resource Center

23. : Organizational structure

24. a: Siemens

25. b: Organic food

26. d: Utopian socialism

27. a: Clean Water Act

28. : Empowerment

29. d: Socialism

30. b: Corporate social responsibility

31. a: Workplace politics

32. : Working poor

33. : Consumerism

34. d: Building

35. : Better Business Bureau

36. c: Affirmative action

37. d: Corporate structure

38. c: Enron

39. a: Organizational culture

40. a: Toxic waste

41. b: Urban sprawl

42. a: Biofuel

43. d: Protestant work ethic

44. : Lead paint

45. a: Organizational ethics

46. b: Referent power

47. : Disclaimer

48. c: Energy policy

49. b: Layoff

50. c: Criminal law

51. a: Undue hardship

52. b: Fraud

53. : Partnership

54. b: Six Sigma

55. b: Sullivan principles

56. a: Medicare fraud

57. a: Business model

58. b: Lanham Act

59. a: Patriot Act

Accounting

1. d: Return on assets

2. c: Ledger

3. c: Balanced scorecard

4. : Internal Revenue Code

5. d: Receivable

6. b: Treasury stock

7. a: Insurance

8. c: American Institute of Certified Public Accountants

9. c: Single Audit

10. b: Benchmarking

11. d: Limited partnership

12. c: MACRS

13. : Transfer pricing

14. b: Payroll

15. d: Supply chain

16. b: Capital account

17. d: Control account

18. : Automated teller machine

19. c: Interest expense

20. d: Self-employment

21. c: Forecasting

22. a: Joint venture

23. c: Revaluation

24. b: Stock Market

25. d: Callable

26. d: Worksheet

27. b: Independent contractor

28. a: Error

29. d: Personal identification number

30. b: Write-off

31. a: Ownership

32. d: Information systems

33. c: Annual report

34. : Accounting records

35. : Internal Revenue Service

36. c: Audit trail

37. c: Sales

38. d: Asset turnover

39. d: Adoption

40. d: Property tax

41. d: Articles of incorporation

42. a: Balance sheet

43. b: Loan

44. d: Securities Exchange Act

45. b: Net investment

46. c: Double taxation

47. a: C corporation

48. a: Cost allocation

49. : Net realizable value

50. d: Tax revenue

51. a: Historical cost

52. c: Residual value

53. d: Trial balance

54. c: Cost driver

55. a: Controversy

56. : Free cash flow

57. a: Promissory note

58. b: Preferred stock

59. a: Probate

CPSIA information can be obtained
at www.ICGtesting.com
Printed in the USA
LVHW011135301019
635717LV00005B/554/P